THE ESSENTIAL
WORDS AND WRITINGS OF
CLARENCE DARROW

The Essential Words and Writings of Clarence Darrow

Edited and with an Introduction by

Edward J. Larson and Jack Marshall

THE MODERN LIBRARY

NEW YORK

2007 Modern Library Paperback Original

Compilation copyright © 2007 by Random House, Inc.
Introduction copyright © 2007 by Edward J. Larson and Jack Marshall

Published in the United States by Modern Library, an imprint of
The Random House Publishing Group, a division of
Random House, Inc., New York.

MODERN LIBRARY and the TORCHBEARER Design are registered
trademarks of Random House, Inc.

ISBN 978-0-8129-6677-0

LIBRARY OF CONGRESS CATALOGING-IN-PUBLICATION DATA
Darrow, Clarence, 1857–1938.
The essential words and writings of Clarence Darrow / edited and
with an introduction by Edward J. Larson and Jack Marshall.
—2007 Modern Library pbk. ed.
p.   cm.—(The Modern Library classics)
ISBN-13: 978-0-8129-6677-0
1. Law—United States. 2. Darrow, Clarence, 1857–1938. 3. Lawyers—United
States—Biography. I. Larson, Edward J. (Edward John) II. Marshall, Jack, 1950–
III. Title.

KF213.D3L37 2007
340.092—dc22   2006046901
[B]

Printed in the United States of America

www.modernlibrary.com

2 4 6 8 9 7 5 3 1

Dedicated to

Y<small>ALE</small> K<small>AMISAR</small>
Clarence Darrow Distinguished University Professor of Law
at the University of Michigan

and

all the trial lawyers inspired by Clarence Darrow's
words and deeds to defend the weak, pursue justice,
and promote liberty

"This is life and all there is of life; to play the game, to play the cards we get; play them uncomplainingly and play them to the end. The game may not be worth the while. The stakes may not be worth the winning. But the playing of the game is the forgetting of self, and we should be game sports and play it bravely to the end."

CLARENCE DARROW,
reflections on his sixty-first birthday

CONTENTS

Introduction

Edward J. Larson and Jack Marshall

The photographs of Clarence S. Darrow invariably show a rumpled, hard-wrinkled man with a large head and a half smile, his most striking feature the lock of oily hair that falls carelessly to his right brow. But his truest and most revealing image is the one painted in his written and spoken words. There are thousands and thousands of them, for Clarence Darrow was no advocate of the unexpressed thought. His words give us a vivid picture of a unique and fascinating American mind; a restless mind, to be sure, and sometimes a mind that was capable of appalling thoughts. But Darrow's was also a mind that explored the mysteries of existence and one that was capable of profound and provocative observations on human nature. To read Darrow is to know Darrow. More than that, it is to become acquainted with one of the most complex and fascinating individuals America has yet produced.

Born in 1857, Darrow was the son of a mother who turned her family home into a "depot" on the Underground Railroad, where runaway Southern slaves were hidden and housed on the way to the

North and freedom. His remote and eccentric father loved books better than people, and was, in Darrow's words, "the village infidel" as well as its undertaker. From his mother he received progressive and humanistic instincts, and from his father a love of history and literature along with an unrestrained delight in voicing unpopular opinions. And from the undertaker's trade Darrow seems to have contracted a strain of dark fatalism that often waged war with his soaring aspirations for the human race.

Clarence Darrow got a late start on his epic career. An unsatisfying stint teaching school reinforced the dislike of authority and institutional power that his parents bequeathed him, but it did not immediately combine with Darrow's rebellious nature and instinctive affinity for the underdog to make him a defense attorney. Until the age of thirty-one, Darrow was seemingly content to be a country lawyer in Ashtabula, Ohio, where his most exciting case was a dispute over a fifteen-dollar harness. But a banker acquaintance in Ashtabula fired Darrow's dormant passion for social reform when he gave him a little book entitled *Our Penal Code and Its Victims,* by Judge John Peter Altgeld of Chicago. It inspired Darrow to move to Chicago, where he became close friends with its author, soon to become the governor of Illinois. And it taught him that powerful words could change minds and lives.

In 1886, a gathering of striking workers from the McCormick Reaper Works turned to violence when a deadly bomb was thrown into the midst of police who had gathered to disperse them. The subsequent trial and harsh punishment of eight labor activists whose only proven connection to the crime was their vocal advocacy of social reforms signaled an intense new stage of labor unrest. Darrow arrived in Chicago in 1888, just as labor conflict was heating to a boil. He quickly leaped into the pot, defending the controversial labor leader Eugene V. Debs in the railroad union strike. Darrow's defense failed, but his skill and passion for the cause impressed Debs's allies, and it proved to be the start of Darrow's twenty-year run as the labor movement's courtroom champion. The often violent clashes between unions and industry during this period produced many high-profile criminal cases. Darrow became a national figure as he dominated sensational trials in which he was called upon to defend labor organizers charged with conspiracy or worse.

His success in opposing these emotion-charged prosecutions reached its zenith with the murder trial of William "Big Bill" Haywood in 1908. Darrow delivered an epic eleven-hour closing argument that persuaded a jury to acquit the flamboyant union leader, who was charged with paying an assassin to kill a strikebreaking former governor of Idaho. Almost immediately after the Haywood victory, Darrow's own life exploded. He developed an ear infection requiring life-threatening surgery that incapacitated him for months, and he lost most of his savings in a stock-market crash. Worst of all, he met with professional disaster, much of it of his own making, when he took on the defense of another pair of union leaders accused of murder. A dynamite explosion at the resolutely antilabor *Los Angeles Times* had killed twenty-one men, and the McNamara brothers, leaders of the printers' union, were charged with the sensational crime. As newspapers pronounced the *Times* bombing "the crime of the century," Debs and another labor icon, Samuel Gompers, persuaded Darrow that it was his duty as labor's advocate to prove the brothers innocent, and thus prevent the public from rejecting the labor movement as the dominion of thugs and criminals. But the evidence against the McNamaras was overwhelming, and when Darrow decided that he could not win acquittals for them, he had no choice but to have them plead guilty.

No choice, that is, after he had been caught attempting to guarantee a deadlocked jury by bribing two jurors.

The labor movement regarded the McNamaras' guilty plea as a capitulation and betrayal by Darrow, who was never again entrusted with a major union client. But that blow paled in comparison to Darrow's travails in escaping Los Angeles with his freedom and his law license. Ultimately, Darrow's argument against conviction in his two trials for jury tampering amounted to a call for jury nullification, as he rhetorically asked if the world would be a better place with Clarence Darrow in prison or fighting for justice. The strategy worked, and at the age of fifty-five he found himself free but facing the massive task of rebuilding a shattered career and reputation.

F. Scott Fitzgerald famously declared that "there are no second acts in American lives." Darrow proved him wrong, for he authored a boffo second act that virtually erased the McNamara debacle from historical memory. Freed from the demanding unions, he applied his skills to a full spectrum of progressive causes: equal rights, intellectual freedom, abolition of capital punishment, pacifism, free speech, and more. Darrow continued to write and speak, in court and out, about these and his own philosophical convictions until his death in 1938.

Although he is primarily remembered today as a trial lawyer (nearly three-quarters of a century after his death, Darrow still routinely tops all surveys and polls as the lawyer most admired by other legal practitioners), he embraced this profession primarily for the opportunities it provided him to do the things he really cared about: arguing, opposing powerful institutions, and pursuing social reform (he didn't mind the money and fame, either). He certainly had no love for the law itself, which he looked upon less as the connective tissue of civilization than as a truncheon wielded by the strong and rich to control the weak and poor. Once, when a prosecutor rebuked Darrow for helping a criminal defendant evade the law, Darrow embraced the rebuke: "The law? To hell with the law! My business is to save this defendant *from* the law!"

Darrow's talents did not extend to financial management, and the dreams of an early retirement that would permit him to devote his full attention to writing never became reality. Nevertheless, many writers would have been satisfied with the number of published works he managed to produce in the moments stolen between speaking engagements, sensational criminal and labor cases, and less glamorous legal work that helped pay the bills, not to mention two marriages and uncounted extramarital affairs. His output included two novels, numerous short stories, dozens of essays, and biographical sketches of those whose achievements or ideas Darrow admired, such as Leo Tolstoy, Voltaire, and John Brown.

In part because his busy legal career did not permit him to concentrate on the writer's craft, Darrow's prose tended to be instinctive and spontaneous rather than polished, often following a vivid, brilliant, passionate, or entertaining passage with a carelessly written one. Sometimes Darrow's writing had the quality of a stream of consciousness that proceeded unedited into published form. This is not surprising. Darrow improvised brilliantly in speech and possessed a master's confidence in his ability to be articulate, witty, and persuasive with a minimum of preparation. Like others with this gift, he tended to write as he spoke, ignoring the fact that a skilled speaker's delivery could significantly improve what might be flawed on the printed page. And, as he was fond of confessing, Darrow could be lazy, or at least unwilling to expend the meticulous effort necessary to refine his writings. Oratory was the talent he had the opportunity and the inclination to perfect, and courtroom oratory was truly Darrow's art.

It is a pity that we have no movies of Darrow delivering his brilliant courtroom orations, because their effectiveness was as much due to performance as content. He enhanced his oratorical skills with those of a natural actor. Many of his closing arguments were delivered with tears streaming down his cheeks, and as every actor knows, tears are contagious. Newspaper accounts of his summations report weeping spectators, weeping juries, even weeping court officials. Still, the content remains impressive without the theatrics. The power of Darrow's speeches jumps off the page, and must have been mesmerizing in court.

Much of their effectiveness comes from the authenticity of the passion Darrow packed into them. He employed a wide variety of tools of persuasion: rationality and logic, analysis, invective, ridicule, humor, sarcasm, sentiment, flattery, despair, inspiration, exhortation, poetry, even religion, but the most powerful quality of his arguments is that they seem genuinely personal and genuinely believed. This is the most treasured quality a trial lawyer can have: the ability to connect with jurors and convince them that the charismatic, articulate, learned, and undeniably wise individual before them is telling the truth.

Darrow *was* telling the truth, at least about the principles he linked so skillfully to every defendant's fate. Indeed, Darrow again and again made the unconventional argument that the principles at issue were more important than that fate. How some of his clients must have flinched in court to hear their lawyer declare that he "didn't care" what happened to them! Darrow's most famous quote, "Hate the sin, never the sinner," could have accurately been paralleled by a sentiment he never stated but often appeared to endorse: "Love the principle, not the person."

His courtroom arguments consistently share the themes of his other writings. Most of these themes had occupied his thoughts for decades, and when he was called upon to expound on them in defense of a client, they emerged fully developed and honed into formidable weapons of advocacy. Of these, the most disturbing to today's readers undoubtedly is Darrow's philosophical embrace of extreme utilitarianism. While telling some juries that he "didn't care" what happened to the defendant, he occasionally added that he "didn't care" whether his client had committed the crime or not "because *his cause was just.*" This is consistent with his speech in praise of the radical abolitionist John Brown, whose spree of violence at Harpers Ferry Darrow celebrated as a courageous act necessary to call attention to the evils of slavery. Darrow's own ethical instincts were driven by results, not values; for all his courtroom eloquence, he was also renowned for tactics in court and out that would warrant serious bar discipline today. But Darrow's tactics followed his view that the powerful make the rules to dominate the powerless, and breaking the rules was sometimes a necessary detour on the road to justice. If he were alive today, he would almost certainly have terrorists as clients.

Perhaps the most significant recurring Darrow theme was the inherent injustice of the criminal justice system. He could barely wait to begin exploring the issue in his autobiography, launching into a full-fledged discussion of it by page 75. Darrow fervently believed that crime was the product of powerful forces the criminal had no chance to avoid: poverty, upbringing, education, reputation, envy, and despair:

> *Who is to blame? To say that it is the fault of the one who goes the luckless way is a travesty upon logic, common sense, and the first elements of*

fair dealing.... And yet people who are discerning and humane can rea-
son out no way to prevent crime excepting by inflicting untold misery,
degradation, and dire vengeance upon the victims who are plainly the
product of our vaunted civilization.

Closely related to this theme was another: Darrow's loathing of capital punishment. It became the dominant theme of his legal career as well, for he defended 102 men facing execution, and not one of them died by the state's hand. His most eloquent and memorable argument against capital punishment was undoubtedly his famous closing plea for mercy in the trial of the teenaged "thrill killers" Nathan Leopold and Richard Loeb in 1925, but Darrow had always attacked this form of punishment with special vigor. He traced his attitude back to a sentiment his father had shared with him when he was no more than eight. Forced by his own father to watch the public hanging of a criminal in the early nineteenth century, the elder Darrow said that he had never stopped feeling shame for participating in the death of another human being. In essays, debates, speeches, and in court, Darrow established himself as twentieth-century America's most prolific and influential opponent of the death penalty.

He also was its most famous agnostic. Darrow's courtroom oratory was often misleading on this point, for he routinely soothed juries with the name of God and other religious imagery. (This apparently fooled the late Supreme Court Justice and liberal icon William O. Douglas, who in his introduction to Arthur Weinberg's collection of Darrow's courtroom performances wrote that "he obviously believed in an infinite God who was the Maker of all humanity.") But Darrow wasn't merely a nonbeliever; he mercilessly ridiculed others for believing in God, reserving special contempt for those who insisted that the Bible was literal truth. Darrow's speeches and essays on the subject vigorously dissected biblical accounts and used logic, science, and humor to declare them myths, impossibilities, or hypocrisy. These arguments were also to serve Darrow in court, as he employed them to great effect when he defended John Scopes, a schoolteacher prosecuted under a Tennessee statute forbidding the teaching of Darwin's theory of human evolution because of its supposed conflict with biblical Christianity. The climax of the Scopes trial was Darrow's aggressive examination of William Jennings Bryan, the orator and former presidential candidate, whose fundamentalist views were ideal targets for Darrow's well-honed attack. Their famous confrontation became legendary, and made Darrow's reasoning a permanent component of the evolution controversy that continues today.

Darrow's absence of belief in the supernatural is the central feature of the great conflict within him, which becomes vividly apparent with any extensive examination of his writings. He was an enthusiastic reader of dour philosophers like Hobbes, Schopenhauer, and Nietzsche, and his reflections on life and mankind were often gloomy to the point of depression. There is no soul, immortality is a myth, mankind is an insignificant speck in a vast unknowable universe, and the future is dust—this sums up the thrust of Darrow's existential musings. Yet few have been more passionate than he in invoking the triumph of the human spirit. There can be no question that Darrow believed that human existence could and should be made more just, merciful, and tolerant; that great advancements in science and medicine were on the horizon; and that every person, given a chance, could accomplish great things.

It seems inconceivable that Darrow could fight so long and so effectively for human lives that he thought were insignificant and human aspirations that he believed were futile fantasies. Perhaps Darrow's writings and speeches exude such vigor because he was arguing with the one adversary he couldn't defeat: himself. The courtroom orations extolling the ideals of mercy, tolerance, justice, and courage had to be more than a brilliant trial lawyer's crafted persuasion. They may have reflected Darrow's spiritual yearnings, which his rational instincts never permitted him to express except on behalf of another. Those copious tears may not have been an actor's trick after all.

In presenting this collection of words from Clarence Darrow, we have aimed to illuminate those passions, ideals, theories, and themes that excited and defined him, while giving the reader a sense of the scope and variety of his work. This necessitated some substantial cuts in the texts, but always in the dual interests of presenting Darrow's concepts with clarity and including as rich a collection of material as possible. For Darrow as a lawyer, words were his stock-in-trade; as a writer and orator, his ideas made him an American icon. We have endeavored to preserve enough of his words and his ideas so that readers can take the full measure of the man.

THE ESSENTIAL
WORDS AND WRITINGS OF
CLARENCE DARROW

CHAPTER 1

LECTURES, SPEECHES, AND ADDRESSES

AUTOBIOGRAPHICAL INTRODUCTION

FROM CLARENCE DARROW, *THE STORY OF MY LIFE*,
CHAPTER 5, "I MAKE A HIT" (1932)

I came to Chicago in 1888. Soon after my arrival I joined the Single
Tax Club, and took part in the second Grover Cleveland campaign,
then going on. This club met regularly every week for several years.
In due time I realized that at every meeting the same faces appeared and reappeared, week after week, and that none of them
cared to hear anything but a gospel which they all believed. It did
not take long for Single Tax to become a religious doctrine necessary to salvation. But, the Single Tax Club furnished a forum for
ambitious young lawyers to win a hearing in; and I generally participated in the debates, which led to my speaking at ward meetings
and other public gatherings from time to time....

One night I was asked to speak at a West Side meeting, called to
discuss some civic problem. The leading speaker was William B.
Mason, who was at that time a state senator, and afterwards became
a United States senator. I had long wanted the newspapers to notice
my existence, but the reporters refused to even look at me. I entered the theater through the back door and noted with joy that the

place was packed. In front of the stage were a half-dozen or more newspaper reporters that gladdened my heart. Easily I sized up the situation and felt that my time had come. After a few preliminaries I was introduced amidst loud calls for Mason. I looked around and over at the audience, trying to gain their attention. The eyes can be very useful for quelling an audience or forcing people to focus on a speaker. I made my speech. I feel sure that it was not very bad. Probably not bad enough. I could see that the audience was waiting for William B. Mason, so I took no chances in delaying them too long. But the one thing that forcibly impressed me while I spoke was that not one of the newspaper men wrote a single line. They leaned back in their chairs and glanced at me with the complacent and sophisticated countenances of newspaper men. They knew why they were there, and whom their editors and the public would want to read about the next day. When I sat down there was slight applause. No speaker can get along without at least a little of that. Such approval as was manifested by the politest and kindliest there was drowned in the cries for "Mason!" They had come to hear him and were not interested in waiting....

After the meeting at the West Side hall I was in gloom amounting almost to despair. If it had been possible I would have gone back to Ohio; but I didn't want to borrow the money, and I dreaded to confess defeat. I did not then know the ways of Fate. I did not know that Fortune comes like the day, sometimes filled with sunshine, sometimes hidden in gloom. I had not then learned that one must accept whatever comes along without regret; that he must not take either gratification or disappointment too seriously. I did not know, as Bret Harte put it, that the only sure thing about luck is that it will change. And luck can change as suddenly as daylight and darkness in a tropical land.

Soon after the blow in connection with the West Side meeting a "Free Trade Convention" was staged in Chicago. The closing session was held in Central Music Hall, at that time the most popular auditorium in the city; Henry George was to be the big drawing-card. Mr. George was then in the zenith of his power. I was invited to appear on the same programme. The great auditorium was

packed, to my satisfaction. I looked out upon the audience with re-
newed hope. Every Single Taxer in Chicago seemed to be present,
and a great throng besides. Mr. George was the first speaker, which
looked ominous to me. I was afraid of either the first or last place;
either one seemed fraught with peril. No one knew the tariff question better than Henry George. More than this, he was a strong idealist, and had the audience in his grasp from the first moment to the
last. Every one but me was carried away with his able address. I was
disappointed. I was sorry that it was so good. I twitched nervously
in my chair until he had finished and the applause began to die
away. I felt that after his wonderful address I would not be able to
hold the audience. I realized that the crowd had come to hear him,
and that but a few among them had ever heard of me.

When the applause subsided people began getting up and going
away. The show was over. I said to the chairman, "For goodness sake
get busy before every one leaves the house!" Quickly he introduced
me, and my friends paused and did their best to give me a good reception. I had discovered enough about public speaking to sense
that unless a speaker can interest his audience at once, his effort
will be a failure. This was particularly true when following a
speaker like Henry George, so I began with the most striking
phrases that I could conjure from my harried, worried brain. The
audience hesitated and began to sit down. They seemed willing to
give me a chance. I had at least one advantage; nothing was expected of me; if I could get their attention it would be easier than if
too much was expected. Not one in twenty of the audience knew
much about me. As a matter of fact, I had taken great pains to prepare my speech. The subject was one that had deeply interested me
for many years, one that I really understood. In a short time I had
the attention of the entire audience, to my surprise. Then came the
full self-confidence which only a speaker can understand; that confidence that is felt as one visits by the fireside, when he can say what
he pleases and as he pleases; when the speaker can, in fact, visit with
the audience as with an old-time friend. I have no desire to elabo-
rate on my talk, but I know that I had the people with me, and that
I could sway those listeners as I wished.

But the crowning triumph had come as I warmed to my subject and waxed earnest in what I had to say, and became aware that the newspaper men down in front were listening, and were plying their pencils, recording my words, or seeming to record them, as fast as they shot past. When I finally finished, the audience was indeed generous and encouraging with its applause and appreciation. Henry George warmly grasped my hand. My friends and others came around me, and it was some time before I could leave the stage.

I have talked from platforms countless times since then, but never again have I felt that exquisite thrill of triumph after a speech. This was forty years ago, and even now I occasionally meet some one who tells me that he heard my speech at Central Music Hall the night I was there with Henry George.

Main Selection

Clarence Darrow, "Crime and Criminals"
An address delivered to prisoners in the Cook County Jail,
Chicago, Illinois (1902)

If I looked at jails and crimes and prisoners in the way the ordinary person does, I should not speak on this subject to you. The reason I talk to you on the question of crime, its cause and cure, is because I really do not in the least believe in crime. There is no such thing as a crime as the word is generally understood. I do not believe there is any sort of distinction between the real moral condition of the people in and out of jail. One is just as good as the other. The people here can no more help being here than the people outside can avoid being outside. I do not believe that people are in jail because they deserve to be. They are in jail simply because they cannot avoid it on account of circumstances which are entirely beyond their control and for which they are in no way responsible.

I suppose a great many people on the outside would say I was doing you harm if they should hear what I say to you this afternoon, but you cannot be hurt a great deal anyway, so it will not matter.

Good people outside would say that I was really teaching you things that were calculated to injure society, but it's worth while now and then to hear something different from what you ordinarily get from preachers and the like. These will tell you that you should be good and then you will get rich and be happy. Of course we know that people do not get rich by being good, and that is the reason why so many of you people try to get rich some other way, only you do not understand how to do it quite as well as the fellow outside.

There are people who think that everything in this world is an accident. But really there is no such thing as an accident. A great many folks admit that many of the people in jail ought not to be there, and many who are outside ought to be in. I think none of them ought to be here. There ought to be no jails, and if it were not for the fact that the people on the outside are so grasping and heartless in their dealings with the people on the inside, there would be no such institution as jails.

I do not want you to believe that I think all you people here are angels. I do not think that. You are people of all kinds, all of you doing the best you can, and that is evidently not very well—you are people of all kinds and conditions and under all circumstances. In one sense everybody is equally good and equally bad. We all do the best we can under the circumstances. But as to the exact things for which you are sent here, some of you are guilty and did the particular act because you needed the money. Some of you did it because you are in the habit of doing it, and some of you because you are born to it, and it comes to be as natural as it does, for instance, for me to be good.

Most of you probably have nothing against me, and most of you would treat me the same as any other person would; probably better than some of the people on the outside would treat me, because you think I believe in you and they know I do not believe in them. While you would not have the least thing against me in the world you might pick my pockets. I do not think all of you would, but I think some of you would. You would not have anything against me, but that's your profession, a few of you. Some of the rest of you, if my doors were unlocked, might come in if you saw anything you wanted—not out of malice to me, but because that is your trade. There is no doubt there are quite a number of people in this jail who would pick my pockets. And still I know this, that when I get outside pretty nearly everybody picks my pocket. There may be some of you who would hold up a man on the street, if you did not happen to have something else to do, and needed the money; but when I want to light my house or my office the gas company holds me up. They charge me one dollar for something that is worth twenty-five cents, and still all these people are good people; they are pillars of society and support the churches, and they are respectable.

When I ride on the street cars, I am held up—I pay five cents for a ride that is worth two and a half cents, simply because a body of men have bribed the city council and the legislature, so that all the rest of us have to pay tribute to them.

If I do not wish to fall into the clutches of the gas trust and choose to burn oil instead of gas, then good Mr. Rockefeller holds me up, and he uses a certain portion of his money to build universities and support churches which are engaged in telling us how to be good.

Some of you are here for obtaining property under false pretenses—yet I pick up a great Sunday paper and read the advertisements of a merchant prince—"Shirt waists for 39 cents, marked down from $3.00."

When I read the advertisements in the paper I see they are all lies. When I want to get out and find a place to stand anywhere on the face of the earth, I find that it has all been taken up long ago before I came here, and before you came here, and somebody says, "Get off, swim into the lake, fly into the air; go anywhere, but get off." That is because these people have the police and they have the jails and judges and the lawyers and the soldiers and all the rest of them to take care of the earth and drive everybody off that comes in their way.

A great many people will tell you that all this is true, but that it does not excuse you. These facts do not excuse some fellow who reaches into my pocket and takes out a five dollar bill; the fact that the gas company bribes the members of the legislature from year to year, and fixes the law, so that all you people are compelled to be "fleeced" whenever you deal with them; the fact that the street car companies and the gas companies have control of the streets and the fact that the landlords own all the earth, they say, has nothing to do with you.

Let us see whether there is any connection between the crimes of the respectable classes and your presence in the jail. Many of you people are in jail because you have really committed burglary. Many of you, because you have stolen something; in the meaning of the law, you have taken some other person's property. Some of you have entered a store and carried off a pair of shoes because you did not have the price. Possibly some of you have committed murder. I cannot tell what all of you did. There are a great many people here who have done some of these things who really do not know themselves why they did them. I think I know why you did them—every one of you; you did these things because you were bound to do them. It looked to you at the time as if you had a chance to do them or not, as you saw fit, but still after all you had no choice. There may be people here who had some money in their pockets and who still went out and got some more money in a way society forbids. Now you may not yourselves see exactly why it was you did this thing, but if you look at the question deeply enough and carefully enough you would see that there were circumstances that drove you to do exactly the thing which you did. You could not help it any more than we outside can help taking the positions that we take. The reformers who tell you to be good and you will be happy, and the people on the outside who have property to protect—they think that the only way to do it is by building jails and locking you up in cells on week days and praying for you Sundays.

I think that all of this has nothing whatever to do with right conduct. I think it is very easily seen what has to do with right conduct. Some so-called criminals—and I will use this word because it is handy, it means nothing to me—I speak of the criminals who get caught as distinguished from the criminals who catch them—some of these so-called criminals are in jail for the first offenses, but nine-tenths of you are in jail because you did not have a good lawyer and of course you did not have a good lawyer because you did not have enough money to pay a good lawyer. There is no very great danger of a rich man going to jail.

Some of you may be here for the first time. If we would open the doors and let you out, and leave the laws as they are today, some of you would be back tomorrow. This is about as good a place as you can get anyway. There are many people here who are so in the habit of coming that they would not know where else to go. There are people who are born with the tendency to break into jail every chance they get, and they cannot avoid it. You cannot figure out your life and see why it was, but still there is a reason for it, and if we were all wise and knew all the facts we could figure it out.

In the first place, there are a good many more people who go to jail in the winter time than in summer. Why is this? Is it because people are more wicked in winter? No, it is because the coal trust begins to get [them] in its grip in the winter. A few gentlemen take possession of the coal, and unless the people will pay seven dollars or eight dollars a ton for something that is worth three dollars, they will have to freeze. Then there is nothing to do but break into jail, and so there are many more in jail in the winter than in summer. It costs more for gas in the winter because the nights are longer, and people go to jail to save gas bills. The jails are electric lighted. You may not know it, but these economic laws are working all the time, whether we know it or do not know it.

There are more people go to jail in hard times than in good times—few people comparatively go to jail except when they are hard up. They go to jail because they have no other place to go. They may not know why, but it is true all the same. People are not more wicked in hard times. That is not the reason. The fact is true all over the world that in hard times more people go to jail than in good times, and in winter more people go to jail than in summer. Of course it is pretty hard times for people who go to jail at any time. The people who go to jail are almost always poor people—people who have no other place to live first and last. When times are hard then you find large numbers of people who go to jail who would not otherwise be in jail.

Long ago Mr. Buckle, who was a great philosopher and historian, collected facts and he showed that the number of people who are arrested increased just as the price of food increased. When they put up the price of gas ten cents a thousand I do not know who will go to jail, but I do know that a certain number of people will go. When the meat combine raises the price of beef I do not know who is going to jail, but I know that a large number of people are bound to go. Whenever the Standard Oil Company raises the price of oil, I know that a certain number of girls who are seamstresses, and who work night after night long hours for somebody else, will be compelled to go out on the streets and ply another trade, and I know that Mr. Rockefeller and his associates are responsible and not the poor girls in the jails.

First and last, people are sent to jail because they are poor. Sometimes, as I say, you may not need money at the particular time, but you wish to have thrifty forehanded habits, and do not always wait until you are in absolute want. Some of you people are perhaps plying the trade, the profession, which is called burglary. No man in his right senses will go into a strange house in the dead of night and prowl around with a dark lantern through unfamiliar rooms and take chances of his life if he has plenty of the good things of the world in his own home. You would not take any such chances as that. If a man had clothes in his clothes-press and beefsteak in his pantry, and money in the bank, he would not navigate around nights in houses where he knows nothing about the premises whatever. It always requires experience and education for this profession, and people who fit themselves for it are no more to blame than I am for being a lawyer. A man would not hold up another man on the street if he had plenty of money in his own pocket. He might do it if he had one dollar or two dollars, but he wouldn't if he had as much money as Mr. Rockefeller has. Mr. Rockefeller has a great deal better holdup game than that.

The more that is taken from the poor by the rich, who have the chance to take it, the more poor people there are who are compelled to resort to these means for a livelihood. They may not understand it, they may not think so at once, but after all they are driven into that line of employment.

There is a bill before the legislature of this state to punish kidnapping of children with death. We have wise members of the legislature. They know the gas trust when they see it and they always see it—they can furnish light enough to be seen, and this legislature thinks it is going to stop kidnapping of children by making a law punishing kidnappers of children with death. I don't believe in kidnapping children, but the legislature is all wrong. Kidnapping children is not a crime, it is a profession. It has been developed with the times. It has been developed with our modern industrial conditions. There are many ways of making money—many new ways that our ancestors knew nothing about. Our ancestors knew nothing about a billion dollar trust; and here comes some poor fellow who has no other trade and he discovers the profession of kidnapping children.

This crime is born, not because people are bad; people don't kidnap other people's children because they want the children or because they are devilish, but because they see a chance to get some money out of it. You cannot cure this crime by passing a law punishing by death kidnappers of children. There is one way to cure it. There is one way to cure all these offenses, and that is to give the people a chance to live. There is no other way, and there never was any other way since the world began, and the world is so blind and stupid that it will not see. If every man and woman and child in the world had a chance to make a decent, fair, honest living, there would be no jails, and no lawyers and no courts. There might be some persons here or there with some peculiar formation of their brain, like Rockefeller, who would do these things simply to be doing them; but they would be very, very few, and those should be sent to a hospital and treated, and not sent to jail, and they would entirely disappear in the second generation, or at least in the third generation.

I am not talking pure theory. I will just give you two or three illustrations.

The English people once punished criminals by sending them away. They would load them on a ship and export them to Australia. England was owned by lords and nobles and rich people. They owned the whole earth over there, and the other people had to stay in the streets. They could not get a decent living. They used to take their criminals and send them to Australia—I mean the class of criminals who got caught. When these criminals got over there, and nobody else had come, they had the whole continent to run over, and so they could raise sheep and furnish their own meat, which is easier than stealing it; these criminals then became decent, respectable people because they had a chance to live. They did not commit any crimes. They were just like the English people who sent them there, only better. And in the second generation the descendants of those criminals were as good and respectable a class of people as there were on the face of the earth, and then they began building churches and jails themselves.

A portion of this country was settled in the same way, landing prisoners down on the southern coast; but when they got here and had a whole continent to run over and plenty of chances to make a living, they became respectable citizens, making their own living just like any other citizen in the world; but finally these descendants of the English aristocracy, who sent the people over to Australia, found out they were getting rich, and so they went over to get possession of the earth as they always do, and they organized land syndicates and got control of the land and ores, and then they had just as many criminals in Australia as they did in England. It was not because the world had grown bad; it was because the earth had been taken away from the people.

Some of you people have lived in the country. It's prettier than it is here. And if you have ever lived on a farm you understand that if you put a lot of cattle in a field, when the pasture is short they will jump over the fence; but put them in a good field where there is plenty of pasture, and they will be law-abiding cattle to the end of time. The human animal is just like the rest of the animals, only a little more so. The same thing that governs in the one governs in the other.

Everybody makes his living along the lines of least resistance. A wise man who comes into a country early sees a great undeveloped land. For instance, our rich men twenty-five years ago saw that Chicago was small and knew a lot of people would come here and settle, and they readily saw that if they had all the land around here it would be worth a good deal, so they grabbed the land. You cannot be a landlord because somebody has got it all. You must find some other calling. In England and Ireland and Scotland less than five percent own all the land there is, and the people are bound to stay there on any kind of terms the landlords give. They must live the best they can, so they develop all these various professions—burglary, picking pockets and the like.

Again, people find all sorts of ways of getting rich. These are diseases like everything else. You look at people getting rich, organizing trusts, and making a million dollars, and somebody gets the disease and he starts out. He catches it just as a man catches the mumps or the measles; he is not to blame, it is in the air. You will find men speculating beyond their means, because the mania of money-getting is taking possession of them. It is simply a disease; nothing more, nothing less. You cannot avoid catching it; but the fellows who have control of the earth have the advantage of you. See what the law is; when these men get control of things, they make the laws. They do not make the laws to protect anybody; courts are not instruments of justice; when your case gets into court it will make little difference whether you are guilty or innocent; but it's better if you have a smart lawyer. And you cannot have a smart lawyer unless you have money. First and last it's a question of money. Those men who own the earth make the laws to protect what they have. They fix up a sort of fence or pen around what they have, and they fix the law so the fellow on the outside cannot get in. The laws are really organized for the protection of the men who rule the world. They were never organized or enforced to do justice. We have no system for doing justice, not the slightest in the world.

Let me illustrate: Take the poorest person in this room. If the community had provided a system of doing justice the poorest person in this room would have as good a lawyer as the richest, would he not? When you went into court you would have just as long a trial, and just as fair a trial as the richest person in Chicago. Your case would not be tried in fifteen or twenty minutes, whereas it would take fifteen days to get through with a rich man's case.

Then if you were rich and were beaten your case would be taken to the Appellate Court. A poor man cannot take his case to the Appellate Court; he has not the price; and then to the Supreme Court, and if he were beaten there he might perhaps go to the United States Supreme Court. And he might die of old age before he got into jail. If you are poor, it's a quick job. You are almost known to be guilty, else you would not be there. Why should anyone be in the criminal court if he were not guilty? He would not be there if he could be anywhere else. The officials have no time to look after these cases. The people who are on the outside, who are running banks and building churches and making jails, they have no time to examine 600 or 700 prisoners each year to see whether they are guilty or innocent. If the courts were organized to promote justice the people would elect somebody to defend all these criminals, somebody as smart as the prosecutor—and give him as many detectives and as many assistants to help, and pay as much money to defend you as to prosecute you. We have a very able man for State's Attorney, and he has many assistants, detectives and policemen without end, and judges to hear the cases—everything handy.

Most of our criminal code consists in offenses against property. People are sent to jail because they have committed a crime against property. It is of very little consequence whether one hundred people more or less go to jail who ought not to go—you must protect property, because in this world property is of more importance than anything else.

How is it done? These people who have property fix it so they can protect what they have. When somebody commits a crime it does not follow that he has done something that is morally wrong. The man on the outside who has committed no crime may have done something. For instance: to take all the coal in the United States and raise the price two dollars or three dollars when there is no need of it, and thus kills thousands of babies and send thousands of people to the poorhouse and tens of thousands to jail, as is done every year in the United States—this is a greater crime than all the people in our jails ever committed, but the law does not punish it. Why? Because the fellows who control the earth make the laws. If you and I had the making of the laws, the first thing we would do would be to punish the fellow who gets control of the earth. Nature put this coal in the ground for me as well as for them and nature made the prairies up here to raise wheat for me as well as for them, and then the great railroad companies came along and fenced it up.

Most all of the crimes for which we are punished are property crimes. There are a few personal crimes, like murder—but they are very few. The crimes committed are mostly against property. If this punishment is right the criminals must have a lot of property. How much money is there in this crowd? And yet you are all here for crimes against property. The people up and down the Lake Shore have not committed crime, still they have so much property they don't know what to do with it. It is perfectly plain why these people have not committed crimes against property; they make the laws and therefore do not need to break them. And in order for you to get some property you are obliged to break the rules of the game. I don't know but what some of you may have had a very nice chance to get rich by carrying the hod for one dollar a day, twelve hours. Instead of taking that nice, easy profession, you are a burglar. If you had been given a chance to be a banker you would rather follow that. Some of you may have had a chance to work as a switchman on a railroad where you know, according to statistics, that you cannot live and keep all your limbs more than seven years, and you get fifty dollars a month for taking your lives in your hands, and instead of taking that lucrative position you choose to be a sneak thief, or something like that. Some of you made that sort of [choice]. I don't know which I would take if I was reduced to this choice. I have an easier choice.

I will guarantee to take from this jail, or any jail in the world, five hundred men who have been the worst criminals and law breakers who ever got into jail, and I will go down to our lowest streets and take five hundred of the most hardened prostitutes, and go out somewhere where there is plenty of land, and will give them a chance to make a living, and they will be as good people as the average in the community.

There is a remedy for the sort of condition we see here. The world never finds it out, or when it does find it out it does not enforce it. You may pass a law punishing every person with death for burglary, and it will make no difference. Men will commit it just the same. In England there was a time when one hundred different offenses were punishable with death, and it made no difference. The English people strangely found out that so fast as they repealed the severe penalties and so fast as they did away with punishing men by death, crime decreased instead of increased; that the smaller the penalty the fewer the crimes.

Hanging men in our county jails does not prevent murder. It makes murderers.

And this has been the history of the world. It's easy to see how to do away with what we call crime. It is not so easy to do it. I will tell you how to do it. It can be done by giving the people a chance to live—by destroying special privileges. So long as big criminals can get the coal fields, so long as the big criminals have control of the city council and get the public streets for street cars and gas rights, this is bound to send thousands of poor people to jail. So long as men are allowed to monopolize all the earth, and compel others to live on such terms as these men see fit to make, then you are bound to get into jail.

The only way in the world to abolish crime and criminals is to abolish the big ones and the little ones together. Make fair conditions of life. Give men a chance to live. Abolish the right of private ownership of land, abolish monopoly, make the world partners in production, partners in the good things of life. Nobody would steal if he could get something of his own some easier way. Nobody will commit burglary when he has a house full. No girl will go out on the streets when she has a comfortable place at home. The man who owns a sweatshop or a department store may not be to blame himself for the condition of his girls, but when he pays them five dollars, three dollars, and two dollars a week, I wonder where he thinks they will get the rest of their money to live. The only way to cure these conditions is by equality. There should be no jails. They do not accomplish what they pretend to accomplish. If you would wipe them out, there would be no more criminals than now. They terrorize nobody. They are a blot upon civilization, and a jail is an evidence of the lack of charity of the people on the outside who make the jails and fill them with the victims of their greed.

SUPPLEMENTARY SELECTION

CLARENCE DARROW, "WHY I AM AN AGNOSTIC"
An address delivered as part of a public symposium
on belief held in Columbus, Ohio, and published in
*Why I Am an Agnostic, Including Expressions of Faith
from a Protestant, a Catholic, and a Jew* (1929)

An agnostic is a doubter.... In a popular way, in the Western world, an agnostic is one who doubts or disbelieves the main tenets of the Christian faith.

I would say that belief in at least three tenets is necessary to the faith of a Christian: a belief in God, a belief in immortality, and a belief in a supernatural book. Various Christian sects require much more, but it is difficult to imagine that one could be a Christian, under any intelligent meaning of the word, with less....

I am an agnostic as to the question of God.... The Christian says that the universe could not make itself; that there must have been some higher power to call it into being.... To say that God made the universe gives us no explanation of the beginning of things. If we are told that God made the universe, the question immediately arises: Who made God? Did he always exist, or was there some power back of that? Did he create matter out of nothing, or is his existence coextensive with matter? The problem is still there. What is the origin of it all? If, on the other hand, one says that the universe was not made by God, that it always existed, he has the same difficulty to confront. To say that the universe was here last year, or millions of years ago, does not explain its origin. This is still a mystery. As to the question of the origin of things, many can only wonder and doubt and guess.

As to the existence of the soul, all people may either believe or disbelieve. Everyone knows the origin of the human being. They know that it came from a single cell in the body of the mother, and that the cell was one out of ten thousand in the mother's body. Before gestation the cell must have been fertilized by a spermatozoon from the body of the father. This was one out of perhaps a billion spermatozoa that was the capacity of the father. When the cell is fertilized a chemical process begins. The cell divides and multiplies and increases into millions of cells, and finally a child is born. Cells die and are born during the life of the individual until they finally drop apart, and this is death.

If there is a soul, what is it, and where did it come from, and where does it go? Can anyone who is guided by his reason possibly imagine a soul independent of a body, or the place of its residence, or the character of it, or anything concerning it? If man is justified in any belief or disbelief on any subject, he is warranted in the disbelief in a soul. Not one scrap of evidence exists to prove any such impossible thing.

Many Christians base the belief of a soul and God upon the Bible. Strictly speaking, there is no such book. To make the Bible sixty-six books are bound into one volume. These books were written by many people at difference times, and no one knows the time or the identity of any author. Some of the books were written by several authors at various times. These books contain all sorts of contradictory concepts of life and morals and the origin of things. Between the first and the last nearly a thousand years intervened; a longer time than has passed since the discovery of America by Columbus....

Can any rational person believe that the Bible is anything but a human document? We now know pretty well where the various books came from, and about when they were written. We know that they were written by human beings who had no knowledge of science, little knowledge of life, and were influenced by the barbarous morality of primitive times, and were grossly ignorant of most things that men know today. For instance, Genesis says that God made the earth, and he made the sun to light the day and the moon to light the night, and in one clause disposes of the stars by saying that "he made the stars also." This was plainly written by someone who had no conception of the stars. Man, by the aid of his telescope, has looked out into the heavens and found stars whose diameter is as great as the distance between the earth and the sun. We now know that the universe is filled with stars and suns and planets and systems. Every new telescope looking further into the heavens only discovers more and more worlds and suns and systems in the endless reaches of space. The men who wrote Genesis believed, of course, that this tiny speck of mud that we call the Earth was the center of the universe, the only world in space, and made for man who was the only being worth considering. These men believed that the stars were only a little way above the earth, and were set in the firmament for man to look at, and for nothing else. Everyone today knows that this conception is not true....

The reasons for agnosticism and skepticism are abundant and compelling. Fantastic and foolish and impossible consequences are freely claimed for the belief in religion. All the civilization of any period is put down as a result of religion. All the cruelty and error and ignorance of the period has no relation to religion. The truth is that the origin of what we call civilization is not due to religion, but to skepticism. So long as men accepted miracles without question, so long as they believed in original sin and the road to salvation—so long as they believed in a hell where man would be kept for eternity on account of Eve, there was no reason whatever for civilization; life was short, and eternity was long, and the business of life was preparation for eternity. When every event was a miracle, when there was no order or system or law, there was no occasion for studying any subject, or being interested in anything except a religion which took care of the soul. As man doubted the primitive conceptions about religion, and no longer accepted the literal, miraculous teachings of ancient books, he set himself to understand nature. We no longer cure disease by casting out devils. Since that time, men have studied the human body, have built hospitals and treated illness in a scientific way. Science is responsible for the building of railroads and bridges, of steamships, of telegraph lines, of cities, towns, large buildings and small, plumbing and sanitation, of the food supply, and the countless thousands of useful things that we now deem necessary to life. Without skepticism and doubt, none of these things could have been given to the world.

The fear of God is not the beginning of wisdom. The fear of God is the death of wisdom. Skepticism and doubt lead to study and investigation, and investigation is the beginning of wisdom.

The modern world is the child of doubt and inquiry, as the ancient world was the child of fear and faith.

SUPPLEMENTARY SELECTION

CLARENCE DARROW, "THE RIGHT OF REVOLUTION"
A widely reprinted extract from a longer address, "The Rights and Wrongs of Ireland," delivered at Central Music Hall, Chicago, Illinois, November 23, 1895

Darrow's address marked the anniversary of the public hanging in 1867 of the so-called Manchester Martyrs, three Irish men convicted in Manchester, England, for killing a British police guard in the course of freeing two captured Fenian revolutionaries.

The right of revolution is planted in the heart of man; it is born of the dignity that causes him to feel his personality and defend his right to a free and independent life; it is nurtured and aided by the unjust oppression that comes from without. Except for this, it would have no chance to grow. . . . All the conspirators and agitators of the world, if left free to speak and act and plan, could not produce a respectable rebellion in the smallest kingdom of the world unless the time was ripe. And all the armies and policemen of the earth could not hold one in check when the time has come. . . .

The world is changing; laws and systems are being tried as they never were before. The spirit of freedom is abroad today upon the earth. Germany is a great military camp, but the tramp of her armed soldiers is lost in the cry of her workmen for the right to live. France is being shaken by a revolution of thought more powerful and logical than that which marked the last century's close. Tyrannical Russia, with all her arbitrary powers, and despotic, cruel force, cannot make the life of the czar safe in his own domain; and the poor, outraged political prisoner in the Siberian mine is greater and better, and more powerful in the world of thought and action than the proudest Cossack, whose iron heel rests on the peasant's neck. England, Italy, Spain, Austria and the Netherlands are struggling with this rising mass of discontent, that demands a portion of the earth and the right to live and breathe....

But these reflections must concern us most as they apply to our own native or adopted land. Most of us, I hope, are patriots; patriots not in the meaning in which that word is chiefly used today. The ordinary fair-weather patriot goes out upon the street corners, and in public places, and proclaims his love for American institutions as a cloak for the support of the existing wrongs, which make him rich and great; he uses his patriotism, as he does the other tools with which he plies his trade; patriotism to him does not mean devotion to his country and the people's highest good, but a blind, unthinking worship of the things that are; the constitution and the laws, to him, are to be either enforced or broken as it may profit at the time; his is the patriotism that flies an American flag from the schoolhouse, and sacrifices the most vital and fundamental principles of liberty for gain....

The patriotism that is worthy of a place in any human heart takes little account of mountains and rivers and forests or of boundary lines, but makes much of the men and women and children of the earth. It loves that country best where freedom is the broadest and opportunity the greatest. It holds fast to all the old guarantees of liberty and ever strives to break down the walls and restrictions of the past. It looks eagerly forward to the time when forts and garrisons, swords and cannons, militias and standing armies, shall no longer disgrace the earth. It longs for the day when nations and individuals shall learn that peace is more profitable and glorious than war; when the walls and boundaries and restrictions which divide nation from nation, and man from man, shall fade like a cruel dream of the past, and liberty and order shall prevail on earth.

America has furnished a bright example of the beneficence of liberty and the wisdom of opportunity. The fathers here established freedom on the broadest plain the world had ever known, and the wide prairies and rich mountains, unfenced and unowned, gave all a chance to obtain the full reward that should ever come to toil. All the nations of the earth sent their disinherited to find a home, and flowing from liberty and opportunity they built here a nation that was the wonder of the world. All the greatness of America, all her marvelous wealth, all the wonders that her short national life can show, are a monument to the wisdom of liberty and the power of opportunity. Wealth has been ever owned by the few and produced by the many; but no nation could create it as we once did unless every workman felt the inspiration that can only come through hope....

In these changing times we have no right to close our eyes to the dangers and responsibilities of the day. No era of the world has ever witnessed such a rapid concentration of wealth and power as the one in which we live. This is no doubt due to the invention of new machinery for the production and distribution of the world's wealth. But while history furnishes no parallel to the rapid centralization of today, it furnishes abundant lessons of the inevitable result that must follow in its path. As liberty produces wealth, and wealth destroys liberty, so power and tyranny have within themselves the seeds of their own destruction. In Rome every function of government was controlled by the rich and strong. After a time the legislature, the courts, the police and finally the army refused to serve this class unless they received a constantly larger contribution from those who had obtained all the empire's wealth. When the levy of blackmail had commenced, the beginning of the end had come.

Injustice, oppression and wrong may always live, but they cannot exist forever in one form or place; and when the evils are great enough, in some way the end will come. With the land and possessions of America rapidly passing into the hands of a favored few; with great corporations taking the place of individual effort; with the small shops going down before the great factories and department stores; with thousands of men and women in idleness and want; with wages constantly tending to a lower level; with the number of women and children rapidly increasing in factory and store; with the sight of thousands of children forced into involuntary slavery at the tender age that should find them at home or in the school; with courts sending men to jail without trial by jury, for daring to refuse to work; with bribery and corruption openly charged, constantly reiterated by the press, and universally believed; and above all and more than all, with the knowledge that the servants of the people, elected to correct abuses, are bought and sold in legislative halls at the bidding of corporations and individuals; with all these notorious evils sapping the foundations of popular government and destroying personal liberty, some rude awakening must come. And if it shall come in the lightning and tornado of civil war, the same as forty years ago, when you then look abroad over the ruin and desolation, remember the long years in which the storm was rising, and do not blame the thunderbolt.

SUPPLEMENTARY SELECTION

CLARENCE DARROW, "THE PROBLEM OF THE NEGRO"
A stenographic report of an address delivered in Chicago to the Men's
Forum, an African-American men's club, May 19, 1901

Probably I do not look at the race problem in as hopeful a way as many of your people do, and I fear that much I shall say this evening will appear discouraging and pessimistic, for I am somewhat pessimistic about the white race, to say nothing about the colored race; when I see how anxious the white race is to go to war over nothing, and to shoot down men in cold blood for the benefit of trade, I am pessimistic about the white race, and when I see the injustice everywhere present and how the colored race are particularly subjected to that injustice and oppression I admit that I am pessimistic as to the future of the colored race, and fear the dreams we have indulged in of perfect equality and of unlimited opportunity are a long way from any realization; but unless we approach these subjects from the right standpoint and go along the right path there is no prospect of ever reaching a right solution....

We hear people say that it is necessary to lynch a Negro in the South, and even to burn a Negro in the South to protect white women, and you find some good, Christian people defending the lynching of Negroes, and even the burning of Negroes in the South, because it is necessary, and I presume they open some of these lynchings with prayer. I do not know why they should not; they defend them.

Now, I do not object to lynchings on account of lynchings especially. We do not always arrive at exact justice in our courts of law; you are not sure because you go through a court that you get at the truth, and I presume that a court organized on the spot, as a body of lynchers are organized, is perhaps quite as apt to get at the truth as a court of justice where lawyers are hired to work a long while to prove that the guilty man is innocent and the innocent man is guilty. I am not especially opposed to the lynchings of Negroes in the South because they do not get a fair trial. A poor man does not get a fair trial anywhere. But this is what I object to: I object to lynching a man because he is a Negro. These men in the South are not lynched because they have committed this crime; they are lynched because the Lord painted their faces black. If the Southern people or the Northern people would enter into an agreement and would stand by it, by which they would try every black man who assaults a white woman by lynch law, and at the same time try every white man who assaults a black woman by lynch law, I would say, "Well and good, we will stand by it." I do not believe in hanging anybody, much less do I believe in burning anybody, but above all things else I believe in equality between all people, no hypocrisy; treat everybody alike, and if the Southern gentlemen, or the Northern gentlemen, believe it is necessary to build bonfires to burn colored men for assaulting white women, well and good, but let them also build bonfires to burn white men for assaulting colored women; treat them all alike. These reasons that are given are excuses, hypocritical excuses, which are not true, and which they know are not true. These lynchings in the South and these burnings in the South are not for the protection of the home and the fireside; they are to keep the Negroes in their place. Of course here and there they are done under some provocation. Crimes are being committed always, everywhere, by whites and blacks, but these particular instances are different. When the offenders are Negroes, or are supposed to be Negroes, then they send out to all the world telling what a dangerous class of citizens these poor unfortunate men and women are....

Now, the South never means to recognize any such thing as social equality between the blacks and the whites, and every single year that passes by there are more and more people in the North who do not propose to recognize any social equality between the blacks and the whites. There are more and more people in the North who propose to say, and who do say that the Negro is one kind of being and the white man is another....

Some time ago I was talking with one of the large employers of labor in Chicago, and he said he liked the colored people, because they are so loyal, they are loyal to you, they will stick to you and they don't "strike." "Well," I said, "are you loyal to them?" Well, he answered, as loyal as he could be. I suggested to him that I had seen men like him, and read of other men like him, and that I had noticed when a body of miners left the mines and struck that they would send South and import a lot of Negroes, and when the strike was over would turn the Negroes loose and send them back again. But here was a man who really said he liked the colored man. Now, he did not. He liked their labor because they worked cheap and they did not have spunk enough to strike; he liked them because they had been slaves and they were still; they still bore the attitude of slavery, and it would be very strange if a race should come up from what you people have come and not in a measure bear the stamp of slavery; it should not be expected that you should be otherwise—and here this man liked colored laborers because he could get them at his own price, and if they did not like the price they would take it anyhow and would not strike.

Now these are the sort of friends that you people have among the rich of the North. Now, let us see what can be done for all of this. It is comparatively easy to tell what is wrong; it is not so easy to say what you are going to do about it, and I am not at all sure of my position on these questions.

NOTA

The path before the colored race is very long and very hard.... This race question can never be finally settled excepting upon one principle, and that is, that all people are equal, that every human being on the earth, white and black and yellow, men and women, are entitled to the same rights, to perfect social equality, and perfect opportunity, the one with the other. It can never be finally settled upon any compromise whatever. Every man must recognize the right of his brother and his sister upon the earth upon equal terms with himself and these people who believe, or profess to believe, in the Christian religion, and believe the Lord has made our souls all alike, show they do not believe it when they say that the Lord has made one set masters and the other slaves. This question may be settled in a hundred years, it may be settled in ten thousand years, but if it is not settled for a million years it will never be settled until every human being is the peer of every other human being, and until nobody will dream of asking the color of your skin, or where you were born, or what is your religion, but will simply ask what are you, and nothing else in the world.

I have no confidence in any plan for improving any class of people that does not teach man his own integrity and worth; you must make each man and each woman understand that they are the peer of any human being on earth. You must respect yourselves or nobody will respect you. No black man, no working man, no red man, ever ought for one single moment to think of himself as being inferior to any human being who treads the earth, no matter who that is. He may be compelled to take an inferior position because he needs to live, and the strong may starve him if he does not, but he ought to carry within his own breast the consciousness that after all he is equal to any man who lives, and if he does not carry that feeling within his breast, then he is not the equal of any man that lives.

And the colored race should learn this: If the white race insults you on account of your inferior position then they also degrade themselves when they do it. Every time a superior person who has position invades the rights and liberties and the dignity of an inferior person, he degrades himself, he retards and debases his own manhood, when he does it. You may be obliged many times to submit to this, but it must always be with the mental reservation that you know you are their equal, or you know that you are their superior, and you suffer the indignity because you are compelled to suffer it, as your fathers were once compelled to do, but after all, your soul is free and you believe in yourself, you believe in your right to live and to be the equal of every human being on the earth.... No people ever were given their liberty from their superiors; you must get it by your own worth, by your own perseverance and by your own work. Nobody will come to boost you up; it is only here and there that some person, out of a feeling of justice, will help you, but you must fight this battle out yourself, many of you must suffer, and many of you must die before the victory will be won.... You have got to help yourself to make the most of every opportunity, and some time, when I do not know, or how, or where, but some time, there will be perfect equality on the earth.

CHAPTER 2

Opening Statements and

Trial Arguments

Autobiographical Introduction

From Clarence Darrow, *The Story of My Life*,
Chapter 9, "How I Fell" (1932)

In 1894 I opened an office and went into private practice. Neither then nor for any considerable time thereafter did I need to worry over business prospects. For many years my practice covered almost all sorts of litigation. When I began, it was with the intention of trying only civil cases. But no one controls his own destiny, and lawyers are no exception to that rule.

I was willing to undertake the injunction case brought by the railroad companies in behalf of the government against Mr. Debs and his associates, or, brought by the government in behalf of the railroad companies, whichever way one chooses to put it. How one puts it depends on how he views public questions. I had never had anything to do with criminal cases, and, like most other lawyers, did not want to take them. But Mr. Debs insisted that I should defend him, so I undertook the case. Naturally the trial attracted a great deal of attention throughout the country, and, as it resulted in victory for the accused, I was asked to enter other labor cases, and criminal cases as well.

Soon afterward I assumed the defense of Thomas I. Kidd, president of the National Association of Wood Workers, and others along with him, all charged with conspiracy, growing out of a strike in the large sash-and-door factories of Oshkosh, Wisconsin. As in all places outside of big cities and industrial centres, the feeling was very bitter on both sides. The division was, as always, the rich of the community on one side and the workers on the other. The case was reported pretty closely by the newspapers of the Northwest, and the fight was intense and long drawn out. I shall not go into the details of this prosecution. It was one of the earliest conspiracy charges against working men growing out of strikes. The jury was drawn from people of all stations, but after short deliberation they returned a verdict of "Not guilty."

From then on I was very busy with all sorts of litigation: labor cases, strikes, condemnation, chancery, criminal cases, and many contests that were submitted to arbitration. I entered my first criminal case in the attitude of the "good" lawyer—the lawyer who attends all the Bar Association meetings and so gravitates as rapidly as he can to the defense of Big Business. The tragedies, the sorrow and despair that were present in the criminal court I knew nothing of, and did not want to know. A verdict of "Not guilty" or a disagreement had been viewed by me as by the general public as a miscarriage of justice and a reflection on the jury system. The jail was a place spoken of as we sometimes mention a leper colony.

Criminal cases receive the attention of the press. The cruel and disagreeable things of life are more apt to get the newspaper space than the pleasant ones. It must be that most people enjoy hearing of and reading about the troubles of others. Perhaps men unconsciously feel that they rise in the general level as others go down. By no effort of mine, more and more of the distressed and harassed and pursued came fleeing to my office door. What could I do to change the situation? I was not responsible for my peculiar organism. It was due to a certain arrangement of cells in which I had no choice that made it impossible to deny help to those in trouble and pain, if I could see or find a way to give them aid. It was really my lively imagination which put me in the other fellow's place and made me suffer with him; so I only relieved him to help myself. Strange as it may seem, I grew to like to defend men and women charged with crime. It soon came to be something more than winning or losing a case. I sought to learn why one man goes one way and another takes an entirely different road. I became vitally interested in the causes of human conduct. This meant more than the quibbling with lawyers and juries, to get or keep money for a client so that I could take part of what I won or saved for him: I was dealing with life, with its hopes and fears, its aspirations and despairs. With me it was going to the foundation of motive and conduct and adjustments for human beings, instead of blindly talking of hatred and vengeance, and that subtle, indefinable quality that men call "justice" and of which nothing really is known....

MAIN SELECTION

FROM *THE STATE OF TENNESSEE V. JOHN THOMAS SCOPES*,
CIRCUIT COURT OF RHEA COUNTY,
DAYTON, TENNESSEE, JULY 13, 1925

Statement in support of a motion to quash the indictment of John Scopes

Earlier in 1925, Tennessee had enacted a statute making it unlawful for any public school teacher "to teach any theory that denies the Story of Divine Creation of man as taught in the Bible, and to teach instead that man has descended from a lower order of animal." The ACLU instigated State v. Scopes *as a means to test the statute's validity under state law by orchestrating the indictment of Dayton, Tennessee, science teacher John Scopes, who had agreed in advance to the arrangement. Along with several leading attorneys from New York City, Darrow volunteered his services for Scopes's defense. He made the following argument on the second day of the eight-day trial. Scopes was convicted of violating the statute, but his conviction was later overturned by the Tennessee Supreme Court.*

This case we have to argue is a case at law, and hard as it is for me to bring my mind to conceive it, almost impossible as it is to put my mind back into the sixteenth century, I am going to argue it as if it was serious, and as if it was a death struggle between two civilizations.

Let us see, now, what there is about it. We have been informed that the legislature has the right to prescribe the course of study in the public schools. Within reason, they no doubt have, no doubt. They could not prescribe it, I am inclined to think, under your [state] constitution, if it omitted arithmetic and geography and writing, neither under the rest of the constitution, if it shall remain in force in the state, could they prescribe it if the course of study was only to teach religion, because several hundred years ago, when our people believed in freedom, and when no men felt so sure of their own sophistry that they were willing to send a man to jail who did not believe them, the people of Tennessee adopted a constitution, and they made it broad and plain, and said that the people of Tennessee should always enjoy religious freedom in its broadest terms, so I assume that no legislature could fix a course of study which violated that. For instance, suppose the legislature should say, we think the religious privileges and duties of the citizens of Tennessee are much more important than education, we agree with the distinguished governor of the state, if religion must go, or learning must go, why, let learning go. I do not know how much it would have to go, but let it go, and therefore we will establish a course in the public schools of teaching that the Christian religion, as unfolded in the Bible, is true, and that every other religion, or mode or system of ethics, is false, and to carry that out, no person in the public schools shall be permitted to read or hear anything except Genesis, *Pilgrim's Progress*, Baxter's *Saint's Rest*, and [William Jennings Bryan's] *In His Image*. Would that be constitutional? If it is, the constitution is a lie and a snare and the people have forgot what liberty means.

I remember, long ago, Mr. Bancroft wrote this sentence, which is true: "That it is all right to preserve freedom in constitutions, but when the spirit of freedom has fled from the hearts of the people, then its matter is easily sacrificed under law." And so it is. Unless there is left enough of the spirit of freedom in the state of Tennessee, and in the United States, there is not a single line of any constitution that can withstand bigotry and ignorance when it seeks to destroy the rights of the individual; and bigotry and ignorance are ever active. Here, we find today as brazen and as bold an attempt to destroy learning as was ever made in the Middle Ages, and the only difference is we have not provided that they shall be burned at the stake, but there is time for that, Your Honor, we have to approach these things gradually.

Now, let us see what we claim with reference to this law. If this proceeding, both in form and substance, can prevail in this court, then Your Honor, no law—no matter how foolish, wicked, ambiguous, or ancient, but can come back to Tennessee. All the guarantees go for nothing. All of the past has gone, will be forgotten, if this can succeed.

I am going to begin with some of the simpler reasons why it is absolutely absurd to think that this statute, indictment, or any part of the proceedings in this case are legal, and I think the sooner we get rid of it in Tennessee the better for the peace of Tennessee, and the better for the pursuit of knowledge in the world, so let me begin at the beginning....

What is this law? What does it mean? Help out the caption and read the law. "Be it enacted by the general assembly of the state of Tennessee that it shall be unlawful for any teacher in any of the universities, normals and all the public schools in the state which are supported in whole or in part by public school funds of the state, to teach any theory that denies the conception of the divine creation of man as put [forth] in the Bible and teach in its stead that man is descended from a lower order of animal."

The statute should be comprehensible. It should not be written in Chinese anyway. It should be in passing English, as you say, so that common human beings would understand what it meant, and so a man would know whether he is liable to go to jail when he is teaching—not so ambiguous as to be a snare or a trap to get someone who does not agree with you. It should be plain, simple and easy. Does this statute state what you shall teach and what you shall not? Oh, no! Oh, no! Not at all. Does it say you cannot teach the earth is round? Because Genesis says it is flat? No. Does it say you cannot teach that the earth is millions of ages old, because the account in Genesis makes it less than six thousand years old? Oh, no. It doesn't state that. If it did you could understand it. It says you shan't teach any theory of the origin of man that is contrary to the divine theory contained in the Bible.

Now let us pass up the word "divine"! No legislature is strong enough in any state in the Union to characterize and pick any book as being divine. Let us take it as it is. What is the Bible? Your Honor, I have read it myself. I might read it more or more wisely. Others may understand it better. Others may think they understand it better when they do not. But in a general way I know what it is. I know there are millions of people in the world who look on it as being a divine book, and I have not the slightest objection to it. I know there are millions of people in the world who derive consolation in their times of trouble and solace in times of distress from the Bible. I would be pretty near the last one in the world to do anything or take any action to take it away. I feel just exactly the same toward the religious creed of every human being who lives. If anybody finds anything in this life that brings them consolation and health and happiness I think they ought to have it, whatever they get. I haven't any fault to find with them at all. But what is it? The Bible is not one book. The Bible is made up of sixty-six books written over a period of about one thousand years, some of them very early and some of them comparatively late. It is a book primarily of religion and morals. It is not a book of science. Never was and was never meant to be. Under it there is nothing prescribed that would tell you how to build a railroad or a steamboat or to make anything that would advance civilization. It is not a textbook or a text on chemistry. It is not big enough to be. It is not a book on geology; they knew nothing about geology. It is not a book on biology; they knew nothing about it. It is not a work on evolution; that is a mystery. It is not a work on astronomy. The man who looked out at the universe and studied the heavens had no thought but that the earth was the center of the universe. But we know better than that. We know that the sun is the center of the solar system. And that there are an infinity of other systems around about us. They thought the sun went around the earth and gave us light and gave us night. We know better. We know the earth turns on its axis to produce days and nights. They thought the earth was created 4,004 years before the Christian Era. We know better. I doubt if there is a person in Tennessee who does not know better. They told it the best they knew. And while [science] may change all you may learn of chemistry, geometry and mathematics, there are no doubt certain primitive, elemental instincts in the organs of man that remain the same: He finds out what he can and yearns to know more and supplements his knowledge with hope and faith.

That is the province of religion and I haven't the slightest fault to find with it. Not the slightest in the world. One has one thought and one another, and instead of fighting each other as in the past, they should support and help each other. Let's see now. Can Your Honor tell what is given as the origin of man as shown in the Bible? Is there any human being who can tell us? There are two conflicting accounts in the first two chapters. There are scattered all through it various acts and ideas, but to pass that up for the sake of argument no teacher in any school in the state of Tennessee can know that he is violating a law, but must test every one of its doctrines by the Bible, must he not? You cannot say two times two equals four or a man is an educated man if evolution is forbidden. It does not specify what you cannot teach, but says you cannot teach anything that conflicts with the Bible. Then just imagine making it a criminal code that is so uncertain and impossible that every man must be sure that he has read everything in the Bible and not only read it but understands it, or he might violate the criminal code. Who is the chief mogul that can tell us what the Bible means? He or they should write a book and make it plain and distinct, so we would know. Let us look at it. There are in America at least five hundred different sects or churches, all of which quarrel with each other and the importance and nonimportance of certain things or the construction of certain passages. All along the line they do not agree among themselves and cannot agree among themselves. They never have and probably never will. There is a great division between the Catholics and the Protestants. There is such a disagreement that my client, who is a school teacher, not only must know the subject he is teaching, but he must know everything about the Bible in reference to evolution. And he must be sure that he expresses his right or else some fellow will come along here, more ignorant perhaps than he, and say, "You made a bad guess and I think you have committed a crime." No criminal statute can rest that way. There is not a chance for it, for this criminal statute and every criminal statute must be plain and simple. If Mr. Scopes is to be indicted and prosecuted because he taught a wrong theory of the origin of life, why not tell him what he must teach. Why not say that you must teach that man was made of the dust; and still stranger, not directly from the dust, without taking any chances on it whatever, that Eve was made out of Adam's rib. You will know what I am talking about.

Now my client must be familiar with the whole book, and must know all about all of these warring sects of Christians and know which of them is right and which wrong, in order that he will not commit crime. Nothing was heard of all that until the fundamentalists got into Tennessee. I trust that when they prosecute their wildly made charge upon the intelligence of some other sect they may modify this mistake and state in simple language what was the account contained in the Bible that could not be taught. So, unless other sects have something to do with it, we must know just what we are charged with doing. This statute, I say, Your Honor, is indefinite and uncertain. No man could obey it, no court could enforce it and it is bad for indefiniteness and uncertainty. Look at that indictment up there. If there is a good indictment I never saw a bad one. Now, I do not expect, your Honor, my opinion to go because it is my opinion, because I am like all lawyers who practice law; I have made mistakes in my judgment of law. I will probably make more of them. I insist that you might just as well hand my client a piece of blank paper and then send the sheriff after him to jail him. Let me read this indictment.

I am reading from a newspaper. I forget what newspaper it was, but am sure it was right: "That John Thomas Scopes on April, 1925, did unlawfully and willfully teach in the public schools of Rhea

County, Tennessee, which public schools are supported in part and in whole"—I don't know how that is possible, but we will pass that up—"in part or in whole by the public school funds of the state a certain theory and theories that deny the story of the divine creation of man as taught in the Bible and did teach instead thereof that man is descended from a lower order of animals." Now then, there is something that is very elementary. That is one of them and very elementary, because the constitution of Tennessee provides and the constitution of pretty near every other state in the United States provide that an indictment must state in sufficient terms so that a man may be apprised of what is going to be the character of charge against him. My friend the attorney-general says that John Scopes knows what he is here for. Yes, I know what he is here for, because the fundamentalists are after everybody that thinks. I know why he is here. I know he is here because ignorance and bigotry are rampant, and it is a mighty strong combination, your Honor, it makes him fearful. But the state is bringing him here by indictment, and several things must be stated in the indictment; indictments must state facts, not law nor conclusions of law. It is all well enough to show that the indictment is good if it charges the offense in the language of the statute. In our state of Illinois, if one man kills another with malice aforethought, he would be guilty of murder, but an indictment would not be good that said John Jones killed another. It would not be good. It must tell more about it and how. It is not enough in this indictment to say that John Scopes taught something contrary to the divine account written by Moses—maybe— that is not enough. There are several reasons for it. First, it is good and right to know. Secondly, after the shooting is all over here and Scopes has paid his fine if he can raise his money, or has gone to jail if he cannot, somebody else will come along and indict him over again. But there is one thing I cannot account for, that is the hatred and the venom and feeling and the very strong religious combination. That I never could account for. There are a lot of things I cannot account for. Somebody may come along next week and indict him again, on the first indictment. It must be so plain that a second case will never occur. He can say to him, "I have cleared that off."

He can file a plea that he has already been put in jeopardy and convicted and paid the fine, so you cannot do it over again. There is no question about that, Your Honor, in the slightest and the books are full of them. I have examined, I think, all the criminal cases in Tennessee on this point. I don't like to speak with too much assurance, because sometimes you get held up on such a thing, but I assume that if they have got anything on the other side I would have heard from them, and I have, with the aid of my assistants and helpers, they doing most of the work, I have examined most all of them, and if there is another indictment in Tennessee like it I haven't found it, and plenty of indictments have been declared void in Tennessee because they did not tell us anything—plenty of them. I do not think there ever was another one like it in Tennessee, and I am not referring to the subject matter now because I know there never was, as far as the subject matter goes, but I am speaking of the form of it. Now, Mr. Scopes, on April 24 did unlawfully and willfully teach in a public school of Rhea County, Tennessee, which public school is supported in whole or in part by the public school fund of the state, certain theories that deny the story of the divine creation of man. What did he teach? What did he teach? Who is it that can tell us that John Scopes taught certain theories that denied the story of the divine—the divine story of creation as recorded in the Bible. How did he know what textbooks did he teach from? Who did he teach? Why did he teach? Not a word—all is silent. He taught, oh yes, the place mentioned is Rhea County. Well, that is some county—Maybe all over it, I don't know where he taught, he might have taught in a half a dozen schools in Rhea County on the one day and if he is indicted next year after this trial is over, if it is, for teaching in District No. 1, in Rhea County, he cannot plead that he has already been convicted, because this was over here in another district and at another place. What did he teach? What was the horrible thing he taught that was in conflict with Moses and what is it that is not in conflict with Moses? What shouldn't he have taught? What is the account contained in the Bible which he ignored, when he taught the doctrine of evolution which is taught by every—believed by every scientific man on earth. Joshua made the sun stand still. The fundamentalists will make the ages roll back. He should have been informed by the indictment what was the doctrine he should have taught and he should have been informed what he did teach so that he could prepare, without reading a whole book through, and without waiting for witnesses to testify—we should have been prepared to find out whether the thing he taught was in conflict with the Bible or what the Bible said about it. Let me call attention, Your Honor, to one case they have heralded here—I don't know why. I will refer to it later. Let me show you a real indictment, gentlemen, in case you ever need to draw another one. You don't mind a little pleasantry, do you? Here is the case we have heard so much about.

Leeper vs. State. My fellow is a leper, too, because he taught evolution. I am going to discuss this case a moment later to show that it has nothing to do with the subject. This man was indicted because under the school book law of this state the commission had decided certain books should be taught, and amongst the rest they decided that Frye's geography should be taught. That any teacher that did not follow the law and taught something else should be fined $25. Of course, it wasn't so bad as to teach evolution, although the statute doesn't say anything about evolution. Now they indicted him and this is what they said in the indictment. This is their leading case. "The grand jury for the state of Tennessee, upon their oaths, present that Edward Leeper, heretofore, to-wit: On the 5th day of October, 1899, in the state and county aforesaid, being then and there a public school teacher and teaching the public school known as school No. 5, Sixth District, Blount County"—they pick that out all right—"did unlawfully use and permit to be used in said public school, after the state textbook commission had adopted and prescribed for use in the public schools of the state Frye's introductory geography as a uniform textbook, another and different textbook on that branch than the one so adopted aforesaid, to-wit: Butler's geography and the new Eclectic elementary geography against the peace and dignity of the state." Now, Your Honor, would that have been a good indictment, if they had left all that out and said he taught some book not authorized by the board? He has got a right to know what he taught and where he taught it and all the necessary things to convict him of crime. Your Honor, he cannot be convicted in this case unless they prove what he taught and where he taught it, and we have got a right to know all that before we go into court—every word of it. The indictment isn't any more than so much blank paper. I insist, your Honor, that no such indictment was ever returned before on land or sea. Some men may pull one on me, but I don't think so—I don't think so. You might just as well indict a man for being no good—and we could find a lot of them down here probably and if we couldn't I could bring them down from Chicago—but only a man is held to answer for a specific thing and he must be told what that specific thing is before he gets into court. The statute is absolutely void, because they have violated the constitution in its caption and it is absolutely uncertain—the indictment is void because it is uncertain, and gives no fact or information and it seems to me the main thing they did in bringing this case was to try to violate as many provisions of the constitution as they could, to say nothing about all the spirit of freedom and independence that has cost the best blood in the world for ages, and it looks like it will cost some more. Let's see what else we have got. This legislation—this legislation and all similar legislation that human ingenuity and malice can concoct, is void because it violates Section 13, Section 12 and Section 3. I want to call attention to that, your Honor, Section 12 is the section providing that the state should cherish science, literature and learning. Now, Your Honor, I make it a rule to try not to argue anything that I do not believe in, unless I am caught in a pretty close corner, and I want to say that the construction of the attorney-general given to that, I think, is correct and the court added a little to it, which I think makes your interpretation correct for what it is good for. It shows the policy of the state. It shows what the state is committed to. I do not believe that a statute could be set aside as unconstitutional simply because the legislature did not see fit to pass proper acts to enlighten and educate the yeomen of Tennessee.

The state by constitution is committed to the doctrine of education, committed to schools. It is committed to teaching and I assume when it is committed to teaching it is committed to teaching the truth—ought to be anyhow—plenty of people to do the other. It is committed to teaching literature and science. My friend has suggested that literature and science might conflict. I cannot quite see how, but that is another question. But that indicates the policy of the state of Tennessee and wherever it is used in construing the unconstitutionality of this act it can only be used as an indication of what the state meant and you could not pronounce a statute void on it, but we insist that this statute is absolutely void because it contravenes Section 3, which is headed "the right of worship free." Now, let's see, your Honor, there isn't any court in the world that can uphold the spirit of the law by simply upholding its letters. I read somewhere—I don't know where—that the letter killeth, but the spirit giveth life. I think I read it out of "The Prince of Peace." I don't know where I did, but I read it. If this section of the constitution which guarantees religious liberty in Tennessee cannot be sustained in the spirit it cannot be sustained in the letter. What does it mean? What does it mean? I know two intelligent people can agree only for a little distance, like a company walking along in a road. They may go together a few blocks and then one branches off. The remainder go together a few more blocks and another branches off and still further someone else branches off and the human minds are just that way, provided they are free, of course, the fundamentalists may be put in a trap so they cannot think differently if at all, probably not at all, but leave two free minds and they may go together a certain distance, but not all the way together. There are no two human machines alike and no two human beings have the same experiences and their ideas of life and philosophy grow out of their construction of the experiences that we meet on our journey through life. It is impossible, if you leave freedom in the world, to mold the opinions of one man upon the opinions of another—only tyranny can do it—and your constitutional provision, providing a freedom of religion, was meant to meet that emergency. I will go further—there is nothing else—since man—I don't know whether I dare say evolved—still, this isn't a school—since man was created out of the dust of the earth—out of hand—there is nothing else, Your Honor, that has caused the difference of opinion, of bitterness, of hatred, of war, of cruelty, that religion has caused. With that, of course, it has given consolation to millions.

But it is one of those particular things that should be left solely between the individual and his Maker, or his God, or whatever takes expression with him, and it is no one else's concern.

How many creeds and cults are there this whole world over? No man could enumerate them. At least as I have said, 500 different Christian creeds, all made up of differences, Your Honor, every one of them, and these subdivided into small differences, until they reach every member of every congregation. Because to think is to differ, and then there are any number of creeds older and any number of creeds younger, than the Christian creed, any number of them, the world has had them forever. They have come and they have gone, they have abided their time and have passed away, some of them are here still, some may be here forever, but there has been a multitude, due to the multitude, and manifold differences in human beings, and it was meant by the constitutional convention of Tennessee to leave these questions of religion between man and whatever he worshipped to leave him free. Has the Mohammedan any right to stay here and cherish his creed? Has the Buddhist a right to live here and cherish his creed? Can the Chinaman who comes here to wash our clothes, can he bring his joss and worship it? Is there any man that holds a religious creed, no matter where he came from, or how old it is or how false it is, is there any man that can be prohibited by any act of the legislature of Tennessee? Impossible? The constitution of Tennessee, as I understand, was copied from the one that Jefferson wrote, so clear, simple, direct, to encourage the freedom of religious opinion, and in substance, that no act shall ever be passed to interfere with complete religious liberty. Now is this it or is not this it? What do you say? What does it do? We will say I am a scientist, no, I will take that back, I am a pseudo-scientist, because I believe in evolution, pseudo-scientist named by somebody who neither knows or cares what science is, except to grab it by the throat and throttle it to death. I am a pseudo-scientist, and I believe in evolution. Can a legislative body say, "You cannot read a book or take a lesson, or make a talk on science until you first find out whether you are saying against Genesis"? It can unless that constitutional provision protects me. It can. Can it say to the astronomer, you cannot turn your telescope upon the infinite planets and suns and stars that fill space, lest you find that the earth is not the center of the universe and there is not any firmament between us and the heaven? Can it? It could—except for the work of Thomas Jefferson, which has been woven into every state constitution of the Union, and has stayed there like the flaming sword to protect the rights of man against ignorance and bigotry, and when it is permitted to overwhelm them, then we are taken in a sea of blood and ruin that all the miseries and tortures and carrion of the Middle Ages would be as nothing. They would need to call back these men once more. But are the provisions of the constitutions that they left, are they enough to protect you and me, and every one else in a land which we thought was free? Now, let us see what it says: "All men have a natural and indefeasible right to worship Almighty God according to the dictates of their own conscience."

That takes care even of the despised modernist who dares to be intelligent. "That no man can of right be compelled to attend, erect or support any place of worship, or to maintain any minister against his consent; that no human authority can in any case whatever control or interfere with the rights of conscience in any case whatever"—that does not mean whatever, that means "barring fundamentalist propaganda." It does not mean whatever, at all times, sometimes may be--and that "no preference shall be given by law to any religious establishment or mode of worship." Does it? Could you get any more preference, Your Honor, by law? Let us see. Here is the state of Tennessee, living peacefully, surrounded by its beautiful mountains, each one of which contains evidence that the earth is millions of years old,—people quiet, not all agreeing upon any one subject, and not necessary. If I could not live in peace with people I did not agree with, why, what? I could not live. Here is the state of Tennessee going along in its own business, teaching evolution for years, state boards handing out books on evolution, professors in colleges, teachers in schools, lawyers at the bar, physicians, ministers, a great percentage of the intelligent citizens of the state of Tennessee evolutionists, have not even thought it was necessary to leave their church. They believed that they could appreciate and understand and make their own simple and human doctrine of the Nazarene, to love their neighbor, be kindly with them, not to place a fine on and not try to send to jail some man who did not believe as they believed, and got along all right with it, too, until something happened. They have not thought it necessary to give up their church, because they believed that all that was here was not made on the first six days of creation, or that it had come by a slow process of developments extending over the ages, that one thing grew out of another. There are people who believed that organic life and the plants and the animals and man and the mind of man and the religion of man are the subjects of evolution, and they have not got through, and that the God in which they believed did not finish creation on the first day, but that he is still working to make something better and higher still out of human beings, who are next to God, and that evolution has been working forever and will work forever—they believe it.

And along comes somebody who says we have got to believe it as I believe it. It is a crime to know more than I know. And they publish a law to inhibit learning. Now, what is in the way of it? First, what does the law say? This law says that it shall be a criminal offense to teach in the public schools any account of the origin of man that is in conflict with the divine account in the Bible. It makes the Bible the yard stick to measure every man's intellect, to measure every man's intelligence and to measure every man's learning. Are your mathematics good? Turn to I Elijah ii. Is your philosophy good? See II Samuel iii. Is your astronomy good? See Genesis, Chapter 2, Verse 7. Is your chemistry good? See—well, chemistry, see Deuteronomy iii-6, or anything that tells about brimstone. Every bit of knowledge that the mind has must be submitted to a religious test. Now, let us see, it is a travesty upon language, it is a travesty upon justice, it is a travesty upon the constitution to say that any citizen of Tennessee can be deprived of his rights by a legislative body in the face of the constitution. Tell me, Your Honor, if this is not good, then what? Then, where are we coming out? I want to argue that in connection with another question here which is equally plain. Of course, I used to hear when I was a boy you could lead a horse to water, but you could not make him drink—water. I could lead a man to water, but I could not make him drink, either. And you can close your eyes and you won't see, cannot see, refuse to open your eyes—stick your fingers in your ears and you cannot hear—if you want to. But your life and my life and the life of every American citizen depends after all upon the tolerance and forbearance of his fellow man. If men are not tolerant, if men cannot respect each other's opinions, if men cannot live and let live, then no man's life is safe, no man's life is safe.

Here is a country made up of Englishmen, Irishmen, Scotch, German, Europeans, Asiatics, Africans, men of every sort and men of every creed and men of every scientific belief; who is going to begin this sorting out and say, "I shall measure you; I know you are a fool, or worse; I know and I have read a creed telling what I know and I will make people go to Heaven even if they don't want to go with me, I will make them do it"? Where is the man that is wise enough to do it?

This statute is passed under the police power of this state. Is there any kind of question about that? Counsel have argued that the legislature has the right to say what shall be taught in the public school. Yes, within limits, they have. We do not doubt it, but they probably cannot say writing and arithmetic could not be taught, and certainly they cannot say nothing can be taught unless it is first ascertained that it agrees with the Scriptures; certainly they cannot say that.

But this is passed under the police power. Let me call Your Honor's attention to this. This is a criminal statute, nothing else. It is not any amendment to the school law of the state. It makes it a crime in the caption to teach evolution and in the body of the act to teach something else, purely and simply a criminal statute.

There is no doubt about the law in this state. Show me that Barber's case will you? *[Taking book from counsel]*.... There isn't the slightest doubt about it. Can you pass a law under the police powers of the state, that a thing cannot be done in Dayton, but they can do it down in Chattanooga? Oh, no. What is good for Chattanooga is good for Dayton; I would not be sure that what is good for Dayton is good for Chattanooga, but I will put it the other way.

Any law passed under the police power must be uniform in its application; must be uniform. What do you mean by a police law? Well, Your Honor, that calls up visions of policemen and grand juries and jails and penitentiaries and eleemosynary establishments, and all that, and wickedness of heart; that is police power. True, it may extend to public health and public morals, and a few other things. I do not imagine evolution hurts the health of anyone, and probably not the morals, excepting as all enlightenment may, and the ignorant think, of course, that it does, but it is not passed for them, Your Honor, oh, no. It is not passed because it is best for the public morals, that they shall not know anything about evolution, but because it is contrary to the divine account contained in Genesis, that is all, that is the basis of it.

Now let me see about that. Any police statute must rest directly upon crime, or what is analogous to it; it has that smack, anyhow. Talk about the police power and the policemen and all the rest of them with their clubs and so on, you shudder and wonder what you have been doing, and that is the police power.

Now, any such law must be uniform in its application, there cannot be any doubt about that, not the slightest. Here, for instance...good people stirred up the community, by somebody, I don't know who, passed a law which said it was a misdemeanor to carry on barbering on Sunday, and that it should be a misdemeanor for anyone engaged in the business of barbering to shave, shampoo and cut hair or to keep open the bathrooms on Sunday. *[Laughter in courtroom.]*

Well, of course, I suppose it would be wicked to take a bath on Sunday, I don't know, but that was not the trouble with this statute. It would have been all right to forbid the good people of Tennessee from taking a bath on Sunday, but that was not the trouble. A barber could not give a bath on Sunday, anybody else could. No barber shall be permitted to give a bath on Sunday, and the Supreme Court seemed to take judicial notice of the fact that people take a bath on Sunday just the same as any other day. Foreigners come in there in the habit of bathing on Sundays just as any other time, and they could keep shops open, but a barber shop, no. The Supreme Court said that would not do, you could not let a hotel get away with what a barber shop can't. *[Laughter.]*

And so they held that this law was unconstitutional, under the provision of the constitution which says laws must be uniform. There is no question about the theory of it. If there were not, why, they would be passing laws against—the fundamentalists would be passing laws against the Congregationalists and Unitarians—I cannot remember all the names—Universalists—they might graduate the law according to how orthodox or unorthodox the church was. You cannot do it; they have to be general. The Supreme Court of this state has decided it and it does not admit of a doubt.

Now, I will just read one section of the opinion: The act is for the benefit of all individuals, barbers excepted; we know that all of the best hotels have bathrooms for the use of guests, that they accept pay for baths and permit them on Sunday.

"that in many cases a barber has his shop and bath-rooms under the roof and parts of the building in which the hotel and its bath-rooms are kept, occupied, and used. So if the act is to be enforced as the law, it will apply alone to barbers with its penalties and punishments, while the inn-keeper may with impunity use and keep open his bath-rooms on the same floor and equally public.

"Under the act, every other individual than one engaged in barbering may establish and keep open on Sunday any number of bath-rooms, and may even buy or rent those now used by the proscribed barber, in or out of a hotel building, continue its use as a bath-room, and keep it open as such on Sunday. The act falls strictly within the ordinances in its tacit but distinct and unequivocal reservation of rights, privileges, immunities, and exemptions to all classes of individuals except those 'engaged in

the business of barbering.' For this and other things, the act is
held void."

That is the case in 2 Pickle that I read from. Why they named
this Pickle I have not found out yet.

But there is another in 16 Cates, page 5. This is a case, Your
Honor, where they passed a law:

> "that it shall be unlawful for any joint-stock company, associa-
> tion, or corporation, organized, chartered, or incorporated by
> and under the laws of this State, or operated or doing business
> in this State under its laws, either as owner or lessee, having
> persons in their service or employees, to discharge any em-
> ployee or employees, or to threaten to discharge employee or
> employees in their service for voting or not voting in any elec-
> tion, State, county, or municipal, for any person as candidate or
> measure submitted to a vote of the people. It shall be unlawful."

If it is unlawful for these corporations to discharge an individual because they didn't vote a certain ticket, this must have been
passed against the wicked Democrats up here. Up in our state it is
the Republicans who do all that, but still, it shall be unlawful to discharge any man if he don't vote a certain way or buy at a certain
place if he did buy at a certain place, that only applied to corporations; if John Smith had a little ranch upon the mountain or had
hired a man he could discharge him all right if he didn't vote the
right ticket or go to the right church or any old reason. And the
Supreme Court of the state said, "Oh, no, you cannot pass that sort
of a law." What is sauce for the goose must be sauce for the gander.
You cannot pass a law making it a crime for a corporation to discharge a man because he voted differently and leave private individuals to do it. And they passed this law.

Let us look at this act, Your Honor. Here is a law which makes it
a crime to teach evolution in the caption. I don't know whether we
have discussed that or not, but it makes it a crime in the body of the
act to teach any theory of the origin of man excepting that con-

tained in the divine account, which we find in the Bible. All right. Now I have seen somewhere a statement of Mr. Bryan's that the fellow that made the pay check had a right to regulate the teachers. All right, let us see. I do not question the right of the legislature to fix the courses of study, but the state of Tennessee has no right under the police power of the state to carve out a law which applies to school teachers, a law which is a criminal statute and nothing else; which makes no effort to prescribe the school law or course of study. It says that John Smith who teaches evolution is a criminal if he teaches it in the public schools. There is no question about this act; there is no question of its origin. Nobody would claim that the act could be passed for a minute excepting that teaching evolution was in the nature of a criminal act; that it smacked of policemen and criminals and jails and grand juries; that it was in the nature of something that was criminal and, therefore, the state should forbid it.

It cannot stand a minute in this court on any theory than that it is a criminal act, simply because they say it contravenes the teaching of Moses without telling us what those teachings are. Now, if this is the subject of a criminal act, then it cannot make a criminal out of a teacher in the public schools and leave a man free to teach it in a private school. It cannot make it criminal for a teacher in the public schools to teach evolution, and for the same man to stand among the hustings and teach it. It cannot make it a criminal act for this teacher to teach evolution and permit books upon evolution to be sold in every store in the state of Tennessee and to permit the newspapers from foreign cities to bring into your peaceful community the horrible utterances of evolution. Oh, no, nothing like that. If the state of Tennessee has any force in this day of fundamentalism, in this day when religious bigotry and hatred is being kindled all over our land, see what can be done?

Now, Your Honor, there is an old saying that nits make lice. I don't know whether you know what it makes possible down here in Tennessee? I know, I was raised in Ohio. It is a good idea to clear the nits, safer and easier.

To strangle puppies is good when they grow up into mad dogs, maybe. I will tell you what is going to happen, and I do not pretend to be a prophet, but I do not need to be a prophet to know. Your Honor knows the fires that have been lighted in America to kindle religious bigotry and hate. You can take judicial notice of them if you cannot of anything else. You know that there is no suspicion which possesses the minds of men like bigotry and ignorance and hatred.

If today...you can take a thing like evolution and make it a crime to teach it in the public school, tomorrow you can make it a crime to teach it in the private schools, and the next year you can make it a crime to teach it to the hustings or in the church. At the next session you may ban books and the newspapers. Soon you may set Catholic against Protestant and Protestant against Protestant, and try to foist your own religion upon the minds of men. If you can do one you can do the other. Ignorance and fanaticism is ever busy and needs feeding. Always it is feeding and gloating for more. Today, it is the public school teachers, tomorrow the private. The next day the preachers and the lecturers, the magazines, the books, the newspapers. After a while, Your Honor, it is the setting of man against man and creed against creed until with flying banners and beating drums we are marching backward to the glorious ages of the sixteenth century when bigots lighted fagots to burn the men who dared to bring any intelligence and enlightenment and culture to the human mind.

SUPPLEMENTARY SELECTION

FROM *STATE OF IDAHO V. WILLIAM D. HAYWOOD*, ADA COUNTY COURTHOUSE, BOISE, IDAHO, JUNE 26, 1907
Opening statement

Labor unrest plagued the mining districts of Idaho, Montana, and Colorado during the late 1800s and early 1900s, with the Western Federation of Miners (WFM) organizing much of the resistance to the mine owners' labor practices. Frank Steunenberg, of Idaho, took a particularly strong stand against striking miners during his term as governor, from 1897 to 1901. In 1905, Harry Orchard dynamited the Steunenberg home in Caldwell, Idaho, killing the former governor. Orchard was quickly arrested and, pressed by the renowned Pinkerton detective James McParland, implicated WFM leaders Big Bill Haywood, Charles Moyer, and George Pettibone in the assassination. These three labor leaders lived in Colorado, where they led the violent 1904 strike by miners at Cripple Creek. Using secretive extradition procedures that Joseph McKenna, associate justice of the United States Supreme Court, later equated to kidnapping, McParland brought Haywood, Moyer, and Pettibone to Bosie, Idaho, for trial in Steunenberg's murder. The state tried Haywood first. His eight-week trial, which began on June 4, 1907, focused the nation's attention on conditions in the Western mining regions. Two leading Idaho trial attorneys, James Hawley and a future United States senator, William Borah, presented the prosecution's case. It rested largely on the dramatic testimony of Harry Orchard, who confessed to killing seventeen people (in addition to Steunenberg) in a series of WFM-sanctioned bombings in Colorado and Idaho, as well as having written articles, for a WFM magazine, that were bitterly critical of Steunenberg. Three weeks into the trial, after the state had presented its evidence, Darrow delivered his opening statement for the defense. He was assisted by the WFM attorney Edmund Richardson, who had cross-examined Orchard without impeaching his story. Darrow's two-day-long opening statement began turning the tide in a case that had appeared hopeless for the defense.

MR. DARROW: If the Court please, and gentlemen of the jury: You have been sitting here a long while, several weeks, and I suppose you would like to have us be as brief as we possibly can. However, sometimes it is a little difficult for lawyers to be brief as you have got to know by this time.

You have listened to the statements of the prosecution and you have listened to the evidence on the part of the state; and the court has told you what you twelve men already know, and you should be careful not to come to any conclusion upon any of this evidence until you hear everything that is in this case, and listen to both sides; and, while it is sometimes difficult, I am certain that each member of this jury will do everything in his power to keep his mind perfectly free from bias until the last word has been spoken and then take it all together in your jury room and decide this case. You have heard the evidence of the state and the theory of the state. It has now come our time to tell you our side of this story. This case, like most everything else, has two sides to its story, and I have no doubt that you twelve men will listen with the same care, attention and honest endeavor to our side that you have given to theirs.

Nominally, William Haywood here is on trial charged with the murder of ex-Governor Steunenberg of this state. There must be some nominal charge, and that is it. The state has gone over a broader field, and, as you know, the charge [is] considerably wider than that. Mr. Hawley laid out their work when he opened this case to this jury and told you what he expected to prove and they have traveled over all that ground; and, of course, we will have to follow over all that ground so far as they have taken us to those different points of the compass. Mr. Hawley told you that they expected to prove that these people, the members and officers of the Western Federation of Miners, from the beginning of their organization had entered into a terrible conspiracy to kill—from the very inception of the organization, as he said, to kill almost anybody, because, he said, the killing of the late Governor Steunenberg was simply an incident in this great conspiracy, whatever it was. He says they had entered into a conspiracy to kill; they had entered into a conspiracy to control politics or take a hand in politics; that they had entered into a conspiracy by means of which large amounts of money are set aside to hire lawyers, and other criminal purposes.

Part of this is true, part of it isn't. It is true that there is a labor organization called the Western Federation of Miners which was nominally organized [in] 1893 and made up of the local unions that before that time had existed in all the industrial centers of this great mining region. It is true that they spend money for lawyers—unfortunate, but most everybody has to do it, and that is where we come in. This organization was really born in 1892 and 1893. It was born down here in the cell below this courtroom, in the very room where these three men are waiting now for the judgment of the jury. When Ed Boyce and some other leading spirits were here in jail, they planned the organization of the Western Federation of Miners, which is the organization which is on trial before you twelve men. And of course they hired a lawyer and paid large fees, and they hired the best they could. They hired Mr. Hawley and he laid it out for them, and advised them, and was the godfather of them, and they thought it was innocent. He was its first attorney and attorney for a long time afterwards. And if there was anything criminal in the appropriation of money for the attorney the miners didn't know it.

They formed this organization in 1893. It was an industrial organization not a murder organization, and we will show by the evidence what was its purpose. The purpose was to organize the men who did the work so that they might have better wages, that they might have shorter hours, that they might have cleaner mines, that they might have better machinery, that they might have better conditions in the smelters, that their widows and their orphan children might be looked after. It was organized for the benefit of the working men and for the families dependent upon them, and they paid some money for lawyers and they are paying some still.

They did take some hand in politics. I trust, gentlemen, that there is no organization that is going to be hanged for taking a hand in politics. If so we probably will have to get after pretty much all of the corporations there are in the United States. This labor union was interested in passing laws and they did all they could to pass the eight-hour laws in Utah, in Colorado, in Montana, and they went down into their treasury to hire lawyers to defend those laws in all the courts of the United States against the mine [owners'] association who tried to defeat them. They endeavored to elect the judges who could look at these questions from the standpoint of the men with the pick and the shovel digging down into the earth, and to elect a United States senator. Among the rest, they tried to elect Mr. Hawley and unfortunately failed on that, and here and there they have taken a hand in politics, to which we plead guilty, gentlemen.

This organization then was formed practically as Mr. Hawley says. It has paid money for lawyers, as he says. It has taken an interest in politics, as he says. But it has never been in any criminal conspiracy to any unlawful act. I don't mean by that that all of its members have always been angels. Angels don't work in the mines. They are mine owners. But as an organization they have had no other purpose, as we will show by this evidence, except the benefitting and uplifting of their class.

It was long after this organization was put together that the defendant, Mr. Haywood, had anything to do with it, or the defendant Mr. Moyer had anything to do with it, years after. It stumbled along from 1893 up to 1902 before Mr. Moyer became president of the organization, nearly ten years, and up to 1901 before the defendant in this case became secretary-treasurer of this organization. One of its first presidents was Mr. Boyce, whom they have called upon the stand. When he became president some ten thousand men were banded together in this organization. When he left it, after about six years of struggle, after six years of constant warfare and flight, as the evidence will show in this case, it had some twenty-five or thirty thousand members, and then he turned over the burden to Mr. Moyer and Mr. Haywood and those who have carried it since. This organization, as the evidence will show, was practically born in jail and a good many of [its leaders] have been there ever since, and it has led a troublous career from the beginning, and we make no effort to conceal it or dispute it.

Whatever else we may do in this case, we are not here to apologize for anything that the Western Federation of Miners has ever done. It has been a fighting organization from the beginning, and if it dies it will die a fighting organization. [Its] purposes and [its] objects were such as I have sketched, and [it] had no sooner begun than [it] met the amity and the opposition and the force and violence of every kind [from the] mine owners' association, which was organized before [it was] born. We will show the reason for this organization and that it was not the criminal conspiracy that [the state's] counsel told this jury in the beginning was its purpose; that before the organization was born men worked from twelve to sometimes fourteen hours in the mines; that in the smelters they worked the same length of time—on an average of only six or seven years to a man. Their teeth fell out. Their bones twisted. They became helpless, crippled and paralytic. That if they bought anything they had to buy it at the company store. That if they needed a doctor they got a company doctor. If they went to a hospital they went to a company hospital where it was pretty sure they could get a release from any injury that they suffered in a mine. That everything they used, needed, ate and wore, came in contact with generally, was furnished by the mine owners. The machinery was unsafe. The smelters vomited forth poison and death. And the [Western Federation] set to work as best [it] could as a great organization to correct these evils, to shorten the hours, to increase the wages, to lengthen their lives, to care for the men who were injured, and to take care of the widows and orphans of the dead. There was one union up here, the Butte union, that since its organization has paid out more than a million dollars to widows and orphans [in] accident benefits and burial benefits, and the Lead union has paid out half as much more while this criminal conspiracy was on. They set to work to form a practical organization that they might get better wages. They set to work to pass legislation that would provide for inspection, for safety equipment and appliances, for doing away with some of the dangers of the smelters, for making an eight-hour work day, for improving conditions generally just the same as any other labor organization on the face of the earth. And they were met, as is usual, by the employers.

Now, gentlemen of the jury, we will show you that these [defendants] have done something since 1903. We will show that they have sometimes been associating with somebody besides Orchard. We will show that they were the head and front of every political movement in Colorado, in Utah, in Montana, for the adoption of the eight-hour day or the eight-hour law, and to amend the constitutions of these states so that the Supreme

Court could not set aside those laws after they were passed. We will show that they have raised the wages of their men. That they have shortened the hours from about twelve to eight. That they have looked after the widows and orphans and taken care of the sick and the maimed. That they have established hospitals in these great camps. That they have established halls and libraries. In many of the mining camps [the Western Federation has] some of the best property there is in the town. They have done these things since Mr. Hawley organized them into one compact mass of men.

[The defendants] have met a great deal of opposition and difficulty, and the evidence will show, as I have said, that they have been in trouble all the time, as they are in trouble now. Wherever they have gone to form their organizations, with a very few exceptions (and there are exceptions), but we will show that in most instances whenever an organizer or an officer of the organization would go into a mining camp to form an organization of the Western Federation they would be met by the most stubborn resistance by the owners and the bosses. The men would be ordered not to attend their meetings. They would be discharged if they attended. Over and over again their jobs have been taken from them, as we will show, because they simply affiliated with the Western Federation of Miners, and they have been blacklisted and set out into the world to tramp because they saw fit to unite their destinies with this organization. We will show that in some instances when the president would go to a mining camp that he would be refused food in the camp, could get nothing to eat in the company boarding house or in the town and be forced to go to some more friendly town before he could get a mouthful to eat or a night's lodging, and arrests, following charges and crimes, real and imaginary, have come thick and fast from the day of [the Federation's] birth until now. In ninety-nine out of a hundred [cases, union organizers] have not even had the grace of a trial, of which we cannot complain in this case.

[We will show] that as soon as this organization was born, the mine owners set to work to destroy it, and that as one of their chief means of destroying it they hired the Pinkerton detective agency, with one McParland at the head in the West. That from the beginning until now that agency has been busy, stealthily following, scheming and working and lying to get these men. We will show that amongst other things [the mine owners] repeatedly hired detectives and placed those detectives in positions of responsibility as secretaries and presidents of local unions, and they sent those detectives out amongst the union men at their meetings to advise strikes, and wherever there was a strike to advise violence and bloodshed and dynamite and murder. We will show that they did it in Telluride, that they did it in Cripple Creek, that they have done it from one end to the other of this mining region, and that most of the talk and most of the inciting to violence and crimes has come from their hired men through the Pinkerton detective agency, which has been the chief factor in this case.

[The mine owners] have also regaled themselves with a campaign of slander, abuse and vilification against the organization. Every deed of violence in the West almost has been charged to [it] indiscriminately. We will show that when in Cripple Creek a cage with sixteen men fell to the bottom because the company did not have proper machinery and the sixteen were killed, it was at once charged to the Western Federation of Miners—that [union agents] had tampered with it and killed the men. When the Moscow [Idaho] university was burned, that was the Western Federation of Miners. That wherever there was a man killed— Lyte Gregory—anybody—it was the Western Federation of Miners. That since [it was] organized, every illegitimate child that was born west of the Mississippi has been bundled up in its swaddling clothes and hurried up to Denver and laid on the front door step of the Western Federation of Miners—for a purpose. That these are a piece of many of the statements that Mr. Orchard has detailed to this jury upon the witness stand.

That [the miners], after they organized this Western Federation, did establish a magazine—gentlemen, no doubt about that. And it is running still—at least it was last week. The Miners' Magazine—you have heard some extracts from it and we will read you more. It has been running for ten years and it is possible that some foolish things have crept into it—[no] different from any other newspaper or magazine that was ever published for that length of time. Mr. Boyce wrote a considerable number of the first articles, but [it] had a regular editor. Mr. Haywood paid little attention to it. He was busy. Mr. Moyer paid little attention to it. He was busy. These articles are not all as polished as my friend Borah might write or even as my friend Hawley would pen, because there are a lot of these miners who haven't got a college education. Some of them haven't even been to high school. So they wrote the best they could. Sometimes possibly intemperate, but we are willing to show you all there are, and we will read you some that have not yet been read. This magazine that [the state] introduced in evidence was a magazine published [by the Federation] for its members and published for its organization, published to help along the cause which some of them at least thought they were working for. We, as I have said, will wish to offer and will read to you, we think, some of the other matters that were not introduced by the state. We will show [that in this magazine, Federation leaders] did not counsel violence, that they had a fair understanding of the economic questions and what was necessary to be done, and that their appeals were appeals to their men and appeals for political acts which they had a right to make.

Now that brings us down to the Coeur d'Alenes....

[Darrow then outlined in great detail the story that defense witnesses would tell about what had happened at Idaho's Coeur d'Alene silver mine and at other Western mines leading up to the trial. In this account, Harry Orchard had his own private reasons for killing Governor Steunenberg and the WFM was not involved. Darrow ultimately brought the story to Steunenberg's hometown of Caldwell, Idaho, where the assassination occurred.]

Orchard came down to Caldwell. He had been pursuing Governor Steunenberg and swearing vengeance upon him for years; that we will show you. He had, during all those years, been connected with a detective association—more with them than with us. Now, again gentlemen, I don't want you to make any mistake. I don't believe for a moment that the detective association or the mine owners association had anything to do with killing ex-Governor Steunenberg. But we will show that so far as this man is concerned, he was more their agent in everything than he could ever by any possibility have been ours, and that this act he did in pursuance of his old private grudge, which we will prove by ten or a dozen people. He fixed this bomb and it was exploded in the most cowardly way that a coward could kill a man. He was arrested, was thrown in jail. He stayed around Caldwell without any excuse for being there; he was caught red handed. He was thrown into jail and brought from there to the penitentiary and turned over to McParland, the head of the Western branch of the Pinkerton detective association. And after manipulations with McParland for a sufficient length of time, he was persuaded that the easiest thing for him to do was to lay his crimes onto somebody else. And so he did it. And this is the biggest reward he is getting—he is going to get the biggest reward for killing these men, if he lands them, than he ever got for anything in his life. He is going to save his own miserable neck.

After the manipulations of McParland he gave out a confession in which he confessed to everything in Colorado and this in Idaho, and implicated these three men in some fifteen or twenty murders in Colorado where they lived, and where they were fighting and had been living and fighting for years. And that [confession] was delivered over to a Pinkerton detective who lived in Colorado and where a judge of the Supreme Court and several of the other officers stay. If the confession is true, then they killed one man here and fifteen or twenty there. Orchard was kept in the penitentiary until one day when the state's attorney of [Idaho's] Canyon County drew up a perjured affidavit swearing that these men were [in Idaho] at the time of this crime. They got a requisition from the [Idaho] Governor who knew the affidavit was a perjury. They kept it from the newspapers and from the light of day. They went down to Colorado and presented it to another Governor who knew it was perjured because [he] knew they were [in Colorado then]. The business was all done in the Pinkerton office, and while the Governor of Colorado, if he believed the story at all, knew that the men were under his jurisdiction and were responsible to that commonwealth for twenty crimes, he allowed the requisition to be issued in secret and in private. It was issued on Thursday. They could not get their men bunched until Saturday, and Saturday night about ten o'clock they grabbed [these] three men and took them to the jail. They denied them the right to go to their lawyer to get a writ of habeas corpus to keep them in that state; denied them the right to consult with their families or their friends; lodged them on a special train in charge of the militia and the Pinkerton detectives and went through Cheyenne at forty miles an hour, passed through every town on the way, changed engines at obscure places, took on coal and water in obscure places, and kidnapped them and brought them down here in this jail for a year and five or six months until a jury might pass upon their case....

Gentlemen, many names have been mentioned by Mr. Orchard—names of members of the Western Federation of Miners whom he has said were connected with some things he has done. Gentlemen, in Cripple Creek [the Federation's] lodges were broken up and the members were scattered throughout the length and breadth of the land after the riots at Cripple Creek. Some of them [went] to Montana, some to California, some to Idaho, some to Nevada, some to Utah, and taking all sorts of names that they could find, but, gentlemen, we will bring before you here—most of those whose names he has given. We will bring you Davis, and Easterly, Malich. Nearly all the men whose names have been given have taken their chance and come here to Idaho to tell their story. There may be some we cannot find, but I think before we get done you will say we have had most of them and that we have had enough of them.

MR. RICHARDSON: Mention the two or three who are dead.

MR. DARROW: Parker, Kennison, and a few others are dead, as we will prove to you; we will account for them, but most of the rest will come.

Gentlemen, we will show you that Moyer, Haywood, Pettibone, not one of them ever had any connection with [Orchard] in any criminal act. Moyer and Haywood were the leading officers of the labor union, doing their best and all they could for that organization. And we will tell you, straight to this jury, that this is not a murder case, and Bill Haywood is not on trial, but that the [mine owners of the] state of Colorado have sent these men to Idaho thinking that conditions and the people were different here. They have sent them here—the mine owners of Colorado—that they might try and hang and execute and kill forever the Western Federation of Miners. And it is that organization and through them all organizations, and not Haywood, that is on trial in this court.

CHAPTER 3

ARTICLES AND ESSAYS

AUTOBIOGRAPHICAL INTRODUCTION

FROM CLARENCE DARROW, *THE STORY OF MY LIFE*, CHAPTER 10, "WAR" (1932)

In all situations, the emotions are the moving forces among men, and through them, of states and all society. Reason has very little to do with human action. Reason is simply a method of comparing and appraising: it is always used to justify what the emotions demand. How far the reason of man can be used to inhibit emotions may be a subject of debate, but it can go a little way. The structure of man determines his course under certain circumstances. An impression occurs, the impression is carried by a nerve to the brain. This is automatic; just as automatic as the response of the organism to the signal.... When sensations that come into an organism produce a reaction we call rage, men will fight. Perhaps, to a small extent, these reactions can be modified by habits, but when the reaction is strong enough the response is certain.

When I read of the German army marching through Belgium I had exactly the same reaction that I would experience if a big dog should attack a little one.... Whatever the cause or whether I was right or wrong, my sympathies were at once with France and England and Russia. This was not due to dislike of Germans. As a matter of fact, I found them in America more tolerant and liberty-loving than any other of our people, and as a consequence I had many friends among them, most of whom I wanted to retain....

When we were once in the contest, I gave nearly all my time to making speeches throughout the United States. It was the first occasion when I had known of a war I believed in....

At no time did I declare my adoration of my country after the manner of a professional patriot. I always distrust those who make a business of loving their country. I knew that many men and women did not believe in the war, and that as a rule they were moved by higher ideals than most of those who supported it. I felt, and still think, that they were wrong. Over and over I went to the Government offices in Chicago to save someone from imprisonment that I knew was not hostile to the United States, but who was accused of disloyalty. In most cases I succeeded because the authorities knew I was for the war and they could trust my honesty in the matter....

Reading and experience have taught me that when governments prepare for war, the first unit they mobilize is the liar's brigade.... Somehow the whole thing did not look so good to me after the war was over. I began to ask myself many questions. I had been roundly denounced by many of my pacifist and radical friends. All of these were like most people: they were positive that they were right. The question did not even admit of reasoning; I soon saw not only the futility of it all but the cost of it all; I knew the effect, direct and indirect, of the torrent of malice and evil that had been let loose upon the world.

Main Selection

Clarence Darrow, "The Myth of the Soul: Is the Belief in Immortality Necessary or Even Desirable?"

From *Little Blue Book* No. 1404, Haldeman-Julius Publications, Girard, Kansas; original version edited by E. Haldeman-Julius

There is, perhaps, no more striking example of the credulity of man than the widespread belief in immortality. This idea includes not only the belief that death is not the end of what we call life, but that personal identity involving memory persists beyond the grave. So determined is the ordinary individual to hold fast to this belief that, as a rule, he refuses to read or think upon the subject lest it cast doubt upon his cherished dream. Of those who may chance to look at this contribution, many will do so with the determination not to be convinced, and will refuse to even consider the manifold reasons that might weaken their faith. I know that this is true, for I know the reluctance with which I long approached the subject and my firm determination not to give up my hope. Thus the myth will stand in the way of a sensible adjustment to facts.

Even many of those who claim to believe in immortality still tell themselves and others that neither side of the question is susceptible to proof. Just what can these hopeful ones believe that the word "proof" involves? The evidence against the persistence of personal consciousness is as strong as the evidence of gravitation, and much more obvious. It is as convincing and unassailable as the proof of the destruction of wood or coal by fire. If it is not certain that death ends personal identity and memory, then almost nothing that man accepts as true is susceptible to proof....

It is customary to speak of a "belief in immortality." First, then, let us see what is meant by the word "belief." If I take a train in Chicago at noon, bound for New York, I believe I will reach that city the next morning. I believe it because I have been to New York, I have read about the city, I have known many other people who have been there, and their stories are not inconsistent with any known facts in my own experience. I have even examined the time tables and I know just how I will go and how long the trip will take. In other words, when I board the train for New York, I believe I will reach that city because I have *reason* to believe it.

If, instead, I wanted to see Timbuktu or some other point on the globe where I had never been, or of which I had only heard, I still know something about geography, and if I did not I could find out about the place I wished to visit. Through the encyclopedia and other means of information, I could get a fair idea of the location and character of the country or city, the kind of people who lived there and almost anything I wished to know, including the means of transportation and the time it would take to go and return. I already am satisfied that the earth is round, and I know about its size. I know the extent of its land and water. I know the names of its countries. I know perfectly well that there are many places on its surface that I have never seen. I can easily satisfy myself as to whether there is any such place and how to get there, and what I shall do when I arrive.

But if I am told that next week I shall start on a trip to Goofville; that I shall not take my body with me; that I shall stay for all eternity: can I find a single fact connected with my journey— the way I shall go, the time of the journey, the country I shall reach, its location in space, the way I shall live there—or anything that would lead to a rational belief that I shall really make the trip? Have I ever known anyone who has made the journey and returned? If I am really to believe, I must try to get some information about all these important facts.

But people hesitate to ask questions about life after death. They do not ask, for they know that only silence comes out of the eternal darkness of endless space. If people really believed in a beautiful, happy, glorious land waiting to receive them when they died; if they believed that their friends would be waiting to meet them; if they believed that all pain and suffering would be left behind: why should they live through weeks, months, and even years of pain and torture while a cancer eats its way to the vital parts of the body? Why should one fight off death? Because he does *not* believe in any real sense; he only hopes. Everyone knows that there is no real evidence of any such state of bliss; so we are told not to search for proof. We are to accept through faith alone. But every thinking person knows that faith can only come through belief. Belief implies a condition of mind that accepts a certain idea. This condition can be brought about only by evidence. True, the evidence may be simply the unsupported statement of your grandmother; it may be wholly insufficient for reasoning men; but, good or bad, it must be enough for the believer or he could not believe.

Upon what evidence, then, are we asked to believe in immortality? There is no evidence. One is told to rely on faith, and no doubt this serves the purpose so long as one can believe blindly whatever he is told. But if there is no evidence upon which to build a positive belief in immortality, let us examine the other side of the question. Perhaps evidence can be found to support a positive conviction that immortality is a delusion.

The belief in immortality expresses itself in two different forms. On the one hand, there is a belief in the immortality of the "soul." This is sometimes interpreted to mean simply that the identity, the consciousness, the memory of the individual persists after death. On the other hand, many religious creeds formulated a belief in "the resurrection of the body," which is something else again. It will be necessary to examine both forms of this belief in turn.

The idea of continued life after death is very old. It doubtless had its roots back in the childhood of the race. In view of the limited knowledge of primitive man, it was not unreasonable. His dead friends and relatives visited him in dreams and visions and were present in his feeling and imagination until they were forgotten. Therefore, the lifeless body did not raise the question of dissolution, but rather of duality. It was thought that man was a dual being possessing a body and a soul as separate entities, and that when a man died, his soul was released from his body to continue its life apart. Consequently, food and drink were placed upon the graves of the dead to be used in the long journey into the unknown. In modified forms, this belief in the duality of man persists to the present day. But primitive man had no conception of life as having a beginning and an end. In this he was like the rest of the animals. Today, everyone of ordinary intelligence knows how life begins, and to examine the beginnings of life leads to inevitable conclusions about the way life ends. If man has a soul, it must creep in somewhere during the period of gestation and growth.

All the higher forms of animal life grow from a single cell. Before the individual life can begin its development, it must be fertilized by union with another cell; then the cell divides and multiplies until it takes the form and pattern of its kind. At a certain regular time the being emerges into the world. During its term of life millions of cells in its body are born, die, and are replaced until, through age, disease, or some catastrophe, the cells fall apart and the individual life is ended.

It is obvious that but for the fertilization of the cell under right conditions, the being would not have lived. It is idle to say that the initial cell has a soul. In one sense it has life; but even that is precarious and depends for its continued life upon union with another cell of the proper kind. The human mother is the bearer of probably ten thousand of one kind of cell, and the human father of countless billions of the other kind. Only a very small fraction of these results in human life. If the unfertilized cells of the female and the unused cells of the male are human beings possessed of souls, then the population of the world is infinitely greater than has ever been dreamed. Of course no such idea as belief in the immortality of germ cells could satisfy the yearnings of the individual for a survival of life after death.

If that which is called a "soul" is a separate entity apart from the body, when, then, and where and how was this soul placed in the human structure? The individual began with the union of two cells, neither of which had a soul. How could these two soulless cells produce a soul? I must leave this search to the metaphysicians. When they have found the answer, I hope they will tell me, for I should really like to know.

We know that a baby may live and fully develop in its mother's womb and then, through some shock at birth, may be born without life. In the past, these babies were promptly buried. But now we know that in many such cases, where the bodily structure is complete, the machine may be set to work by artificial respiration or electricity. Then it will run like any other human body through its allotted term of years. We also know that in many cases of drowning, or when some mishap virtually destroys life without hopelessly impairing the body, artificial means may set it in motion once more, so that it will complete its term of existence until the final catastrophe comes. Are we to believe that somewhere around the stillborn child and somewhere in the vicinity of the drowned man there hovers a detached soul waiting to be summoned back into the body by a pull-motor? This, too, must be left to the metaphysicians.

The beginnings of life yield no evidence of the beginnings of a soul. It is idle to say that something in the human being which we call "life" is the soul itself, for the soul is generally taken to distinguish human beings from other forms of life. There is life in all animals and plants, and at least potential life in inorganic matter. This potential life is simply unreleased force and matter—the greatest storehouse from which all forms of life emerge and are constantly replenished. It is impossible to draw the line between inorganic matter and the simpler forms of plant life, and equally impossible to draw the line between plant life and animal life, or between other forms of animal life and what we human beings are pleased to call the highest form. If the thing which we call "life" is itself the soul, then cows have souls; and, in the very nature of things, we must allow souls to all forms of life and to inorganic matter as well.

Life itself is something very real, as distinguished from the soul. Every man knows that his life had a beginning. Can one imagine an organism that has a beginning and no end? If I did not exist in the infinite past, why should I, or could I, exist in the infinite future? "But," say some, "your consciousness, your memory may exist even after you are dead. This is what we mean by the soul." Let us examine this point a little.

I have no remembrance of the months I lay in my mother's womb. I cannot recall the day of my birth nor the time when I first opened my eyes to the light of the sun. I cannot remember when I was an infant, or when I began to creep on the floor, or when I was taught to walk, or anything before I was five or six years old. Still, all of these events were important, wonderful, and strange in a new life. What I call my "consciousness," for lack of a better word and a better understanding, developed with my growth and the crowding experiences I met at every turn. I have a hazy recollection of the burial of a boy soldier who was shot toward the end of the Civil War. He was buried near the schoolhouse when I was seven years old. But I have no remembrance of the assassination of Abraham Lincoln, although I must then have been eight years old. I must have known about it at the time, for my family and my community idolized Lincoln, and all America was in mourning at his death....

"Ah, yes," say the believers in the soul, "What you say confirms our own belief. You certainly existed when these early experiences took place. You were conscious of them at the time, even though you are not aware of it now. In the same way, may not your consciousness persist after you die, even though you are not aware of that fact?"

On the contrary, my fading memory of the events that filled the early years of my life leads me to the opposite conclusion. So far as these incidents are concerned, the mind and consciousness of the boy [I was] are already dead. Even now, am I fully alive? I am seventy-one years old. I often fail to recollect the names of some of those I knew full well. Many events do not make the lasting impression that they once did. I know that it will be only a few years, even if my body still survives decay, when few important matters will even register in my mind. I know how it is with the old. I know that physical life can persist beyond the time when the mind can fully function. I know that if I live to an extreme old age, my mind will fail. I shall eat and drink and go to my bed in an automatic way. Memory—which is all that binds me to the past—will already be dead. All that will remain will be a vegetative existence; I shall sit and doze in the chimney corner, and my body will function in a measure even though the ego will already be practically dead. I am sure that if I die of what is called "old age," my consciousness will gradually slip away with my failing emotions! I shall no more be aware of the near approach of final dissolution than is the dying tree....

In primitive times, before men knew anything about the human body or the universe of which it is a part, it was not unreasonable to believe in spirits, ghosts, and the duality of man. For one thing, celestial geography was much simpler then. Just above the earth was a firmament in which the stars were set, and above the firmament was heaven. The place was easy of access and in dreams the angels were seen going up and coming down on a ladder. But now we have a slightly more adequate conception of space and the infinite universe of which we are so small a part. Our great telescopes reveal countless worlds and planetary systems which make our own sink into utter insignificance in comparison. We have every reason to think that beyond our sight there is endless space filled with still more planets, so infinite in size and number that no brain has the smallest conception of their extent. Is there any reason to think that in this universe, with its myriads of worlds, there is no other life so important as our own? Is it possible that the inhabitants of the earth have been singled out for special favor and endowed with souls and immortal life? Is it at all reasonable to suppose that any special account is taken of the human atoms that forever come and go upon this planet?

If man has a soul that persists after death, that goes to a heaven of the blessed or to a hell of the damned, where are these places? It is not so easily imagined as it once was. How does the soul make its journey? What does immortal man find when he gets there, and how will he live after he reaches the end of endless space? We know that the atmosphere will be absent; that there will be no light, no heat—only the infinite reaches of darkness and frigidity....

These conceptions were formed early in the history of man; in fact, it has only been in recent years that we have had any knowledge or vision of the immensity of space and the impossibility of any such place as is envisioned by the credulous and trusting. We know now that the earth revolves upon its axis at a terrific speed. This motion makes a complete revolution in twenty-four hours. We know down to the second of time that no spot bears the same relation to space as it did before. If one who dies at midnight has a soul and starts on his trip to Heaven, he goes in an opposite direction from one who dies at noon, and chances to meet under any circumstances which can be conceived would grow less as they traveled on. Besides this revolution on its axis, the earth is traveling at an inconceivable speed around the sun, which, at times, is about ninety-three million miles away. This complete journey is made once a year. In its orbit around the sun it travels more than a thousand miles a minute. This constant appalling speed would evidently add to the confusion of two mortals locating themselves in the same spot in space, even though they had souls. The atmosphere, even in its most attenuated form, does not reach over five hundred miles away from the earth, and for only a small fraction of that space could life as we conceive it exist. And when the earth leaves a given spot in space the atmosphere is carried along with it. In addition to the motion of the earth on its axis and its unthinkable speed in its circuit around the sun, the whole solar system is traveling around the pole star, accompanied no doubt by many other systems like our own; no one can tell how fast it goes or how far it goes, in what seems endless space. And these systems travel in turn around some other central point in the far-off Milky Way, and no one knows how many other apparently central points somewhere off amongst the stars and worlds and suns furnish foci around which the earth and all the systems constantly revolve. What possible means of locomotion could be furnished for mortals to find a place of rest, and what possible unimaginable guide could pilot individuals going in different directions at all times of the day and night and all portions of the year and century, and other greater periods of time, to this haven of the blessed? All of these conceptions beggar any sort of imagination and make and substitute the wildest unthinkable dreams in place of real beliefs....

Two thousand years ago, in Palestine, little was known of man, of the earth, or of the universe. It was then currently believed that the earth was only four thousand years old, that life had begun anew after the deluge about two thousand years before, and that the entire earth was soon to be destroyed. Today it is fairly well established that man has been upon the earth for a million years. During that long stretch of time the world has changed many times; it is changing every moment. At least three [or] four ice ages have swept across continents, driving death before them, carrying human beings into the sea or burying them deep in the earth. Animals have fed on man and on each other. Every dead body, no matter whether consumed by fire or buried in the earth, has been resolved into its elements, so that the matter and energy that once formed human beings has fed animals and plants and other men. As the great naturalist, Fabre, has said: "At the banquet of life each is in turn a guest and a dish." Thus the body of every man now living is in part made from the bodies of those who have been dead for ages.

Yet we are still asked to believe in the resurrection of the body.

By what alchemy, then, are the individual bodies that have successfully fed the generations of men to be separated and restored to their former identities? And if I am to be resurrected, what particular *I* shall be called from the grave, from the animals and plants and the bodies of other men who shall inherit this body I now call my own? My body has been made over and over, piece by piece, as the days went by, and will continue to be so made until the end. It has changed so slowly that each new cell is fitted into the living part, and will go on changing until the final crisis comes. Is it the child in the mother's womb or the tottering frame of the old man that shall be brought back? The mere thought of such a resurrection beggars reason, ignores facts, and enthrones blind faith, wild dreams, hopeless hopes, and cowardly fears as sovereign of the human mind....

These natural processes of change, which in the human being take the forms of growth, disease, senility, death, and decay, are essentially the same as the processes by which a lump of coal is disintegrated in burning. One may watch the lump of coal burning in the grate until nothing but ashes remains. Part of the coal goes up the chimney in the form of smoke; part of it radiates through the house as heat; the residue lies in the ashes on the hearth. So it is within human life. In all forms of life nature is engaged in combining, breaking down, and recombining her store of energy and matter into new forms. The thing we call "life" is nothing other than a state of equilibrium which endures for a short span of years between the two opposing tendencies of nature—the one that builds up, and the one that tears down. In old age, the tearing-down process has already gained the ascendancy, and when death intervenes, the equilibrium is finally upset by the complete stoppage of the building-up process, so that nothing remains but complete disintegration. The energy thus released may be converted into grass or trees or animal life; or it may lie dormant until caught up again in the crucible of nature's laboratory. But whatever happens, the man... the *You* and the *I*... like the lump of coal that has been burned, is gone, irrevocably dispersed. "All the King's horses and all the King's men" cannot restore it to its former unity.

The idea that man is a being set apart, distinct from all the rest of nature, is born of man's emotions, of his loves and hates, of his hopes and fears, and of the primitive conceptions of undeveloped minds. The *You* and the *I* which is known to our friends does not consist of an immaterial something called a "soul" which cannot be conceived. We know perfectly well what we mean when we talk about this *You* and this *Me:* and it is equally plain that the whole fabric that makes up our separate personalities is destroyed, dispersed, disintegrated beyond repair by what we call "death."

As a matter of fact, does *anyone* really believe in a future life? The faith does not simply involve the persistence of activity, but it has been stretched and magnified to mean a future world infinitely better than the earth. In this far-off land no troubles will harass the body or the soul. Eternity will be an eternity of bliss: Heaven, a land made much more delightful because of the union with those who have gone before. This doctrine has been taught so persistently through the years that men and women of strong faith in their dying moments have seen relatives and friends, long since dead, who have come to lead them to their heavenly home.

Does this conduct of the intense disciple show that he really believes that death is a glad deliverance? Why do men and women who are suffering torture on earth seek to prolong their days of agony? Why do victims of cancer being slowly eaten alive for months and years prefer enduring such pain rather than going to a land of bliss? Why will the afflicted travel all over the world and be cut to pieces by inches that they may stay a few weeks longer, in agony and torture? The one answer that is made to this query is that the afflicted struggle to live because it is their duty to hang fast to mortal life, no matter what the pain or the expected joy in heaven. The answer is not true. The afflicted cling to life because they doubt their faith, and do not wish to let go of what they have, terrible as it is.

Those who refuse to give up the idea of immortality declare that their nature never creates a desire without providing the means for its satisfaction. They likewise insist that all people, from the rudest to the most civilized, yearn for another life. As a matter of fact, nature creates many desires which she does not satisfy; most of the wishes of men meet no fruition. But nature does not create any emotion demanding a future life. The only yearning that the individual has is to keep on living—which is a very different thing. This urge is found in every animal, in every plant. It is simply the momentum of a living structure: or, as Schopenhauer put it, "the will to live." What we long for is a continuation of our present state of existence, not an uncertain reincarnation in a mysterious world of which we know nothing. The idea of another life is created after men are convinced that this life ends....

Is it possible that any sort of proof could prove the existence of an individual after his decay? Suppose that some good fairy, distressed at my unbelief, should come to me with the offer to produce any evidence that I desired to satisfy me that I would see my loved ones after death. Suppose I should tell this fairy that my father had been dead for twenty years; that I followed his lifeless body to the crematory where he was converted into ashes; that I desired to have him brought back to me as a living entity, and to stay in my house for a year, that I might not be deceived. Assume that when the year had passed I should go out and tell my neighbors and friends that my father had been living in my house, although he died two score years ago *[sic]*; suppose that they believed implicitly in my integrity and my judgment. Even then, could I convince one person that my statement was true? Would they be right in doubting my word? After all, which is the more reasonable, that the dead have come back to life, or that I have become insane? All of my friends would say: "Poor fellow, I am sorry he has lost his mind." Against the universal experience of mankind and nature, the dementia or the insanity of one man, or a thousand men, could count as nothing. The insane asylums of the world are filled with men who have these dreams and visions which are realities to them, but which no one else believes, because they are entirely at variance with well-known facts.

All men recognize the hopelessness of finding any evidence that the individual will persist beyond the grave. As a last resort, we are told that it is better that the doctrine be believed even if it is not true. We are assured that without this faith, life is only desolation and despair. However that may be, it remains that many of the conclusions of logic are not pleasant to contemplate; still, so long as men think and feel, at least some of them will use their faculties as best they can. For if we are to believe things that are not true, who is to write our creed? Is it safe to leave it to any man or organization to pick out the errors that we must accept? The whole history of the world has answered this question in a way that cannot be mistaken.

And after all, is the belief in immortality necessary or even desirable for man?

... The things that really affect the happiness of the individual are the matters of daily living. They are the companionship of friends, the games and contemplations. They are misunderstandings and cruel judgments, false friends and debts, poverty and disease. They are our joys in our living companions and our sorrows over those who die. Whatever our faith, we mainly live in the present—in the here and now. Those who hold the view that man is mortal are never troubled by metaphysical problems. At the end of the day's labor we are glad to lose our consciousness in sleep; and intellectually, at least, we look forward to the long rest from the stresses and storms that are always incidental to existence.

When we fully understand the brevity of life, its fleeting joys and unavoidable pains; when we accept the facts that all men and women are approaching an inevitable doom: the consciousness of it should make us more kindly and considerate of each other. This feeling should make men and women use their best efforts to help their fellow travelers on the road, to make the path brighter and easier as we journey on. It should bring a closer kinship, a better understanding, and a deeper sympathy for the wayfarers who must live a common life and die a common death.

SUPPLEMENTARY SELECTION

CLARENCE DARROW, "HOW TO PICK A JURY," *ESQUIRE*, MAY 1936

Darrow often expounded on the topic of how to pick a jury, both orally and in written form, in varying detail and with more or less of his tongue pressed firmly against his cheek. This version, his last, appeared in Esquire *magazine in May 1936.*

Whether a jury is a good one or a bad one depends on the point of view. I have always been an attorney for the defense. I can think of nothing, not even war, that has brought so much misery to the human race as prisons. And all of it so futile!

... The stage, the arena, [and] the court are alike in that each has its audience thirsting to drink deeply of the passing show. Those playing the parts vie for success and use whatever skill and talent they possess. An actor may fumble his lines, but a lawyer needs to be letter-perfect; at least, he has to use his wits, and he may forget himself, and often does, but never for a moment can he lose sight of his client....

If it is a criminal case, or even a civil one, it is not the law alone or the facts that determine the results. Always the element of luck and chance looms large. A jury of twelve men is watching not only the evidence but the attitude of each lawyer, and the parties involved, in all their moves. Every step is fraught with doubt, if not mystery.

Selecting a jury is of the utmost importance.... Every knowing lawyer seeks for a jury of the same sort of men as his client; men who will be able to imagine themselves in the same situation and realize what verdict the client wants....

Choosing jurors is always a delicate task. The more a lawyer knows of life, human nature, psychology, and the reactions of the human emotions, the better he is equipped for the subtle selection of his so-called "twelve men, good and true." In this undertaking, everything pertaining to the prospective juror needs to be questioned and weighed: his nationality, his business, religion, politics, social standing, family ties, friends, habits of life and thought; the books and newspapers he likes and reads, and many more matters that combine to make a man; all of these qualities and experiences have left their effect on ideas, beliefs and fancies that inhabit his mind. Understanding of all this cannot be obtained too bluntly. It usually requires finesse, subtlety and guesswork. Involved in it all is the juror's method of speech, the kind of clothes he wears, the style of haircut, and, above all, his business associates, residence and origin.

To the ordinary observer, a man is just a man. To the student of life and human beings, every pose and movement is a part of the personality and the man.

It is obvious that if a litigant discovered one of his dearest friends in the jury panel he could make a close guess as to how certain facts, surrounding circumstances, and suppositions would affect his mind and action; but as he has no such acquaintance with the stranger before him, he must weigh the prospective juror's words and manner of speech and, in fact, hastily and cautiously "size him up" as best he can. The litigants and their lawyers are supposed to want justice, but in reality there is no such thing as justice, either in or out of court. In fact, the word cannot be defined. So, for lack of proof, let us assume that the word "justice" has a meaning, and that the common idea of the definition is correct, without even seeking to find out what is the common meaning. Then how do we reach justice through the courts? The lawyer's idea of justice is a verdict for his client, and really this is the sole end for which he aims.

...It is not the experience of jurors, neither is it their brain power that is the potent influence in their decisions. A skillful lawyer does not tire himself hunting for learning or intelligence in the box; if he knows much about man and his malting, he knows that all beings act from emotions and instincts, and that reason is not a motive factor. If deliberation counts for anything, it is to retard decision. The nature of the man himself is the element that determines the juror's bias for or against his fellow-man. Assuming that a juror is not a half-wit, his intellect can always furnish fairly good reasons for following his instincts and emotions. Many irrelevant issues in choosing jurors are not so silly as they seem, matters that apparently have nothing to do with the personality and the man. There is no sure rule by which one can gauge any person. A man may seem to be of a certain mold, but a wife, a friend, or an enemy, entering into his life, may change his most vital views, desires and attitudes, so that he will hardly recognize himself as the man he once seemed to be.

In the last analysis, most jury trials are contests between the rich and poor. If the case concerns money, it is apt to be a case of damages for injuries of some sort claimed to have been inflicted by someone. These cases are usually defended by insurance companies, railroads, or factories. If a criminal case, it is practically always the poor who are on trial. The most important point to learn is whether the prospective juror is humane. This must be discovered in more or less devious ways.... Next to this, in having more or less bearing on the question, is the nationality, politics, and religion of the person examined for the jury. If you do not discover this, all your plans may go awry....

Let us assume that we represent one of "the underdogs" because of injuries received, or because of an indictment brought by what the prosecutors name themselves, "the state." Then what sort of men will we seek?

An Irishman is called into the box for examination. There is no reason for asking about his religion; he is Irish; that is enough. We may not agree with his religion, but it matters not, his feelings go deeper than any religion. You should be aware that he is emotional, kindly and sympathetic. If he is chosen as a juror, his imagination will place him in the dock; really, he is trying himself. You would be guilty of malpractice if you got rid of him, except for the strongest reasons.

An Englishman is not so good as an Irishman, but still, he has come through a long tradition of individual rights, and is not afraid to stand alone; in fact, he is never sure that he is right unless the great majority is against him. The German is not so keen about individual rights except where they concern his own way of life; liberty is not a theory, it is a way of living. Still, he wants to do what is right, and he is not afraid. He has not been among us long, his ways are fixed by his race, his habits are still in the making. We need inquire no further. If he is a Catholic, then he loves music and art; he must be emotional, and will want to help you; give him a chance.

If a Presbyterian enters the jury box and carefully rolls up his umbrella, and calmly and critically sits down, let him go. He is cold as the grave; he knows right from wrong, although he seldom finds anything right. He believes in John Calvin and eternal punishment. Get rid of him with the fewest possible words before he contaminates the others; unless you and your clients are Presbyterians you probably are a bad lot, and even though you may be a Presbyterian, your client most likely is guilty.

If possible, the Baptists are more hopeless than the Presbyterians... you do not want them on the jury, and the sooner they leave the better. The Methodists are worth considering; they are nearer the soil. Their religious emotions can be transmuted into love and charity. They are not half bad; even though they will not take a drink, they really do not need it so much as some of their competitors for the seat next to the throne. If chance sets you down between a Methodist and a Baptist, you will move toward the Methodist to keep warm.

Beware of the Lutherans, especially the Scandinavians; they are almost always sure to convict. Either a Lutheran or Scandinavian is unsafe, but if both in one, plead your client guilty and go down the docket. He learns about sinning and punishing from the preacher, and dares not doubt. A person who disobeys must be sent to hell; he has God's word for that.

As to Unitarians, Universalists, Congregationalists, Jews and other agnostics, don't ask them too many questions; keep them anyhow, especially Jews and agnostics. It is best to inspect a Unitarian, or a Universalist, or a Congregationalist with some care, for they may be prohibitionists; but never the Jews and the real agnostics! And do not, please, accept a prohibitionist; he is too solemn and holy and dyspeptic. He knows your client would not have been indicted unless he were a drinking man, and anyone who drinks is guilty of something, probably much worse than he is charged with, although it is not set out in the indictment. Neither would he have employed you as his lawyer had he not been guilty.

I have never experimented with Christian Scientists; they are much too serious for me. Somehow, solemn people seem to think that pleasure is wicked. Only the gloomy and dyspeptic can be trusted to convict. Shakespeare knew: "Yon Cassius has a lean and hungry look; he thinks too much; such men are dangerous."

You may defy all the rest of the rules if you can get a man who laughs. Few things in this world are of enough importance to warrant considering them seriously. So, by all means, choose a man who laughs. A juror who laughs hates to find anyone guilty. Never take a wealthy man on a jury. He will convict, unless the defendant is accused of violating the anti-trust law, selling worthless stocks or bonds, or something of that kind. Next to the Board of Trade, for him, the penitentiary is the most important of all public buildings. These imposing structures stand for capitalism. Civilization could not possibly exist without them. Don't take a man because he is a "good" man; this means nothing. You should find out what he is good for. Neither should a man be accepted because he is a bad sort. There are too many ways of being good or bad. If you are defending, you want imaginative individuals. You are not interested in the morals of the juror. If a man is instinctively kind and sympathetic, take him.

Then, too, there are the women. These are now in the jury box. A new broom sweeps clean. It leaves no speck on the floor or under the bed, or in the darkest corners of life. To these new jurors, the welfare of the state depends on the verdict. It will be so for many years to come. The chances are that it would not have made the slightest difference to the state if all cases had been decided the other way. It might, however, make a vast difference to the unfortunates facing cruel, narrow-minded jurors who pass judgment on their fellow-men. To the defendants it might have meant the fate of life rather than death.

But what is one life more or less in the general spawning? It may float away on the tide, or drop to the depths of oblivion, broken, crushed and dead. The great sea is full of embryo lives ready to take the places of those who have gone before. One more unfortunate lives and dies as the endless stream flows on, and little it matters to the wise judges who coldly pronounce long strings of words in droning cadence; the victims are removed, they come and go, and the judges keep on chanting senseless phrases laden with doom

upon the bowed heads of those before them. The judge is as uncon-
cerned about the actual meaning of it all as the soughing wind
rustling the leaves of a tree just outside the courthouse door.

Women still take their new privilege seriously. They are all
puffed up with the importance of the part they feel they play, and
are sure they represent a great step forward in the world. They believe that the sex is cooperating in a great cause. Like the rest of us,
they do not know which way is forward and which is backward, or
whether either one is any way at all. Luckily, my services were almost over when women invaded the jury box. . . .

Judges and jurors are like the rest of humans. Now and then
some outstanding figures will roll up their sleeves, as it were, and
vigorously set to work to reform the courts and get an efficient administration of justice. This will be ably seconded by the newspapers, lashing courts and jurors, past, present and prospective, into a
spasm of virtue that brings down the innocent and guilty together,
assuming always that there are innocent and guilty. Then, for a
time, every defendant is convicted; and soon the campaign reaches
the courts; after ruining a few lives and reputations, the frenzy is
over, and life goes on smoothly and tranquilly as before.

When I was a boy in the country, one of the standard occupa-
tions was whittling. It became as mechanical as breathing. Since
then I have decided that this is as good a way to live as any other.
Life depends on the automatic taking in and letting out of breath,
but in no way is it lengthened or made happier by deep thinking or
wise acting. The one big word that stands over courts and other
human activities is FUTILITY.

The courts may be unavailing, lawyers stupid, and both as dry
as dust, but the combination makes for something interesting and
exciting, and it opens avenues that seem to lead somewhere. Liberty, lives, fortunes often are at stake, and appeals for assistance and
mercy rend the air for those who care to hear. In an effort to help,
often a casual remark may determine a seemingly vital situation,
when perhaps the remark, of all the palaver, was the least important
one breathed forth. In all questions men are frequently influenced
by some statement which, spoken at the eventful time, determines

fate. The most unforeseen, accidental meetings sometimes result in seemingly new and strangely fateful family lines. In fact, all that occurs in life is an endless sequence of events resulting from the wildest chance.

Amongst the twelve in a jury box are all degrees of alertness, all sorts of ideas, and a variety of emotions; and the lawyers, too, are important factors in the outcome. They are closely observed by the jurors. They are liked or disliked; mayhap because of what they say, or how they speak, or pronounce their words, or part their hair. It may be that a lawyer is disliked because he talks too little or too much, more often the latter. But a lawyer of subtlety should know when to stop, and when to go on, and how far to go. As a rule, he must not seem to be above the juror, nor below him. He must not too obviously strive for effect. He often meets baffling situations not easily explained. Sometimes it is better for him to talk of something else. Explanations must not be too fantastic or ridiculous. It does no harm to admit the difficulty of the situation, to acknowledge that this circumstance or that seems against him. Many facts point to guilt, but in another light these facts may appear harmless.

Lawyers are apt to interpret deeds and motives as they wish them to appear. As a matter of fact, most actions are subject to various inferences, sometimes quite improbable, but nonetheless true. Identifications show common examples of mistakes. Many men are in prison and some are sent to death through mistaken identifications. One needs but recall the countless errors he himself has made. How many have met some person whom they believed to be an old-time friend, and have found themselves greeting a total stranger? This is a common mistake made in restaurants and other public places. Many identifications in court are made from having seen a person but once, and under conditions not critical. Many are made from descriptions and photographs, and urged on by detectives, lawyers, and others vitally interested in the results. From all of this it is easy to see that many are convicted who are guiltless of crime. In situations of strong agitation, acquittals are rare, and sentences made long and barbarous and inhuman.

The judge is, of course, an important part of the machinery and administration of the court. Like carpenters and lawyers, brick-layers and saloon-keepers, they are not all alike. No two of them have the same fitness for their positions. No two have the same education; no two have the same natural understanding of themselves and their fellow-man, or are gifted with the same discernment and balance.

Not that judges are lacking in knowledge of law. The ordinary rules for the administration of law are rather simple and not difficult to follow. But judges should be students of life, even more than of law. Biology and psychology, which form the basis of understanding human conduct, should be taken into account. Without a fair knowledge of the mechanism of man, and the motives and urges that govern his life, it is idle to venture to fathom a situation; but with some knowledge, officers and the public can be most useful in preserving and protecting those who most need such help. The life of almost any unfortunate, if rightly understood, can be readjusted to some plan of order and system, instead of left to drift on to ruin, the victim of ignorance, hatred and chance.

If the physician so completely ignored natural causes as the lawyers and judges, the treatment of disease would be relegated to witchcraft and magic, and the dungeon and rack would once more hold high carnival in driving devils out of the sick and afflicted. Many of the incurable victims of crime are like those who once were incurable victims of disease; they are the product of vicious and incompetent soothsayers who control their destinies....

No scientific attitude toward crime can be adopted until lawyers, like physicians and scientists, recognize that cause and effect determine the conduct of men.

When lawyers and courts, and laymen, accept the scientific theory which the physicians forced upon the world long years ago, then men will examine each so-called delinquency until they discover its cause, and then learn how to remove the cause. This requires sympathy, humanity, love of one's fellow-man, and a strong faith in the power of knowledge and experience to conquer the maladies of men. The forum of the lawyers may then grow smaller, the courthouse may lose its spell, but the world will profit a thousandfold by a kindlier and more understanding relation toward all humankind.

SUPPLEMENTARY SELECTION

CLARENCE DARROW, "ABSURDITIES OF THE BIBLE"
From *Little Blue Book* No. 1631, Haldeman-Julius Publications, Girard,
Kansas; original version edited by E. Haldeman-Julius

... Is the Bible the work of anything but man? Of course, there is no such book as the Bible. The Bible [is] made up of sixty-six books, some of them written by various authors at various times, covering a period of about 1,000 years—all the literature that they could find over a period longer than the time that has elapsed since the discovery of America down to the present time....

What about its accounts of the origin of the world? What about its account of the first man and the first woman? Adam was the first, made less than 6,000 years ago. Well, of course, every scientist knows that human beings have been on the earth at least a half-million years, probably more. Adam got lonesome and they made a companion for him. That was a good day's work—or a day's work, anyhow. They took a simple way to take one of Adam's ribs and cut it out and make it into a woman.

Now, is that story a fact or a myth? ... If it isn't true, then what is? How much did they know about science in those days? How much did they know about the heavens and the earth? The earth was flat: did God write that down, or did the old Hebrew write it down because he didn't know any better and nobody else then knew any better?

What were the heavens? The sun was made to light the day and the moon to light the night. The sun was pulled out in the day time and taken in at night and the moon was pulled across after the sun was taken out. I don't know what they did in the dark of the moon. They must have done something.

The stars: all there is about the stars [is] "the stars he made also." They were just "also." Did the person who wrote that know anything whatever about astronomy? Not a thing! They believed they were just little things up in the heavens, in the firmament, just a little way above the earth, about the size of a diamond in an alderman's shirt stud. They always believed it until astronomers came along and told them something different.

Adam and Eve were put in a garden where everything was lovely and there were no weeds to hoe down. They were allowed to stay there on one condition, and that was that they didn't eat of the tree of knowledge. That has been the condition of the Christian church from then until now. It hasn't eaten as yet; as a rule it does not.

[Adam and Eve] were expelled from the Garden; Eve was tempted by the snake, who presumably spoke to her in Hebrew. And she fell for it, and of course Adam fell for it, and then they were driven out. How many believe that story today? If the Christian church doesn't believe it, why doesn't it say so? You do not find it saying that. If it does not believe it, here and there someone says it. That is, he says it at great danger to his immortal soul, to say nothing of his good standing in his church.

The snake was cursed to go on his belly after that. How he went before, the story doesn't say. And Adam was cursed to work. That is why we have to work—that is, some of us. Not I. And Eve and all of her daughters to the end of time were condemned to bring forth children in pain and agony. Lovely God, isn't it? Lovely!... If that story was necessary to keep me out of hell and put me in heaven... I wouldn't believe it because I couldn't believe it. I do not think any God could have done it and I wouldn't worship a God who would. It is contrary to every sense of justice that we know anything about....

"And Joshua Said to the Sun, 'Stand Still.'" "Is that true or is it a story?

And Joshua; you remember about Joshua. He was a great general. Very righteous... he was killing a lot of people [but] he hadn't quite finished the job, and so he turned to the mountain top and said to the sun, "Stand still till I finish this job," and it stood still.

... There are several things that [this story] does. It shows how little they knew about the earth, and day and night. Of course, they thought that if the sun stood still it wouldn't be pulled along any further and the night wouldn't come on. We know that if it had stood still from that day to this it wouldn't have affected the day or night; that is affected by the revolution of the earth on its axis.

Is [the story] true? Am I wicked because I know it cannot possibly be true? Have you got to get rid of all your knowledge and all your common sense to save your soul? Wait until I am a little older; maybe I can [believe it] then....

Here was a child born of a virgin. What evidence is there? What evidence? Do you suppose you could get any positive evidence that would make anyone believe that story today or anybody, no matter who it was?

Child, born of a virgin! There were at least four miraculous births recorded in the Testament. There was Sarah's child, there was Samson, there was John the Baptist, and there was Jesus. Miraculous births were rather a fashionable thing in those days, especially in Rome, where most of the theology was laid out. Caesar had a miraculous birth, Cicero, Alexander from Macedonia: nobody was in style or great unless he had a miraculous birth. It was a land of miracles.

What evidence is there of it? How much evidence would it require for intelligent people to believe such a story?...Nobody would believe it anyway, and yet some people say that you must believe that without a scintilla of evidence of any sort....

But let's look at some things charged to [Jesus]. He walked on the water. Now how does that sound? Do you suppose Jesus walked on the water? Joe Smith tried it when he established the Mormon religion. What evidence have you of that?

[Jesus] found some of His disciples fishing and they hadn't gotten a bite all day. Jesus said, "Cast your nets down there," and they drew them in full of fish. The East Indians couldn't do better than that. What evidence is there of it?

He was at a performance where there were 5,000 people and they were out of food, and He asked them how much they had; five loaves and three fishes, or three fishes and five loaves, or something like that, and he made the five loaves and three fishes feed all the multitude and they picked up I don't know how many barrels after-ward. Think of that! How does that commend itself to intelligent people, coming from a land of myth and fable as all Asia was, a land of myth and fable and ignorance in the main, and before anybody knew anything about science? And yet that must be believed, and is, to save us from our sins.

What are these sins? What has the human race done that was so bad, except to eat of the tree of knowledge? Does anybody need to save man from his sins in a miraculous way? It is an absurd piece of theology which they themselves say that you must accept on faith because your reason won't lead you to it....

I know the weakness of human reason...but it is all we have, and the only safety of man is to cultivate it and extend his knowl-edge so that he will be sure to understand life and as many of the mysteries of the universe as he can possibly solve....

Did [Jesus] raise a dead man to life? Why, tens of thousands of dead men and women have been raised to life, according to all the stories and all the traditions. Was this the only case? All Europe is filled with miracles of that sort, the Catholic Church performing miracles almost to the present time. Does anybody believe it, if they use their senses? I say no. It is impossible to believe it if you use your senses....

I am asked to say why I am an agnostic. I am an agnostic be-cause I trust my reason. It may not be the greatest that ever existed. I am inclined to admit that it isn't. But it is the best I have. That is a mighty sight better than some other people's at that.

I am an agnostic because no man living can form any picture of any God, and you can't believe in an object unless you can form a picture of it. You may believe in the force, but not in the object. If there is any God in the universe I don't know it. Some people say they know it instinctively. Well, the errors and foolish things that men have known instinctively are so many we can't talk about them.

As a rule, the less a person knows, the surer he is. He gets it by instinct, and it can't be disputed, for I don't know what is going on in another man's mind. I have no such instinct.

Let me give you just one more idea of a miracle of this Jesus story which has run down through the ages and is not at all the sole property of the Christian. You remember when Jesus was born in a manger, according to the story, there came wise men from the east to Jerusalem. And they were led by a star.

Now the closest star to the earth is more than a billion miles away. Think of the star leading three moth-eaten camels to a manger! Can you imagine a star standing over any house? Can you imagine a star standing over the earth even?... Well, if any star came that near the earth or anywhere near the earth, it would immediately disarrange the whole solar system. Anybody who can believe those old myths and fables isn't governed by reason.

CHAPTER 4

DEBATES

AUTOBIOGRAPHICAL INTRODUCTION

FROM CLARENCE DARROW, *THE STORY OF MY LIFE*, CHAPTER 41,
"A NEW HABIT" (1932)

Before I was of age I began speaking and debating. No doubt early environment was largely responsible for this. Before I was old enough to go to school at the academy I used to go up to the building every Friday night in the autumn and winter months. For several years, while I was in my later teens, the Literary Society met in the schoolhouse. My older brother Everett and my sister Mary were members of the organization, and before I was old enough to join I used to go to hear the essays and debates. It was some very pressing interference that caused me ever to miss one of these meetings. Our father always encouraged us to go, and sometimes he went along. As soon as possible I became a member and participated in the scholarly activities.

My interest in these exercises was stimulated by my father. The fact that he was a heretic always put him on the defensive, and we children felt that it was only right and natural and loyal to echo and champion his cause. Even in our little shop the neighbors heard vigorous discussions and found my father willing to meet all comers on the mysteries of life and death.

As a listening youth, my moral support was with my father. I never doubted that he was right, and the fact that most of the community was on the other side made me feel surer that his was the just cause. But in spite of the majority of the people being against his views, most of them respected him and his sincerity and recognized his learning and ability. Perhaps that early and exciting environment implanted a certain liking for exchange of ideas and the evolving of whatever mentality and personality that it thus brought about....

I cannot remember that I ever looked for a chance to talk. I am sure that neither directly nor indirectly did I ever challenge any one to debate, or seek to draw any one into debating. I have always been called on for much more than I wanted to do, or could do. For a great many years I spoke in various parts of the country without taking any compensation except expenses; and often, for some certain cause, where my interest and sympathy were strong and the urge was high and the treasury low, I have even paid the expenses myself. For the past forty years I have spoken in Chicago frequently and have never asked for money, and seldom received it.

From time to time, over a period of years, I debated at the Garrick Theatre on Sunday afternoons with George Burman Foster, a professor in the University of Chicago, and with Frederick Starr, also at the head of a department of the Chicago University, and others equally well known here and elsewhere. These debates were solely for the benefit of a free-thought organization that had a hard enough time to get along. I never accepted a penny for myself, but did insist that the others should always be paid a moderate amount.

I debated then as I do now, because of my interest in certain public questions. But since I have retired from business, and the demand upon my time and strength has grown from month to month, I lately have taken a fee for speaking and debating in connection with forums of various organizations, almost always outside Chicago. Especially has this come about since the panic, when I, in common with so many others, met marked losses and needed to do something to bridge the situation or else have to seriously cut down my living expenses, which in any event were never exorbitant....

My public talks have been mainly about politics, economics, labor, religion, prohibition, crime, and now and then on literary celebrities and what they have said and done. My debates have been on prohibition, religion, politics, and science. As a man's life consists largely of his ideas, I have felt free to present these questions as a part of myself and my life. Even this I have stated in my addresses and debates, so that my hearers would understand me and my attitudes from the start....

There is scarcely a city or town in the United States with a population of one hundred thousand or over where I have not spoken... and I have been in many of much smaller size. Most of the larger cities I have visited over and over again. In 1930 and 1931 I did more of this than ever before; I know of no reason for it but that I could lend myself to more engagements than when I had been otherwise occupied.

I spent a good deal of the winter of 1930 and 1931 in the South. I seem much like the Northern evangelists who are specially concerned over the souls of the Southern crackers in the winter time, but do not worry so much about them in the summer. During that season I visited most of the Southern States, in most of their large towns. On almost all occasions the audiences were large and decidedly responsive. In the debates there were generally a Rabbi and a Protestant and a Catholic. I alone represented the unrighteous, although I frequently had some consolation, and sometimes aid, from the Rabbi....

Main Selection

"Are We Machines?"

Debate between Clarence Darrow, affirmative, and Will Durant, negative, held at the New York League for Public Discussion (1927)

Powerfully giving voice to a socialist sense of progress in civilization, Will Durant was an enormously popular historian and lecturer whose books sold more than 17 million copies. At the time of this debate, Darrow was at the height of his fame following the Scopes and Sweet brothers trials, and Du-

rant's breakthrough popular book, The Story of Philosophy, *was a national bestseller. More than two thousand people were turned away from the overcrowded public auditorium where the debate was staged.*

Negative Presentation Address

WILL DURANT:...It was the Industrial Revolution that filled the world with the strange notion that man is a machine. For first of all it accustomed the mind to dealing with machines and induced it more and more to think of causes not as biological, but as mechanical. The worker within the factory wall, seeing the busy activity slip about him on pulleys and revolve on wheels, forgot that older existence in which life had seemed to be a matter of seeds spontaneously sprouting from the soil, responding eagerly to every encouragement, and multiplying with an astounding and bountiful fertility. The world, which had once been a picture of growing plants and wilful children, of loving mothers and ambitious men, became for the modern mind a vast array of mechanisms, from the planets that circled mechanically around the sun to the crowds that flocked mechanically to be in at the death of a moving-picture star. Science was sure now that it had at last been admitted behind the curtains of the cosmic drama. It marveled at the unsuspected machinery which had shifted a thousand scenes and created a million delusions. It concluded in modest admiration that the property man was the real dramatist and that the wires were the play.

But again, the Industrial Revolution made cities, and cities made crowds, and crowds unmade men. Once again in the modern metropolis those conditions appeared which in the ancient Orient had shorn the individual of personality, reduced him to insignificance, and led him to a similar philosophy of fatalism and despair. In this teeming welter of city population one became a number or a hand; the mind became an instrument for measuring, for weighing, for counting. A man became part of the machines he fed with fuel. Democracy, which had proposed to liberate the individual, became itself a mechanism, an enslaving chain of machines leading mindless masses to the ballot box. It was as useless for the individual to rebel against this system of wires and pulls and pushes as it had been for the individual to assert himself against the crushing conformities and crowds of the distant East. Even the leaders became a half-inanimate portion of the new contraption, almost as will-less and blind as the deluded people whose noses were quadrennially counted (or not counted) at the polls....

Was it necessary to yield so utterly? Is human behavior of the same order as the erosion of the hills, or the flight of the winds, or the obstinate tides of the sea? Is the inexhaustible solicitude of motherhood, the eager ambition of youth, the quiet tenderness of love merely a mechanical redistribution of physical force? Are the power and exuberance of life an appearance only? Is the passionate striving for beauty and perfection only a blind and fatal compulsion? Is the efficacy of consciousness only a delusion? Is the reality of will only a dream? Is man only a machine?

That is our question. It may comfort you to know that at the very moment when the theory of mechanism has reached down into popular favor, it is being abandoned in a great many of the sciences, in biology (not in psychology), in physiology, even in physics itself....

Yet, don't imagine for a moment that I wish to rest my case on authorities. Let us do our own thinking and face the phenomena directly for ourselves. Let us observe the unmechanical spontaneity, and purposiveness and selectiveness of life in locomotion, in digestion, in growth, in regeneration, in reproduction, in consciousness, and in genius.

Consider locomotion. Take some mechanism, say a toy automobile which will run resolutely enough when its spring has been wound and released by a human hand. Set it upon a smooth floor directly facing a slightly distant wall. Wind the spring, and release it. The car plunges forward against the wall. If the conditions are perfect it will rebound in the same line by which it advanced. It will stop for a moment and it will advance again and rebound in that same straight line, and continue forward and back in the same straight line until its artificial energy is completely spent.

By contrast let us perform in imagination an experiment that has been repeated time and again in biological laboratories. Take a glass bowl and fill it with water. Across the center put a perfectly transparent glass partition just short enough to leave a narrow slit at either side. Into one half drop food. Into the other half drop some lowly organism, as simple as possible. Observe it under the microscope. It moves directly forward toward the food. It does not see the glass. It strikes the glass and rebounds in a straight line: apparently it is a machine. But suddenly it veers about, to the left or the right, and moves forward now at an angle, strikes the glass, rebounds. It veers again in the same direction. If it veered left the first time, it veers left again. It moves forward, strikes the glass, rebounds, again goes forward, goes through the partition, and finds the food. I ask you, can you conceive of a mechanical contraption of any kind that could possibly rival that judicious veering about, this appearance of self-directive purpose in the lowliest organism known to man? ...

Consider growth. How could a machine grow? Why should it wish to grow? Was there ever a mechanism so marvelous that it might offer an analogy to the astounding self-development of life? Consider the lilies of the field: what enchanting power is it that frees them from their prison in the soil and lifts them, slowly, longingly toward the sun? ...

Consider regeneration. Cut off one ray of a starfish and the center will regrow it. Cut off all of them, and the center will regrow them all. Cut out the center and the rays will regrow it. A machine out of order cannot repair its parts; it waits stupidly and senselessly for some living hand to come and restore it to order and efficacy. ...

Therefore, consider reproduction. ... Now, ladies and gentlemen, imagine a machine that cohabits with another machine to produce a third machine. Imagine that each machine is composed of millions of parts, each of which has the power of reproduction, and divides and multiplies and grows. Imagine that each machine separates one special part of itself to coalesce with a special part of another machine to form the model of a new machine.... I ask you, was there ever a jollier hoax in science or philosophy? Was there ever in any religion, ancient, medieval or American, any miracle that could compare with this majestic and monstrous myth? ...

Let us in conclusion consider genius. Here is the creative power of life in its clearest and highest form. Here is the last product of that glorious vitality which dances in the atom and fills the soil and the sea and the air with living and growing things. Here, in genius, mind turns around and remolds the environment in which it grew. Man, the supposed machine, invents and operates machines, and craves beauty, and seeks truth, and creates social order, and rises to the loftiest reaches of morality and love. And I am asked to believe that the philosophic frenzy of Plato, the fine passion of Beethoven or Shakespeare, the divine intoxication of Spinoza, the godlike grandeur of Leonardo da Vinci's mind are mechanical processes, that the thoughts and the aspirations of these men were put into them with some mysterious time attachment by that mythical nebula a million millennia ago!

Well, I refuse to believe it. I cannot understand how any cautious and skeptical mind can so far forget itself as to accept so ridiculous a fairy story; and I wonder does Mr. Darrow realize how much credulity lies behind his unbelief, how much simple faith in untested and fallible authority? I do not believe that Chicago's leading citizen is a machine mechanically meditating upon its own machinery, an automaton automatically reflecting upon its own automatism. If I could believe that I could accept every fairy story ever told and every legend in every Bible ever written. After escaping from the infallibility of a church and from the infallibility of a book I refuse to surrender to the infallibility of a physicist who tries to squeeze into his test tubes and his narrow formulae all this budding and teeming world. It is time we should put an end to this new age of faith, and come to doubt even our scientists when they speak to us of miracles in terms of a childish mythology....

Affirmative Presentation Address

CLARENCE DARROW:...My friend over here has been talking for forty minutes telling us what life is not, but not uttering a single word as to what it is.... If one seriously does not believe that man is a machine, then it is up to him as a matter of fairness to tell us what man is—if he can—which he can't. I will be honest with you in this matter. I cannot prove to you that man is a machine. I cannot demonstrate to you just what process makes life. I cannot demonstrate to you as a mathematician would demonstrate a problem just what process of mechanism brings consciousness, if there be such a thing, which is very doubtful.

What I do contend is this: That the manifestation of the human machine and of living organisms is very like unto what we know as a machine, and that if we could find it all out we would probably find that everything had a mechanistic origin....

Now, what is a machine, first? I will not especially quarrel with my friend's definition of a machine, for I never deal in technicalities, and I have no short cut in this question. I am here to learn. I only wish I had a chance! *[Laughter.]* One definition of a machine which appeals to me as pretty good is this: "An apparatus so designed that it can change one kind of energy to another for a purpose." Coal may be taken out of a mine and fed into a machine and it may produce power in the shape of steam or electricity. It was all in the coal before, but it has been transferred to something else. Nothing is lost, no forces, no power of any sort is lost, no matter is lost. It is simply changed into something else.

Is man this sort of a machine? Let's examine it. I don't know so much about the nobility and grandeur of man as my friend seemed to think perhaps he knows. I do not think that I am degrading him when I place him in the category of machines. If anybody complains it ought to be the machine!

What do we know about the human machine? We know that it takes one form of energy and transposes it into another. We know that we give it food which in the human system is broken up and the energy that results is transferred into something else. Let us look at the process that the human machine goes through in this transformation of energy and see whether it resembles any other machine, and if it doesn't, then what? Is there some mysterious thing about man which for lack of some other word, or for lack of any word that any human being can understand, we call a soul? Does he stand out here separated from nature, and stand alone? Let us see what man does.

We feed him, or he can't live and he can't work. We place food in his mouth. What happens to it? It is digested. The energy in the food is released and goes into the body just exactly the same as the energy placed in the coal box of an engine is released and makes steam. How does it go? It is first taken care of by certain juices and is digested. It passes into the intestine. Then what happens? This digested food is power, just like the coal; it is energy. If a man is to work, if the body is to live, this energy must become a part of him. It must go to his brain, if he has any, to his feet, to every part of him. How does it get there? Man has a circulatory system made of arteries and blood vessels. The artery at the intestine is separated by only a very small lining from the intestine. The juices of the intestine pass into the blood, some of the blood to the intestines. As it goes by these juices are absorbed; this food is absorbed; this energy is absorbed; the power is absorbed—a simple, plain, obviously mechanical process.

Then what happens? These arteries and blood vessels reach every part of the body. They carry to every part of the body the strength that it needs and the power that it needs.

But the system must have oxygen just exactly the same as an engine must have oxygen for combustion. One thing is turned into another. This food is turned into starch, sugar, and one or two other things and consumed to produce this power. The blood is pumped by the heart. We call it pumped; that isn't exactly the process. I don't need to describe the process—in fact, I can't. But for all conveniences everybody calls the heart a pump. Anyhow, by its constant action it pushes the blood out and in. It is carried to the lungs. As it passes through the lungs just for a brief second it comes in contact with the air, which is necessary to complete the fuel. The power is carried to every part of the human body; perfectly mechanical, like an engine, like a machine that a man has built—the whole process the same....

Is there anything that a man presents in his conduct, in his actions, in the uses of his abilities, that isn't performed in exactly the same way as a machine? I think there is not.... My friend talks about the absurdity of a machine writing poetry. Well now, I think that is just what machines do, as a rule. Nothing but a machine can turn out the metrical stuff that passes as poetry....

If we were standing somewhere out in space and saw this planet moving as if it was in a devil of a hurry to get along with its journey, we'd say it had free will and knew where it was going. Of course, we'd say it, because we don't know any better, and somebody standing out somewhere and watching all the automobiles come into New York in the morning and go out at night would say the drivers have free will, too. They have neither freedom nor will, or they wouldn't do it. *[Laughter.]* ...

When it comes to man you can find out every single thing that is in him. There isn't a single thing in him you can't buy at the drug store for about ninety-five cents, and a good many of them aren't worth it at that! *[Laughter.]* Why is it, pray tell me, that all the investigation, with closed eyes, that theologians have always given these problems, with all the thought and all the speculation, down through all the ages they have never found a single thing that isn't mechanical, never found a single thing in man, or the manifestation of a single thing, that isn't a mechanism? And when we get to man and understand him, we understand what the mechanism is. It is man's body....

His body isn't a perfect thing in any way. It is full of maladjustments. No two bodies are equally good, but no two are perfect. Even his eyes are a botched job. His nervous system is a bad job. His whole internal organism is bad. At that, it is better than most machines, perhaps than any. But why? Why is it bad? I will tell you why. Let me give you a few simple illustrations. Men get varicose veins in their legs. Why? Because the small veins in the legs won't hold up all the blood of the body and they were made as they are when he walked on all fours. The veins didn't need to hold up any such weight of blood. His whole apparatus goes back to a primitive time and more simple arrangement. He used what he could use of the old while he was getting the new. How long has he been doing this? Nobody knows. As a human being he has been here at least a half million years. As a descendant of earlier organisms he has been here since the earth was cool enough for life to exist. He is constantly changing.

Is there anybody who can tell us where the first form of life began, or how it began? If he can, he ought to. It would be very interesting. Can you tell when or where or how? Nobody knows. They don't know when or where or how, but they do know this. We read it in the rocks, we read it in man; we read it in all animal life that this first was an inorganic world floating in space, made for nobody so far as we can see, unless someone was playing football with it, and it was hardly large enough for that, or interesting enough. It circulated in space for millions of ages without any form of what we call life, and gradually, as it cooled, and probably through heat and moisture, vegetable life appeared. Vegetable life had the field alone for ages. Vegetable life created inorganic matter into organic matter. How? Because it had a soul? Nobody knows anything about the soul of a cabbage, although they think they know about the soul of a cabbage head! I can't see any difference. Nobody knows a thing about it. Animals came, and they lived upon vegetable life, more primitive forms first. Man is the last and perhaps the most complex of all. We know enough about the past, we know enough about evolution, we know enough about man himself, we know enough about the mechanical constructions of things to be warranted in believing that when we have all the facts and are wise enough we will find that all is of one pattern. *[Applause.]*

Negative Refutation

DR. DURANT:... Mr. Darrow tells me that no fact has been discovered that proves anything except that all life is mechanical. Well, I can only believe that he had a good nap while I was talking. I thought I had loaded the atmosphere down with facts about locomotion and digestion and growth and almost everything conceivable. I observed the care with which he avoided touching upon the facts that I had enumerated! *[Applause.]*

I don't remember his attempting to meet any one of the points made, but I have hopes that an attempt will be made before the night is over. He says with the audacity of a young student that we have never found a single thing that isn't a mechanism. Well, of course, that is the begging of a question. We are discussing that question, we are not assuming it. He tells us there is not a single thing in you that cannot be bought in a drug store. I don't think you could buy the raw materials that would make a Clarence Darrow unless you had some life potency to work upon those materials and build them up! *[Applause.]* ...

Why, I submit that the merest sensation going on in these living organisms here tonight is something that Mr. Darrow has not begun to reduce into a mechanical process. A machine doesn't repair itself that way, never could possibly begin to create blood in itself. Always that power of life is hard in a living thing, which distinguishes it from mechanisms....

Now, when I speak of this power of life, it is in that sense that I consider myself free. I do not say I have free will. I submit that I never used that phrase, except to ridicule it in my first address. I quite recognize that my will is the sum total of my desires, my aptitude, my dispositions, my tendencies. I recognize that I was subjected to thousands of molding forces even before I was born. But there is that thing, that quota, that iota, that particle of life that is subjected to these things. It is a neglected part of the determining conditions. That is the whole point....

Affirmative Refutation

MR. DARROW: ... I want to repeat again that I can't explain the mystery of life, but I think I know enough about it to believe that when it is all told, human life and animal life and plant life will be just like everything else that exists, and all come within the same great general realm of law, that no miracle was wrought when these things made a human being. Man wasn't made out of the earth in the image of God, with a bone furnished to make a wife. Nothing of that. He is a matter of evolution from the first forms, and where those come from I don't know, but I do believe that it all works in a mechanistic way. *[Applause.]* . . .

I think that the theory of mechanism is growing very rapidly in the world. There are only two theories that I can conceive. There may be a hundred others that no man knows about, but there are only two theories that can be conceived. Now my friend talks about vitalism. What in the dickens does he mean by vitalism? Change the word spirit to vital, and it means nothing. . . .

We know now that the earth is one of the most insignificant spots of mud in the whole untraversed universe; that there are an infinite number of suns and planets and stars that are as much bigger than the earth as we are bigger than a fly speck. We know it, and yet, we hang on to the idea that somehow or other we are going to be cheated unless we live forever!

I am not here to give you any consolation. I am not going to give you any consolation excepting this, that in a world of egotistic people who have nothing to brag about excepting their ignorance, a frame that is capable of some joy but of much pain, a life of vicissitudes whose end is death and pain, and whose constant accompaniment is pain, in a world of that sort it ought to be some consolation to know that you haven't got to live forever.

Why am I interested in this subject, and why should you be interested? Because, as my friend puts it, man is an inquiring animal. Can any being something like man be an inquiring animal? Oh, yes. All the animals are, and I suspect in the same sense all the plants are. You see them poking their noses into the most unheard of places, and for no reason on earth excepting curiosity as far as I can see. We can't correctly translate the actions of plants and animals. The only thing I ever saw that to my limited knowledge seemed to have free will was an electric pump I had once on a summer vacation. Every time we wanted it to go, it stopped. I couldn't think of anything except free will, and all of a sudden when we knew nothing about it, it started again. *[Laughter.]* Now, I suspect that there was a reason for it. I suspect there was just as much reason for it as there is for the most intelligent being, if we could find such a person, and such an action....

As far as we know and can see and understand, this is a monistic universe. It is all of one piece. The farthest star that our telescope sees is made from exactly the same material as the earth. One law rules, and it rules the living and the dead. There are no living, and there are no dead, because there is action in the dead as well as the living, simply of a different form as the decay of the body and sending forth of the gases is all one thing, and it is idle to try to separate it. *[Applause.]*

Negative Rebuttal

DR. DURANT: I doubt if the first speaker in a debate has any right to this third appearance. I have protested against it, but they have asked me to obey the Queensbury Rules, and so I should like to say (now that Mr. Darrow has no chance of answering me) that all his talk about the immortality or non-immortality of the soul is irrelevant to this debate, and I put it aside. *[Applause.]* ...

Let us be honest and clear-headed with ourselves. Do we treat ourselves as machines? Do we treat our friends as machines? Does Clarence Darrow treat people as machines, or as living, growing, groping, feeling personalities? I leave his life to answer that.

He tells me that life is stupid, that it is often suicidal.... Yes, life is full of maladjustments, of sufferings, but what I see in it is that it ran a tremendous gamut from the amoeba to Clarence Darrow, and I do not believe that we can understand that effortful struggle of life to reach from that lowly condition to this culminating condition unless you see in it something that could not possibly be explained in mechanical terms. And when I say vital I do not use a mystical term. Let me remind you that we are more directly aware of vitality than of any other fact in the world. If that is not a fact, nothing is. And yet, we die, which I remind you again a machine cannot do. But sometimes before we die we reproduce, and through reproduction life cheats death and passes on. We individuals are the cells of the body of life; we drop off like the epidermal cells of our hands, but the living power goes on, reaching ever higher.

Mr. Darrow wants my theory. My theory is not vitalism. I never used the word tonight, but he has chosen to put that theory into my mouth. Vitalism is the theory of Bergson that, in addition to matter and absolutely distinct from it, [there] is this thing called life which he believes can exist without matter. I disagree with all those propositions. I do not say that life exists in matter and distinct from it. I say matter is alive. I say that life and matter are one in inextricable unity, and matter is a word that describes only one side of that complicated and throbbing fact. *[Applause.]* I suspect that if we could get into the inside of the matter, we should have to use in order to understand it that concept of the organism and vitality which I have suggested to you. That is all.

SUPPLEMENTARY SELECTION

"IS LIFE WORTH LIVING?"

Debate between George Burman Foster, a religion professor at the University of Chicago, affirmative, and Clarence Darrow, negative, held at the Garrick Theatre, Chicago, Illinois, March 11, 1917

Deeply influenced by the pragmatic philosophy of John Dewey and German biblical higher criticism, Foster was a prominent member of the so-called Chicago School of Theology, which promoted scientific modernism within the liberal wing of American Protestantism. He died in 1918.

Opening Speeches

GEORGE BURMAN FOSTER:... The day has come when that which the race has most commonly appealed to in the long human story, i.e., some superhuman agency, some reservoir of power not our own, which we can tap, and from which we can draw living waters of strength and courage and hope, is what is most in doubt on the part of needy souls. If I mistake not, many men, in their religious beliefs, are in a tight place. They think the environmental odds, in the absence of the gods, are too much for them. It only takes Darrow to assure them that this is so, and life is not only overcast with the pale hue of thought, but sinks into abysmal darkness, and men ask what is the good....

But, there is another item in this religion problem still. Men have said, "I can endure my situation now with resignation, fortitude, in view of the sure and certain hope of immortality where the scales will be turned and the environment will be plastic and malleable in my hands and there will be nothing in it that does not lead to facile organization into those verities and values and virtues which I may enjoy in an eternity of unruffled bliss, and, in view of that fact, my hope of the immortal life encourages me, so that I can at least endure now if I cannot triumph." I do not know what Darrow is going to do with that, but we shall see.

Meantime, as a matter of fact, this two-fold belief has obtained in ninety-nine cases out of every hundred—no, I think I could go further and say that in the history of the human race, this two-fold belief has obtained in nine hundred and ninety-nine cases out of every thousand up to the present time. And, although I admit that in certain forms of it, it is under decay today, yet, up to the present, in view of the strength it has given to men, in view of the satisfaction and cheerfulness and fortitude it has brought to the human heart in all kinds of trying and despairing situations, in view of these things up to the present time, I say the vast majority of the human race has had an adequate basis for a consistent opposition to a fundamental pessimistic judgment of the worth of life, of the value of man, and of the appraisal of the universe. Up to this time that is true. But there is some corrosive that is undermining these beliefs. Yet I do not say if they are corroded and undermined that I have no chance to make out a case against pessimism, for I have.

I think that I can surrender both of these beliefs and yet make out a case against pessimism in this world. But I am not going to surrender them until I have to. Meantime, I am to urge upon you and upon my friend Mr. Darrow that up to this date, in view of the persistence of these two beliefs with nine hundred and ninety-nine out of every thousand of the human race, there has been a consistent basis for hope, for encouragement, that can rob life of its terror and the grave of its gloom. So life in all the past has had a good basis for rejecting the deadening influence of a pessimistic unfaith. But what of the future? Even now there are those who are so sure that they have experienced the direct intervention of God in their own lives that they are on that account safe from pessimistic doubt. Others find the essence of faith in the will, and are willing to will a reality whose existence cannot be proved or refuted. These believe along the line of their deepest needs. I think I must belong to this class. Others still believe only what can be scientifically verified. To them religion is a dead issue, and by them pessimism is sometimes espoused. Mr. Darrow's task is to make out a case for scientific pessimism, and I shall retire and let him do so....

CLARENCE DARROW: I am going to admit, from Professor Foster's statement, that he has almost proven his case. Perhaps up to the present there have been more men to whom life was worth while than to whom it was not. The cheerful idiot has been plentiful in the past. But when I admit that, he also suggests that the foundations of faith are tottering and the world is waking up, and when it loses its heaven and its god, there will be pessimists, or we must get hold of some new delusion.

I think that no one can be an optimist unless he believes in a future life, and a future life which must be an improvement on this one. Every religion I am familiar with—and religion is my long suit—every one of them is practically based upon the idea that life is not worth while unless God is in heaven and all is well with the world. He is going to pay us for what he has done to us here. Now, that does not satisfy for two reasons: First, there is no proof of either God or heaven, and, second, if you assume it, you have no reason to assume that the Lord will do better in the next world than he did in this! Without those two propositions, I can see nothing to be cheerful over—except temporarily when indulging in excessive drink or something of the sort, giving a delusion of optimism, seeing things as things are not. Optimism is really seeing things. And I do not object to anybody seeing things if they can. But, if they point me to some wonderful thing and I cannot see it, then I cannot be an optimist on that account. . . .

Wherever you find consciousness, you must find pain and suffering. Then, perhaps we balance up—is there more pain or more pleasure? This question is not an easy one, perhaps, to prove. It can scarcely be proven by my friend Foster.

Take all the good things in this world that bring joy, and figure out all the horrible things that bring suffering. Perhaps there is a broader basis to place it on than that. It is hard to find a single place, save for the moment, where suffering is not present with consciousness and it is hard to find a chance to get out of the suffering until you lose consciousness forever and forever. . . .

Man invented heaven so that life might be good; so that life might be better than non-existence. Take the whole Christian world. Tell them for a moment so they will understand it and believe it, that there is no future, that the grave ends all. How many optimists would be left? Then they would ask the question, what is their religion for? It is a crutch to lean on. And when it ceases to be a crutch, that is the end of it.

Practically all real optimism rests upon the idea that there is something good in the universe, which neither the eye or the reason of man can take hold of. Somewhere we will get paid for what we suffer. Now, if you believe it, you can be an optimist. The world that has believed it, perhaps is optimistic. But, we are growing intelligent. We are increasing knowledge, until one can no longer pin his faith to a heaven that cannot be proven, to something that cannot stand the investigation of science,—in fact, to a lie. . . .

Men have turned to every delusion in the world to satisfy their desire to find something better, to keep on living, to find life worth while. Why, they even turn to socialism! And Single Tax!

DR. FOSTER: And prohibition.

MR. DARROW: Yes, and prohibition, the Professor says. But I can get more optimism without prohibition than I can with it. The socialist says sometime we will have an ideal state, where everybody will be rich and happy, and won't have to work—I have tried that—and I got over that, too. In the first place, the ideal state was too far away to create any emotion in me, and, in the second place, I know you cannot get happy by getting rich. I have tried that, too.

If you make everybody equally rich or equally poor, it does not bring happiness, for that is mostly within you, and the reason it is within you is because you must find some sort of dope within you to square yourself with life. It is a mental attitude, believing something. If I am not an optimist, it does not mean that I haven't tried. I am willing to try any new scheme or old. Of course there are many kinds of dope that will work on some people that will not work on others. All I contend for is to let each person take his individual dope and see if it will work. Once in a while a glass of whisky will make me an optimist. Sometimes making a speech will make me fairly optimistic. Morphine will do it. Smoking any kind of a pipe will do it, more or less, mental or physical. But I never could find anything that would do it except smoking a pipe, nothing else, for any length of time....

Let me give you one more thought. I am a pessimist, but I am a cheerful pessimist. I sometimes think that pessimism is my dope. I would hate to live without it. I don't know what I would do.

Is it all black? Why, it is the only good philosophy of life; it prepares you for the worst. I am never disappointed unless I am happy. Nothing can come out any worse than I expect.... It is a pleasant thought!

Closing Speeches

DR. FOSTER: Mr. Chairman, Ladies and Gentlemen: It is as I expected! I now know what a pessimist is. A pessimist is a man who, when he has to choose between two evils, takes both! I really expected that you would be led into an inclement, dismal region of pessimism where there are fifty-seven varieties of weather, at least,—all bad! Bad, did I say? All the worst possible!...

I want to call your attention in this connection to a fact characteristic of his entire speech, and characteristic of all pessimism wherever you find it. Pessimism cannot make out its case save upon the basis of a reduction, an impoverishment, a mutilation of human nature as we know it in actual experience. It has to leave out and be blind to whole regions of us. Darrow did it. He reduced us to the pleasure or pain ingredient. And then he was blind to the pleasure. And, by that process of decimation, he got us down to a content of pain, and said, what's the good? But human nature, as we know it, has pleasure and pain, not as its essential content at all. We are greater than that. There are other sides to us than that. There is the content of moral worth. So surely is this true that we sacrifice our pleasure and suffer pain to achieve ends that we set ourselves, whether God sets them or not—ends that we think are worth while. Pleasure is no more than Nature's bribe to keep the race going. Joy is far higher, pointing out the direction in which the driving force of life is urging. Every creative act brings joy....

I deny that there is a theoretical basis for pessimism. Let me look into this a little more closely.

Now, add up your column of pain and your column of pleasure. Take a single day. The pleasure side would run this way: Today: Had a good night's sleep. Enjoyed ham and eggs at breakfast. Read a chapter out of the Bible. Had a nice special delivery letter from a friend. Debated with Darrow. And so forth.

Then, on the pain side: Coffee was scorched. Read horrible murder story in the newspaper. Had to listen to the neighbor across the way play the piano. Debated with Darrow. And so forth.

Now, my friends, add up the columns. Draw the balance. Draw up a calculus of pleasures and pains, and show that in the balance the pains exceed the pleasures. The thing can't be done.

It can't be done for a single day, much less for a whole life. How is it possible to fix a standard or unit of pleasure-value? There is no common measure. Besides, pleasures are different in quality. How can I say which is ten, which twenty, or five, or six percent? Here is Darrow's stomach-ache; here is the death of my friend. You see that when this matter is reduced, as Mr. Darrow did it, to a calculus of pleasure-pain, he can get nowhere. You cannot affirm, demonstrably, pessimism—for it is utterly impossible for you to get a standard or unit of measure of pleasure or pain by which you can solve the problem....

If I might bear my personal testimony as against the position of Mr. Darrow, who would not live his life over again, I stand before this audience as a man that has had not a few of what many a man would call the blind blows of what seem to be a cruel fate—not infrequently have I received these blows—and I declare to you that my soul still believes in the final balance of the best, is not crushed, and in the face of all that has been endured, if I had a chance to live my life over again, I would do it again and again!...

MR. DARROW: My good friend, Professor Foster, if he keeps on debating, will become an orator! The only trouble about oratory is that it is not true. I used to work at it some. Now, I liked his speech. I always like his talks: Almost thou persuadeth me to say that I am an optimist. I would like to be one. Let's see what it amounts to.

Is life worth living? Does that have anything to do with pleasure and pain? I am not at all sure that pleasure and pain are the correct measures of existence. However, I think they come the nearest to it. What else can you test it by as well as pleasure and pain?

Is life worth living to me? To you? Would it have been better for you had you never been born, or is it better for you as it is? That is the question. And I think there is no other test excepting pleasure and pain. Has it been worth while? It is not a question of whether you are master of your soul—which you are not, excepting in rhetoric. In the first place you have no soul, and in the second place, you are not master. The blind forces are master. It is not a question of whether you will be heroic while tied to the stake with a fire built around you for maintaining your convictions. That sounds good, but I cannot imagine there is much fun in it. . . .

How do we live? Does anybody live it honestly? Or do we live it by everlastingly deceiving ourselves? Do we live upon facts or do we live upon feelings, emotions, dreams and imaginings? I have not many illusions left. I think I might get a new one, I don't know. Like him, I love clever men and intellectual, interesting women—especially interesting. I love all the good things of life. Have I ever lived the truth? Let me be honest for a moment. I have not lived on today; neither have you; neither has the Professor. I have lived on tomorrow; on next summer; on next year. The man does not live who can open his eyes upon the facts of life and live. He lives upon what is created by his dreams, and he can live in no other way. . . .

Do I want the truth? Do I live on it? Not for a moment. Nobody lives on it. If I suspect that somebody has some nasty criticism to make do I try to hear it? Or do I run away? If the newspapers say something unpleasant, as they generally do, and I see it first, I don't look at it. If, per chance, some friend of mine sneaks something into the papers that is favorable, I read it three or four times. Even if I know it isn't true! Do I live on facts or illusions? Nobody lives on facts; and they cannot live on facts. The trouble with intelligence is that it is hard to keep illusions with intelligence. It is hard for a man as intelligent as I am to be an optimist! . . .

Would you live your life over?

I would not live mine. And, as lives go, I have no complaint to make of mine. Life is about the same with one and all. Schopenhauer compared it to sitting in the box at the play; the people are the same, you see it, and it is done. I have seen the play, into the fourth act, and I think I will stay to the fifth, though I know it will end with a tragedy. We do not live because we expect to be happy or unhappy. We live because Nature has planted in us the will to live and we cannot die, and however heroically we may live, it does not change the question as to whether life is good or life is bad. . . .

SUPPLEMENTARY SELECTION

"IS THE HUMAN RACE PERMANENTLY PROGRESSING
TOWARD A BETTER CIVILIZATION?"
Debate between University of Chicago professor
John C. Kennedy, affirmative, and Clarence S. Darrow, negative,
held at the Garrick Theatre, Chicago, Illinois, March 23, 1919

A proponent of socialist economic reforms, Kennedy served as a Chicago city alderman. At the time of this debate, he was optimistic about the potential of the Russian Revolution and was preparing for a trip to Moscow.

Opening Speeches

JOHN C. KENNEDY: Mr. Chairman, Mr. Darrow, Comrades and Friends: Lester F. Ward has defined social progress as "Whatever increases the sum total of human happiness." For the purpose of this debate I am willing to accept this definition given by Mr. Ward and to endeavor to show that social evolution has been following along lines which, on the whole, have been increasing the sum total of human happiness. There are certain conditions which I think all of us will agree to be necessary for the advancement of human happiness.

In the first place, for most of us, at least, it is necessary to have a good subsistence, to have the necessaries of life before we can enjoy any great amount of happiness. We must have plenty of food—a variety of food; must have adequate clothing and shelter. These are fundamental requisites for happiness for the masses of the people.

Then, again, we need freedom; freedom to pursue some line of activity which gives us satisfaction; freedom of thought; freedom of expression; freedom to develop our personality so that our various talents and capacities will have an opportunity to manifest themselves.

In addition to this freedom, if we are to enjoy happiness, I think most of us must have leisure—we must have the time to enjoy the fine arts, to enjoy music, sculpture, painting, literature, the drama—we must have the time, opportunity and means to travel and enjoy the beauties of Nature.

These are some of the requirements of happiness for the human race. And just insofar as any civilization makes it possible for an increasingly large number of people to get the necessities of life, to enjoy freedom, self-expression, to participate in the fine arts, and enjoy the fine arts, I would say that we are making progress toward a higher civilization....

There is the key to human history and the one who masters that interpretation of history and applies it to the development from the primitive savage stage up to the present, can see that as the tools developed; as man's understanding of the forces of Nature developed; as the industrial system developed; civilization moved forward. And, it is only when something happens to that industrial system that you make any lasting progress. And, the whole lesson of history is this, that economically, we have been progressing from a very simple, crude stage of production up to a higher and higher stage of production, which makes possible, what? It makes possible a vast amount of wealth; which makes possible a great amount of leisure; which makes possible for the first time in all human history real freedom. It is only by the conquest of the forces of Nature—by the organization of the productive forces—by the application of science to the natural resources and the powers of the universe: it is only thus, that we get the foundation for a real civilization, a real freedom.

And, the lesson of all human history is, despite all the superstition, despite all of the tyranny, despite all of the sufferings of the past, we have been marching forward toward that goal, getting an economic foundation for a real civilization. And, today, we are just about at the point where it is within the grasp of humanity to build a co-operative commonwealth where all will be free; where all will enjoy the fruits of human progress; where all will be free, not only economically, but intellectually and spiritually; where the fogs of superstition will pass away; where freedom of thought will prevail and where mankind really will enjoy happiness.

And, it is because I believe that; because I see what has been already achieved, I am ready to say here today, we are making permanent progress toward a higher civilization!

CLARENCE DARROW: ... I do not know whether the civilized man of today is happier than the savage or not. I fancy that I am happier here in Chicago than I would be in Tierra del Fuego, but I kind of fancy that those natives are happier there than they would be here! I would hate to be a barn-yard hog, but I fancy if they had any brains—which they have not—they would hate to be men. I am inclined to think, on the whole, they are happier, while it lasts, and it does not last very long either way so I do not see there is much in that. The question that I am interested in is not the one that my friend discussed—I do not mean that his discussion was not interesting. It was both interesting and learned, especially learned, and still it does not get anywhere.

Now, I really do not know how to prove that a civilized man is less happy than a savage; in fact, I do not know how to prove which is the civilized man and which is the savage! That question depends upon your standpoint, like everything else in this world. Of course, there is only one really civilized man that I know. There are a lot of them who think they are, but they are not.

I am willing to accept [Professor Kennedy's] definition of progress. That is one thing we agree on. I believe that progress is purely a question of the pleasure units that we get out of life. The pleasure and pain theory is the only correct theory of morality and the only way to judge life. Many of us might debate for a great while about the meaning of the word progress, but I think he has come closer to it than anybody else could have got at it and I am going to accept it just as he stated it.

Progress means how much fun we get out of it. If the human race today is getting more fun out of it than it was five hundred years ago, then there has been progress between that time and this. If it was getting more fun out of it two thousand years ago, than it was one thousand years ago, then there was no progress between the two thousand years ago and one thousand years ago. If, at a certain time it got more pleasure and then something happened so it got less, then there has not been progress between those two dates. If there is a permanent law of progress it means we are forever going toward a point where the human race is getting more and more pleasure out of life. That is what I dispute. I presume there are periods in the human race when men got along more comfortably than at other periods, but we are not always getting along more comfortably year after year or age after age. We go forward and we go backward and we go up and we go down and bob around and think we are getting somewhere and we are not. That is what I contend: I do not think we are getting anywhere....

For instance, [Professor Kennedy] tells us they used to be very superstitious. Used to be? We have the same God the first savage had, and He does just the same things, and we believe in Him just as much. His method of action has taken a different form, that is all. Now, I suppose there were half a million people, more or less, today who went to church in Chicago and at least pretended that they believe in God. A thoroughly civilized city! The savages had something to look at that represented their god; but the Chicago people did not—they just talked into the air! And, we are civilized! We have all the charms and incantations and so on.

Why, I went to a banquet the other night, a Victory banquet, on account of our triumph over German autocracy, and some "fool" preacher talked to God before we had a chance to talk, and he thanked God for ending the war! The preacher did not think it funny. I fancy I was pretty nearly the only one there that did. Of course, he did not thank Him for starting the thing; just for stopping it....

Then, to come back to the savage.... Really, is there any way to tell [who is happier]? We just assume these things, you know.

Now, if a savage wrote books, he would tell how much better off they were than we civilized people are. If the mosquitoes wrote them they would tell; if the flies wrote them, they would tell us how all these fool people waste their time preparing food for them to eat. We only see the world from the standpoint of civilized human beings, or semi-civilized, whatever it is, and we cannot judge the other fellow's pleasure or his pains; but I fancy that the savage had some advantages over us, and I don't care to emphasize this for the sake of making this side seem stronger than it really is: The relative pleasures of the savage and the civilized man are fair subjects for discussion and are worth thinking about, and it is of no importance to me which side you take. I don't know which side I am on. All I can say is people assume too much entirely. Now, even though I may have been descended from an ape, still my children might be—well, Methodists. I know which side I am on as to the permanent progress. But as to whether the savage or civilized man is better off, you can say things in favor of each of them....

As a matter of science and of philosophy, is there something in the universe which in and of itself means that the world will always be getting happier? That is purely a religious doctrine. It can rest upon nothing excepting religion. My friend and I, neither of us being orthodox, of course, we cannot take it from that angle. As a religious doctrine it rests with the orthodox, first, on the assumption that there is a God, and, secondly, that He is good. Well, you have to prove both of them to me. Every fact in life and science is against both, and there is no use talking about them. Scientific men do not talk about it any more than they talk about hobgoblins.

Now, suppose you do not believe in it, then progress rests upon another religious dogma, which in some way is hitched up to science: That the law of evolution is beneficent; that the world is changing and there is something inherent in the law of evolution which takes the human race higher and higher and makes it happier. Why? Why should you not say that the law of evolution is demoniac; that it carries us lower? It is a pure matter of faith that it takes us higher and higher. Faith, a religious faith, whether the religion is God or evolution, it does not make a particle of difference; you get back to the same thing.

Are you going to base it on facts? I take a telescope and look out into the heavens. I find a countless number of worlds that are dead, have been burned to cinders that were once worlds like ours. I find others that are in the forming; others like ours that seem plainly to have passed their highest stage and the deserts appear and they seem to be going toward the sunset. Worlds are found in their birth; in every stage; life and death are there as they are everywhere and there is no chance for any permanence.

Turn to the race. Civilization, as we call it, is not very old; perhaps some vestige of civilization for five or six thousand years. And yet nations have risen and flourished and decayed. We have had the civilization of Persia; of Arabia; of Egypt; of Mesopotamia; and through all these places there are desert wastes where the owl hoots at night, and where beasts pursue their prey in those spots which once were fertile lands and where once lived civilized people, so-called. They were born, and they lived, and they died. The everlasting cycle of the earth going around the sun; the everlasting law of change, that is not the law of progress, but simply a law of change and nothing more. There is no chance to prove anything more. The savage looked at the rising tide and thought it would rise forever; but it went back again; it goes back just as it rises. It changes as the seasons change. An everlasting change, that is all there is to it....

Closing Speeches

PROF. KENNEDY: When we attempt to judge whether or not human beings are more or less happy, it is very difficult of course to get a standard by which we can register an accurate judgment. Happiness is a subjective matter. You cannot tell exactly from looking at a person whether he is happy or not. You cannot tell by reading about a certain place or civilization whether those people were happy or not. So, when Mr. Darrow says that perhaps if the savages were considering our civilization, they would say they were a whole lot happier under savagery than here, perhaps he is right. But, really, that has no bearing on the debate.

We are not interested in what savages think about our civilization. We are doing the judging ourselves. It is up to us to decide whether we think our civilization is better than savagery. If we do, we want to keep it and improve it. If we do not, we can get back to savagery pretty fast! It is a whole lot easier to drop from civilization to savagery than to come from savagery to civilization! If we come to the conclusion that we do not like to have three meals a day, it is very easy to go without, isn't it? I do not need to argue about that. . . .

Remember [the story of] the countryman who said to the engineer, when he saw the first locomotive: "You will never get the darn thing started." And, then as the locomotive rolled off he turned to him and said: "You will never get the darn thing stopped." That is very much the position our friend Darrow takes [toward happiness]. If you do get it you can not keep it, and even if you are happy you will never be satisfied, and whatever progress you get will not be progress after all. Well, I believe that it makes Brother Darrow happy to think that way. He gets the pleasure out of his pessimism that the rest of us get out of our optimism.

But, to get back to what I believe to be the fundamental and essential key to the whole situation. The question of the higher civilization rests on that proposition of the technique to control the forces of Nature; that is fundamental, and as that advances, your civilization advances; if that goes down, your civilization goes down. You can satisfy yourself, if you will make the investigation that there has been great advance in the past. If you will look over the various institutions and agencies for perpetuating and advancing the achievements that have been made, I think you will be satisfied that there is a promising future for the human race. . . .

MR. DARROW: Mr. Kennedy does not quote me quite right in saying the machine will not start or stop. I believe it will start and I believe it will stop. Then it will start again and speed up and slow down and stop and start again and stop, world without end— Amen!...

Let me put this question a little plainer, if I can. Civilization has in itself the seeds of its decay. As long as man lives, he must have legs and arms and a stomach. He can get along with very little brains. Most of them do, and they have too much brains at that, for they do not use them, they do not need them. But, his stomach and his legs are necessary. Now, it is a fool world that they should be necessary but, there they are, and you cannot help it. What man ought to have had was brain and wings. That is all he ever should have had; but Nature, not knowing how to do the job, loaded him up this way. But, he cannot live without putting food down into his stomach and running around so that it will digest. And, when you get your flying machines, and your automobiles and your railroads, and man stops running around to hunt his prey, he is going to die, that is all, and he always has, I think. He can only live until this physical part of him gets so far up and then he comes down to earth, for that is whither he draws his supply. That law has been at work forever. Mankind only gets a certain distance from the earth when he comes back just as gravitation draws the balloon back when it goes up. An everlasting round. From work, running, eating and digesting, man develops a certain brain power, and when he is overloaded with that, he goes back again to the earthly things to pull himself up.

Take this with you as a suggestion: The intellect keeps you always thinking and dreaming. Suppose the people of this world learn just one thing, which they are learning very fast; suppose they learn birth control. Then the human race is done for; it is done for, unless there are just a few savages left who will build it up again. Nature tricked man into life; she lied to him and cheated him and defrauded him and tricked him so that life would be born everlastingly upon the earth. And, when man is intelligent enough to learn the cheat, and the fraud and the lie, and to control it, then the race is going to die. The Catholics are right on that proposition. You can only go up in the air a certain distance; gravity calls you back. The old pendulum is swinging around forever. The eternal recurrence of things in the physical world, in the spiritual world, in matter and in life, prevails forever!

CHAPTER 5

WITNESS EXAMINATIONS

AUTOBIOGRAPHICAL INTRODUCTION

FROM CLARENCE DARROW, *THE STORY OF MY LIFE*, CHAPTER 31, "THE BRYAN FOUNDATION" (1932)

When Mr. Bryan took the stand, I began by asking him concerning his qualifications to define religion, and especially fundamentalism, which was the state religion of Tennessee. In response to my questions he said that he had been a student of religion all his life, that he was familiar with a great deal of the literature concerning Christianity and the Bible; that he had lectured on religious subjects at religious meetings and Chautauqua gatherings for years; that for a long time he had been conducting a Bible class at Miami on Sundays during the winter season, and that for a number of years he had written weekly syndicate letters for various publications extending over the country; that he had spoken on evolution in many college towns in the North and had been active in getting the Tennessee statute through the legislature and in urging similar statutes in various other States.

Then I proceeded with questions that brought out points illustrating the fundamentalists' ideas of the Bible and religion. These questions were practically the same that I had prepared and had published in a Chicago paper two years earlier. These questions were prepared because Mr. Bryan had submitted a list of questions through the press to the President of Wisconsin University, which appeared in the Chicago *Tribune* in July, 1923. My questions were presented in the same month, in reply to Mr. Bryan's. Needless to say, when I ventured those questions two years before I got no answer. *The Tribune* had interviewed him at Winona Lake, Ind., where he was attending a religious convention, and he replied that he had not read my questions; that Mr. Darrow was an agnostic, and that he had no quarrel with agnostics, that his controversy was with men who pretended to be Christians but were not Christians. Even had he read the questions propounded two years before he would have been compelled to choose between his crude beliefs and the common intelligence of modern times.

Now Bryan twisted and dodged and floundered, to the disgust of the thinking element, and even his own people. That night an amount of copy was sent out that the reporters claimed was unprecedented in court trials. My questions and Bryan's answers were printed in full, and the story seems to have reached the whole world.

When court adjourned it became evident that the audience had been thinking, and perhaps felt that they had heard something worth while. Much to my surprise, the great gathering began to surge toward me. They seemed to have changed sides in a single afternoon. A friendly crowd followed me toward my home. Mr. Bryan left the grounds practically alone. The people seemed to feel that he had failed and deserted his cause and his followers when he admitted that the first six days might have been periods of millions of ages long. Mr. Bryan had made himself ridiculous and had contradicted his own faith. I was truly sorry for Mr. Bryan. But I consoled myself by thinking of the years through which he had busied himself tormenting intelligent professors with impudent questions about their faith, and seeking to arouse the ignoramuses and bigots to drive them out of their positions. It is a terrible transgression to intimidate and awe teachers with fear of want.

The next morning I reached court prepared to continue the examination all that day. The judge convened court down in the yard, and another preacher asked the blessing and guidance of the Almighty. After allowing time for taking pictures, the judge arose, rested one hand on the statutes and the other on the Oxford Bible, and said that he had been thinking over the proceedings of the day before AND—in spite of Mr. Bryan's willingness again to take the stand—he believed that the testimony was not relevant, and he had decided to refuse to permit any further examination of Mr. Bryan and should strike the whole of his testimony from the record.

Mr. Bryan and his associates forgot to look surprised.

MAIN SELECTION

FROM *THE STATE OF TENNESSEE V. JOHN THOMAS SCOPES*, CIRCUIT COURT OF RHEA COUNTY, DAYTON, TENNESSEE, JULY 17, 1925
Direct examination of William Jennings Bryan

During the highly publicized trial of John Scopes for teaching evolution, Clarence Darrow called William Jennings Bryan as an expert witness on the Bible. One of America's leading political and religious orators, Bryan had taken up the cause of outlawing the teaching of the theory of human evolution in public schools, leading to the passage of the Tennessee antievolution law in 1925. Scopes agreed to challenge that new law in a test case instigated by the ACLU, with Darrow as his lead attorney. Bryan joined the prosecution team led by state's attorney Tom Stewart, and agreed to take Darrow's questions on the trial's last full day. It became one of the most famous encounters in American legal history, as Darrow sought to discredit Bryan's reliance on the Bible as a basis for public school science education, and Bryan sought to defend it.

DARROW: You have given considerable study to the Bible, haven't you, Mr. Bryan?

BRYAN: Yes, sir, I have tried to....

DARROW: Do you claim that everything in the Bible should be literally interpreted?

BRYAN: I believe everything in the Bible should be accepted as it is given there; some of the Bible is given illustratively. For instance:

"Ye are the salt of the earth." I would not insist that man was actually salt, or that he had flesh of salt, but it is used in the sense of salt as saving God's people.

DARROW: But when you read that Jonah swallowed the whale—or that the whale swallowed Jonah—excuse me please—how do you literally interpret that?

BRYAN: When I read that a big fish swallowed Jonah—it does not say whale.

DARROW: Doesn't it? Are you sure?

BRYAN: That is my recollection of it. A big fish, and I believe it, and I believe in a God who can make a whale and can make a man and make both do what He pleases....

DARROW: Now, you say, the big fish swallowed Jonah, and he there remained how long—three days—and then he spewed him upon the land. You believe that the big fish was made to swallow Jonah?

BRYAN: I am not prepared to say that; the Bible merely says it was done.

DARROW: You don't know whether it was the ordinary run of fish, or made for that purpose?

BRYAN: You may guess; you evolutionists guess.

DARROW: But when we do guess, we have a sense to guess right.

BRYAN: But do not do it often.

DARROW: You are not prepared to say whether that fish was made especially to swallow a man or not?

BRYAN: The Bible doesn't say, so I am not prepared to say.

DARROW: You don't know whether that was fixed up specially for the purpose?

BRYAN: No, the Bible doesn't say.

DARROW: But do you believe He made them—that He made such a fish and that it was big enough to swallow Jonah?

BRYAN: Yes, sir. Let me add: One miracle is just as easy to believe as another.

DARROW: It is for me ... just as hard.

BRYAN: It is hard to believe for you, but easy for me. A miracle is a thing performed beyond what man can perform. When you get beyond what man can do, you get within the realm of miracles;

and it is just as easy to believe the miracle of Jonah as any other miracle in the Bible....

DARROW: Do you consider the story of Joshua and the sun a miracle?

BRYAN: I think it is.

DARROW: Do you believe Joshua made the sun stand still?

BRYAN: I believe what the Bible says. I suppose you mean that the earth stood still?

DARROW: I don't know. I am talking about the Bible now.

BRYAN: I accept the Bible absolutely.

DARROW: The Bible says Joshua commanded the sun to stand still for the purpose of lengthening the day, doesn't it, and you believe it?

BRYAN: I do.

DARROW: Do you believe at that time the entire sun went around the earth?

BRYAN: No, I believe that the earth goes around the sun.

DARROW: Do you believe that the men who wrote it thought that the day could be lengthened or that the sun could be stopped?

BRYAN: I don't know what they thought.

DARROW: You don't know?

BRYAN: I think they wrote the fact without expressing their own thoughts.

DARROW: Have you an opinion as to whether or not the men who wrote that thought—

STEWART: I want to object, Your Honor; it has gone beyond the pale of any issue that could possibly be injected into this lawsuit, except by imagination. I do not think the defendant has a right to conduct the examination any further and I ask Your Honor to exclude it.

THE COURT: I will hear Mr. Bryan.

BRYAN: It seems to me it would be too exacting to confine the defense to the facts; if they are not allowed to get away from the facts, what have they to deal with?

THE COURT: Mr. Bryan is willing to be examined. Go ahead.

DARROW: Have you an opinion as to whether whoever wrote the book, I believe it is Joshua, the Book of Joshua, thought the sun went around the earth or not?

BRYAN: I believe that he was inspired.

DARROW: Can you answer my question?

BRYAN: When you let me finish the statement.

DARROW: It is a simple question, but finish it.

BRYAN: You cannot measure the length of my answer by the length of your question. *[Laughter in the courtyard.]*

DARROW: No, except that the answer be longer. *[Laughter in the courtyard.]*

BRYAN: I believe that the Bible is inspired, an inspired author, whether one who writes as he was directed to write understood the things he was writing about, I don't know.

DARROW: Whoever inspired it? Do you think whoever inspired it believed that the sun went around the earth?

BRYAN: I believe it was inspired by the Almighty, and He may have used language that could be understood at that time... instead of using language that could not be understood until Darrow was born. *[Laughter and applause in the courtyard.]*

DARROW: So, it might not, it might have been subject to construction, might it not?

BRYAN: It might have been used in language that could be understood then.

DARROW: That means it is subject to construction?

BRYAN: That is your construction....

DARROW: ... Can you answer my question directly? If the day was lengthened by stopping either the earth or the sun, it must have been the earth?

BRYAN: Well, I should say so.

DARROW: Now, Mr. Bryan, have you ever pondered what would have happened to the earth if it had stood still?

BRYAN: No.

DARROW: You have not?

BRYAN: No; the God I believe in could have taken care of that, Mr. Darrow.

DARROW: I see. Have you ever pondered what would naturally happen to the earth if it stood still suddenly?

BRYAN: No.

DARROW: Don't you know it would have been converted into a molten mass of matter? ...

BRYAN: I would want to hear expert testimony on that.

DARROW: You have never investigated that subject?

BRYAN: I don't think I have ever had the question asked.

DARROW: Or ever thought of it?

BRYAN: I have been too busy on things that I thought were of more importance than that.

DARROW: You believe the story of the [Noachian] flood to be a literal interpretation?

BRYAN: Yes, sir.

DARROW: When was that flood? ...

BRYAN: I never made a calculation.

DARROW: A calculation from what?

BRYAN: I could not say.

DARROW: From the generations of man?

BRYAN: I would not want to say that.

DARROW: What do you think?

BRYAN: I do not think about things I don't think about.

DARROW: Do you think about things you do think about?

BRYAN: Well, sometimes. *[Laughter in the courtyard.]* ...

DARROW: How long ago was the flood, Mr. Bryan?

BRYAN: Let me see [Bishop] Usher's calculation about it?

DARROW: Surely. *[Handing a Bible to the witness.]*

BRYAN: I think this does not give it.

DARROW: It gives an account of Noah. Where is the one in evidence? I am quite certain it is there.

BRYAN: Oh, I would put the estimate where it is, because I have no reason to vary it. But I would have to look at it to give you the exact date.

DARROW: I would, too. Do you remember what book the account is in?

BRYAN: Genesis. ...

DARROW: The [Bible] in evidence has it.

BRYAN: It is given here, as 2348 years B.C.

DARROW: Well, 2348 years B.C. You believe that all the living things that were not contained in the ark were destroyed.

BRYAN: I think the fish may have lived.

DARROW: Outside of the fish?

BRYAN: I cannot say.

DARROW: You cannot say?

BRYAN: No, except that just as it is, I have no proof to the contrary.

DARROW: I am asking you whether you believe?

BRYAN: I do.

DARROW: That all living things outside of the fish were destroyed?

BRYAN: What I say about the fish is merely a matter of humor.

DARROW: I understand.

BRYAN: Due to the fact a man wrote up here the other day to ask whether all the fish were destroyed, and the gentleman who received the letter told him the fish may have lived.

DARROW: I am referring to the fish, too.

BRYAN: I accept that, as the Bible gives it and I have never found any reason for denying, disputing, or rejecting it.

DARROW: Let us make it definite, 2,348 years?

BRYAN: I didn't say that. That is the time given there *[indicating a Bible]* but I don't pretend to say that is exact.

DARROW: You never figured it out, these generations, yourself?

BRYAN: No, sir; not myself.

DARROW: But the Bible you have offered in evidence, says 2,340, something, so that 4,200 years ago there was not a living thing on the earth, excepting the people on the ark and the animals of the ark and the fishes?

BRYAN: There have been living things before that.

DARROW: I mean at that time?

BRYAN: After that.

DARROW: Don't you know there are any number of civilizations that are traced back to more than 5,000 years?

BRYAN: I know we have people who trace things back according to the number of ciphers they have. But I am not satisfied they are accurate.

DARROW: You are not satisfied there is any civilization that can be traced back 5,000 years?

BRYAN: I would not want to say there is because I have no evidence of it that is satisfactory.

DARROW: Would you say there is not?

BRYAN: Well, so far as I know, but when the scientists differ, from 24,000,000 to 306,000,000 in their opinion, as to how long ago life came here, I want them nearer, to come nearer together before they demand of me to give up my belief in the Bible.

DARROW: Do you say that you do not believe that there were any civilizations on this earth that reach back beyond 5,000 years?

BRYAN: I am not satisfied by any evidence that I have seen....

DARROW: You have never in all your life made any attempt to find out about the other peoples of the earth—how old their civilizations are—how long they had existed on the earth, have you?

BRYAN: No, sir. I have been so well satisfied with the Christian religion that I have spent no time trying to find arguments against it.

DARROW: Were you afraid you might find some?

BRYAN: No, sir. I am not afraid now that you will show me any....

DARROW: Have you any idea how old the earth is?

BRYAN: No.

DARROW: The [Bible] you have introduced in evidence tells you, doesn't it?

BRYAN: I don't think it does, Mr. Darrow.

DARROW: Let's see whether it does; is this the one?

BRYAN: That is the one, I think.

DARROW: It says B.C. 4004?

BRYAN: That is Bishop Usher's calculation....

DARROW: Would you say that the earth was only 4,000 years old?

BRYAN: Oh, no; I think it is much older than that.

DARROW: How much?

BRYAN: I couldn't say.

DARROW: Do you say whether the Bible itself says it is older than that?

BRYAN: I don't think the Bible says itself whether it is older or not.

DARROW: Do you think the earth was made in six days?

BRYAN: Not six days of twenty-four hours.

DARROW: Doesn't it say so?

BRYAN: No, sir.

STEWART: I want to interpose another objection. What is the purpose of this examination?

BRYAN: The purpose is to cast ridicule on everybody who believes in the Bible, and I am perfectly willing that the world shall know that these gentlemen have no other purpose than ridiculing every Christian who believes in the Bible.

DARROW: We have the purpose of preventing bigots and ignoramuses from controlling the education of the United States and you know it, and that is all.

BRYAN: I am glad to bring out that statement. I want the world to know that this evidence is not for the view Mr. Darrow and his associates have filed affidavits here stating, that the purposes of which I understand it, is to show that the Bible story is not true....

DARROW: Then, when the Bible said, for instance, "and God called the firmament heaven. And the evening and the morning were the second day," that does not necessarily mean twenty-four hours?

BRYAN: I do not think it necessarily does....

DARROW: You do not think that?

BRYAN: No. But I think it would be just as easy for the kind of God we believe in to make the earth in six days as in six years or in 6,000,000 years or in 600,000,000 years. I do not think it important whether we believe one or the other.

DARROW: Do you think those were literal days?

BRYAN: My impression is they were periods, but I would not attempt to argue as against anybody who wanted to believe in literal days.

DARROW: Have you any idea of the length of the periods?

BRYAN: No; I don't.

DARROW: Do you think the sun was made on the fourth day?

BRYAN: Yes.

DARROW: And they had evening and morning without the sun?

BRYAN: I am simply saying it is a period.

DARROW: They had evening and morning for four periods without the sun, do you think?

BRYAN: I believe in creation as there told, and if I am not able to explain it I will accept it. Then you can explain it to suit yourself....

DARROW: Yes, all right. Do you believe the story of the temptation of Eve by the serpent?

BRYAN: I do.

DARROW: Do you believe that after Eve ate the apple, or gave it to Adam, whichever way it was, that God cursed Eve, and at that time decreed that all womankind thenceforth and forever should suffer the pains of childbirth in the reproduction of the earth?

BRYAN: I believe what it says, and I believe the fact as fully—

DARROW: That is what it says, doesn't it?

BRYAN: Yes.

DARROW: And for that reason, every woman born of woman, who has to carry on the race, the reason they have childbirth pains is because Eve tempted Adam in the Garden of Eden?

BRYAN: I will believe just what the Bible says. I ask to put that in the language of the Bible, for I prefer that to your language. Read the Bible and I will answer.

DARROW: All right, I will do that: "And I will put enmity between thee and the woman"—that is referring to the serpent?

BRYAN: The serpent.

DARROW: *[Reading]* "and between thy seed and her seed; it shall bruise thy head, and thou shalt bruise his heel. Unto the woman he said, I will greatly multiply thy sorrow and thy conception; in sorrow thou shalt bring forth children; and thy desire shall be to thy husband, and he shall rule over thee." That is right, is it?

BRYAN: I accept it as it is.

DARROW: And you believe that came about because Eve tempted Adam to eat the fruit?

BRYAN: Just as it says.

DARROW: And you believe that is the reason that God made the serpent to go on his belly after he tempted Eve?

BRYAN: I believe the Bible as it is, and I do not permit you to put your language in the place of the language of the Almighty. You read that Bible and ask me questions, and I will answer them. I will not answer your questions in your language.

DARROW: I will read it to you from the Bible: "And the Lord God said unto the serpent, because thou has done this, thou art cursed above all cattle, and above every beast of the field; upon thy belly shalt thou go and dust shalt thou eat all the days of thy life." Do you think that is why the serpent is compelled to crawl upon its belly?

BRYAN: I believe that.

DARROW: Have you any idea how the snake went before that time?

BRYAN: No, sir.

DARROW: Do you know whether he walked on his tail or not?

BRYAN: No, sir. I have no way to know. *[Laughter in audience.]*

DARROW: Now, you refer to the cloud that was put in the heaven after the flood, the rainbow. Do you believe in that?

BRYAN: Read it.

DARROW: All right, Mr. Bryan, I will read it for you.

BRYAN: Your Honor, I think I can shorten this testimony. The only purpose Mr. Darrow has is to slur at the Bible, but I will answer his question. I will answer it all at once, and I have no objection in the world. I want the world to know that this man, who does not believe in a God, is trying to use a court in Tennessee—

DARROW: I object to that.

BRYAN: *[Continuing]* to slur at it, and while it will require time, I am willing to take it.

DARROW: I object to your statement. I am examining you on your fool ideas that no intelligent Christian on earth believes.

THE COURT: Court is adjourned until 9 o'clock tomorrow morning.

SUPPLEMENTARY SELECTION

FROM *STATE OF IDAHO V. WILLIAM D. HAYWOOD,*
ADA COUNTY COURTHOUSE, BOISE, IDAHO, JUNE 26, 1907
Direct examination of C. W. Aller

When a bomb rigged to his home's front gate blew former Idaho governor Frank Steunenberg to bits on December 20, 1905, suspicion immediately fell on the leadership of the Western Federation of Miners, which Steunenberg had vigorously opposed. Of the union leaders who were accused of plotting the murder, the best known was Big Bill Haywood, who was a vocal and radical force in the organized-labor movement and the Federation's secretary-treasurer. The prosecution's star witness was Harry Orchard, a confessed killer-for-hire, who admitted rigging the bomb and claimed that the assassination was the result of an organized labor conspiracy that included Haywood, Darrow's client. C. W. Aller was one of several witnesses presented by the defense to lay a foundation for an alternative theory holding that the railroads recruited Orchard to perform the sensational murder in order to implicate and discredit the labor movement.

Note the way Darrow gets Aller to repeat answers that he wants to make an impression on the jury; the way he manages to lead the witness despite vigorous objections from prosecutors James H. Hawley and William E. Borah against this improper means of direct examination; and especially the way he slips in the word "what" (quickly correcting it to "who") in reference to Orchard. Darrow continued to dehumanize Orchard as the trial progressed.

DARROW: What is your business?

ALLER: Railroading.

DARROW: In what way are you railroading?

ALLER: Well, in the last year I've been in the train service and about seven years before that I was a telegraph operator, a station man, and in the clerical department.

DARROW: Did you used to live in Cripple Creek?

ALLER: Yes, sir.

DARROW: When?

ALLER: I went there in June 1899, left October 4, 1906.

DARROW: What did you do there?

ALLER: I was working in the office in Cripple Creek, the Florence & Cripple Creek Railroad office.

DARROW: Do you know Mr. D. C. Scott?

ALLER: I do.

DARROW: What was his position at that time?

ALLER: He was what was called a "special agent" for the railroad. In other words, a detective.

DARROW: Did he have charge of that district for the Florence & Cripple Creek Railroad?

ALLER: Yes, sir.

DARROW: You have seen him here in Boise, too, haven't you?

ALLER: Yes.

DARROW: He had charge while you were there, and has since, I suppose.

ALLER: Yes, sir. Well I wouldn't say now whether he has or not since I left there.

DARROW: Do you know K. C. Sterling?

ALLER: Yes, sir.

DARROW: What was he?

ALLER: He was also a detective, and I think employed by the mine owners.

BORAH: We object to what he thinks, unless he knows.

DARROW: Well, from what was generally reported there.

BORAH: No, we object to what was generally reported.

DARROW: It has already been testified to.

BORAH: We ask to have that answer stricken out as it is not proper evidence.

THE COURT: It may be stricken out unless he knows.

DARROW: You don't need to know by bringing a witness who's seen someone hire him. He may know a man as a judge because everybody points him out as a judge.

BORAH: That is a different proposition! There is a way to prove an official position.

THE COURT: You may prove what he knows about it, Mr. Darrow—not by giving his opinion.

DARROW: What do you know about Mr. Sterling's business?

ALLER: I don't believe I understand.

DARROW: I say, what do you know about what was Mr. Sterling's business? K. C. Sterling.

ALLER: Well, he associated with Scott and I was told...

BORAH: Wait a moment.

THE COURT: You need not tell what you were told....

DARROW: I will ask you whether you ever saw Scott and Sterling together.

ALLER: Yes, sir.

DARROW: About how frequently?

ALLER: Well, in the whole time that I was there it was a great number of times, but I don't know just how many times. They came in and out of the office there two or three times a day together.

DARROW: And that was during the time of the strike?

ALLER: Yes.

HAWLEY: We object to that as leading.

DARROW: Well, what time was it that they came in and out of the office so many times?

ALLER: Well, it was during the winter of 1904 and also in 1905 and also as far as 1906 until I left there.

DARROW: You meant the early winter of 1904—January and February—or the whole winter?

ALLER: Well, during the winter of 1903, 1904, 1905, 1906—well, all the time.

DARROW: You remember the time of the strike?

ALLER: Yes, but I don't remember the year now.

DARROW: Well, you remember the fact of it?

ALLER: Yes.

DARROW: And whether you saw them together during that time?

ALLER: Oh, yes.

DARROW: Do you know whether Mr. Scott and Mr. Sterling—or Mr. Sterling, I will strike out Scott—were interested in the strike at that time?

HAWLEY: Do you know of your own knowledge?

DARROW: From what you saw of him?

HAWLEY: We don't want an opinion, we want facts.

ALLER: Well, in what way do you mean?

DARROW: Whether he had anything to do with him at all.

BORAH: We will ask him to state what he did.

DARROW: Yes, what he did.

THE COURT: State first whether he knows.

ALLER: Not from personal knowledge, no, but from hearsay, I did.

DARROW: What did you see them do?

ALLER: I seen him around Scott several times and he always had a gun on him, and I have seen him examining his gun several times.

DARROW: Where was he? In what part of the district?

ALLER: He was right in Cripple Creek—well, he was all over the district but he lived in Cripple Creek.

DARROW: I show you some pictures marked defendants' exhibits one and two. I will ask you whether you recognize these.

ALLER: Well, I believe I do. It is a good likeness of a man I know.

DARROW: Did you ever see this man in Boise?

ALLER: Yes, sir.

DARROW: Whereabouts?

ALLER: Several times on the witness stand here.

DARROW: Yes. What is his name?

ALLER: Harry Orchard.

DARROW: That is the name he goes by?

ALLER: Yes, and that is what he went by when I knew him.

DARROW: Where did you see him before that?

ALLER: I saw him at Cripple Creek.

DARROW: Whereabouts?

ALLER: At the depot.

DARROW: Did you ever see him anywhere else in Cripple Creek?

ALLER: Not that I remember, no, I can't say that I did.

DARROW: For what purpose did he come to the depot?

ALLER: To see Mr. Scott.

DARROW: The same D. C. Scott you've spoken of?

ALLER: Yes.

DARROW: Do you know how many times you saw him at the depot to see Mr. Scott?

ALLER: Well, some three or four times.

DARROW: And do you know about when it was?

ALLER: Well, it was within six months before that explosion. He was there three or four times that I know of positively. I don't remember the dates.

DARROW: Do you remember any special time that you saw him at the depot?

ALLER: I do one time in particular, and that was when Mr. Scott told me...

BORAH: Wait a minute...

ALLER: Well, it was on Sunday.

DARROW: On Sunday?

ALLER: Yes.

DARROW: How long before the Independence depot was blown up?

ALLER: Well, it was not over three weeks.

DARROW: And what is the shortest time it might have been before that?

ALLER: I believe it was the second or third Sunday before the Independence blow-up....

DARROW: Had you any engagement with Mr. Scott that day?

ALLER: Yes.

DARROW: For dinner or something like that? A five o'clock dinner?

ALLER: Yes, a five o'clock dinner.

DARROW: Did Mr. Scott... what did he speak to you about? You need not say what he said, but was it in reference to anybody?

ALLER: When he left the depot, do you mean?

DARROW: Yes.

BORAH: We object to what he told him as hearsay.

DARROW: He spoke to you in reference to some man, did he not?

ALLER: Yes, sir, he did.

DARROW: What was it, or who was it?

ALLER: Harry Orchard.

DARROW: What time was it in the day?

ALLER: Well, it was just about two o'clock....

DARROW: Did Scott go away, or did he stay there?

ALLER: Scott went uptown.

DARROW: And how long before he came back?

ALLER: About thirty minutes. Possibly forty minutes.

DARROW: Did anybody else come in the meantime?

ALLER: Mr. Orchard.

DARROW: What?

ALLER: Mr. Orchard!

DARROW: Yes, and did he inquire for anybody?

ALLER: He inquired for Mr. D. C. Scott.

DARROW: Of you?

ALLER: Of me. Yes, sir.

DARROW: And what did you do with Mr. Orchard? Where did you see him?

ALLER: He came in the office and sat down and waited for Mr. Scott.

DARROW: Afterwards, did he meet Scott?

ALLER: He did.

DARROW: Where did they go?

ALLER: Up to Scott's room.

DARROW: Was anybody else there with them?

ALLER: Not at that time, no, sir.

DARROW: Or later?

ALLER: There were later, yes, sir.

DARROW: Who?

ALLER: K. C. Sterling.

DARROW: What is the name?

ALLER: K. C. Sterling.

DARROW: About what time did K. C. Sterling come?

ALLER: Well, I did not see him come in. The first I saw of Sterling was five o'clock when I went up to Scott's room.

DARROW: First, what time did Mr. Scott and Orchard go up to the room? About what time?

ALLER: Well, about half past two.

DARROW: Now, you did not see Sterling when he came in?

ALLER: No, I did not see Sterling when he came in.

DARROW: And then when did you see any of them again?

ALLER: Five o'clock.

DARROW: Five o'clock?

ALLER: Yes, sir.

DARROW: And where did you see them?

ALLER: In Scott's room....

DARROW: Who all was in there?

ALLER: Scott, Sterling and Harry Orchard.

DARROW: Yes, and that was about five o'clock?

ALLER: Yes, that was just at five o'clock because we were going to a five o'clock dinner, Scott was going to dinner with me, and I went up to get him to go.

DARROW: Did he go?

ALLER: No, he did not....

DARROW: You had a conversation with Mr. Scott, did you?

ALLER: Yes, I did.

DARROW: And did you go out?

ALLER: I did. I left and I went to dinner.

DARROW: And then did you go back?

ALLER: I did.

DARROW: At what time?

ALLER: I got back about six o'clock. I worked from six until eleven.

DARROW: And where were they at that time?

ALLER: Well, I did not see them at that time, I saw them a little after that.

DARROW: What time?

ALLER: There is a train leaves there at 8:15 and the next I saw of either of them was when that train was leaving, 8:15.

DARROW: Whereabouts?

ALLER: Mr. Scott was the only one I saw at that time, and he was on the depot platform.

DARROW: Do you know when he left the office?

ALLER: No, I could not say as to that.... I did not see any of them coming down the stairs leaving Scott's room.

DARROW: And you don't know whether they got their dinner, or where they went or what they did?

ALLER: No.

DARROW: And was anything said to you about taking dinner—you must not say what it was.

ALLER: There was.

DARROW: And then you went off after that and got your dinner alone. Did you?

ALLER: Yes.

DARROW: Then you saw Scott again at eight o'clock?

ALLER: Yes.

DARROW: That is all.... Well, the other time you saw Mr. Orchard with Mr. Scott, where were they?

ALLER: Well, Mr. Orchard came to the depot and asked for Mr. Scott, and Scott was either in the depot or he asked for him and turned around and talked to Scott in the depot there and they went off together.

DARROW: Where did they go?

ALLER: I think they went to Scott's room.

DARROW: Yes, and that was before this time or after?

ALLER: That was before that time they were all three together.

DARROW: Do you know whether Mr. Sterling was present or not?

ALLER: No. I never saw the three of them together but once, and that is the only time.

DARROW: *[To the state]* You may cross-examine.

SUPPLEMENTARY SELECTION

FROM *THE PEOPLE OF MICHIGAN V. OSSIAN SWEET AND TEN OTHERS,* RECORDERS COURT, DETROIT, MICHIGAN, NOVEMBER 5, 1925
Cross-examination of Inspector Norton N. Schuknecht

On September 8, 1925, three months after buying a house in a predominantly white neighborhood of Detroit, the African-American physician Ossian Sweet moved into the dwelling with his wife and infant daughter. That year, white mobs, calling themselves Improvement Associations, had driven two other African-American families from their newly purchased homes in predominantly white Detroit neighborhoods, and Sweet's new neighbors had organized a similar reception for him. A police contingent under the command of Inspector Norton N. Schuknecht was assigned to control the situation but instead observed passively as the mob surrounding the Sweet home grew in size to several hundred whites, who became progressively more hostile over the course of two days. Rumors spread that the mob would attack the home on the second night. Sweet was joined by ten family members and friends intent on defending the premises, with guns if necessary. After the white mob began pelting the house with stones, gunshots were heard—with at least some of them apparently fired by Sweet's younger brother, Henry, from within the house. Schuknecht then entered the house to admonish Dr. Sweet for the gunfire. When he later learned that bullets had hit two members of the crowd, one of whom died, Schuknecht arrested Sweet and his ten companions, including Mrs. Sweet. At the ensuing murder trial, prosecution witnesses denied that a hostile mob had surrounded the house prior to the shooting. The following testimony elicited by prosecutor Robert M. Toms from Schuknecht was typical.

TOMS: There was no one there when you got there? The time of your arrival is about 7:30?

SCHUKNECHT: There were people on the street, but they were walking up and down and there was no congregating....

TOMS: Did you see anyone armed with clubs or other weapons?

SCHUKNECHT: Not any time.

TOMS: What happened at 8:15?

SCHUKNECHT: Suddenly a volley of shots was fired from the windows of Dr. Sweet's home.

TOMS: What could you see?

SCHUKNECHT: I saw flashes of guns.

TOMS: How many shots?

SCHUKNECHT: About fifteen or twenty.

Seeking to show that there was in fact a hostile crowd that the police failed to control, Darrow subjected Schuknecht to an extended cross-examination. Darrow similarly pressed other prosecution witnesses as he attempted to establish that Sweet and the other defendants acted in reasonable self-defense. The trial ended in a hung jury. When a second jury subsequently acquitted Henry Sweet for his part in the shooting, Judge Frank Murphy, who later was appointed to the United States Supreme Court, dismissed the charges against Ossian Sweet and the remaining defendants. The following excerpts are taken from Darrow's cross-examination of Schuknecht.

DARROW: How do you pronounce your name, Officer?

SCHUKNECHT: Schuknecht.

DARROW: Schuknecht. That is a new name to me.

SCHUKNECHT: Yes.

DARROW: How long have you been on the police force, Officer?

SCHUKNECHT: Twenty-four and a half years....

DARROW: Now, what was your purpose in going out [to Dr. Sweet's neighborhood] on the eighth?

SCHUKNECHT: What was the purpose?

DARROW: Yes.

SCHUKNECHT: To protect Dr. Sweet's home....

DARROW: How many did you have there when you went on the eighth, how many people, officers?

SCHUKNECHT: The morning of the eighth?

DARROW: Yes.

SCHUKNECHT: When he moved in there?

DARROW: Yes.

SCHUKNECHT: We had four men and a sergeant.

DARROW: What time did you get there?

SCHUKNECHT: That morning?

DARROW: Yes, that day the eighth.

SCHUKNECHT: Oh, I was there three or four different times through the day....

DARROW: What time did you get there in the evening, to the best of your recollection?

SCHUKNECHT: About seven o'clock.

DARROW: You stayed from seven o'clock until midnight on the eighth?

SCHUKNECHT: Yes, sir.

DARROW: That is as near as you can put it? I do not mean to pin you down to minutes or anything. Were there any more policemen excepting those four, at any time on the eighth?

SCHUKNECHT: There was.

DARROW: Where did the rest come from?

SCHUKNECHT: They changed shifts at three o'clock. That was when we put eight men on there in charge of the sergeant.

DARROW: You put eight men and a sergeant there? Anybody else?

SCHUKNECHT: Myself and the lieutenant were there....

DARROW: At no time while you were there, up to the time you went into Dr. Sweet's house after the firing of the shot, at no time did you make any effort to see him or talk with him?

SCHUKNECHT: I did not.

DARROW: Or anybody else in the house?

SCHUKNECHT: No, sir.

DARROW: Or send any word to him?

SCHUKNECHT: I did not. He could see us outside.

DARROW: You sent him no word, however, as to why you were there?

SCHUKNECHT: I did not.

DARROW: Do you know whether any policemen sent into the house, or communicated with him in any way?

SCHUKNECHT: I could not say....

DARROW: Now, there were some 200 people, around about Dr. Sweet's place on both sides of the street, as near as you can get at it, on the eighth?

SCHUKNECHT: People sitting out on their porches, and people walking.

DARROW: Were going back and forth on the street, weren't they?

SCHUKNECHT: The same people?

DARROW: Yes.

SCHUKNECHT: I couldn't say that.

DARROW: You couldn't say?

SCHUKNECHT: No, sir.

DARROW: Did you try to find out?

SCHUKNECHT: I didn't.

DARROW: And you asked nobody what their business was in that vicinity? If you had to?

SCHUKNECHT: No, they had a right to be walking by, hadn't they?

DARROW: You are the officer in charge?

SCHUKNECHT: Yes.

DARROW: Did you ask anybody?

SCHUKNECHT: I did not.

DARROW: You were there to find out whether anything was going on that would imperil Dr. Sweet's property and whoever was there, weren't you?

SCHUKNECHT: Yes, sir.

DARROW: Would people pass the store, and walk back past the store, whether it was the same people or not, I do not care; I mean, whether there were people there?

SCHUKNECHT: Oh, sure, there were people there walking.

DARROW: There were people on the school house lawn, weren't there?

SCHUKNECHT: Yes.

DARROW: Was that a sodded lawn?

SCHUKNECHT: Part of it was sodded.

DARROW: Do you know how many there were?

SCHUKNECHT: There may have been eighteen or twenty.

DARROW: There might have been fifty, or 200, mightn't there?

SCHUKNECHT: No, sir.

DARROW: Did you count them?

SCHUKNECHT: What?

DARROW: Did you count them?

SCHUKNECHT: I could see them from where I was standing.

DARROW: Did you go up there? Did you go to them?

SCHUKNECHT: I didn't count them.

DARROW: Did you talk to anybody there?

SCHUKNECHT: I did not.

DARROW: Now, on the other side where this apartment building was, were there people congregated?

SCHUKNECHT: People on private property on the lawn there.

DARROW: Were there people there?

SCHUKNECHT: Yes, sir.

DARROW: How many?

SCHUKNECHT: Oh, there may have been seven or eight.

DARROW: Did you talk to any of them?

SCHUKNECHT: I did not.

DARROW: Did you make any effort to find out why they were there?

SCHUKNECHT: That was not any of my business. They were on private property.

DARROW: I didn't ask you that. I asked you if you made any effort?

SCHUKNECHT: I did not.

DARROW: You did not know them, did you?

SCHUKNECHT: No, sir.

DARROW: And you did not know where any of these people that came out of the automobiles came from, or where they went to, did you?

SCHUKNECHT: No, I couldn't say that I did.

DARROW: And you made no effort to find out?

SCHUKNECHT: No, sir....

DARROW: Can you mention anything that you heard from anybody, outside of officers, in the two days and two nights that you were there until you met Dr. Sweet?

SCHUKNECHT: No, because I didn't talk to any of them.

DARROW: You heard no stones against Dr. Sweet's house?

SCHUKNECHT: Not before the shooting.

DARROW: Not before the shooting?

SCHUKNECHT: No.

DARROW: Did you afterwards?

SCHUKNECHT: I did.

DARROW: How many?

SCHUKNECHT: When I was at his front door, there was two stones on the porch.

DARROW: When you were at his front door?

SCHUKNECHT: Yes.

DARROW: Do you know where they came from?

SCHUKNECHT: I do not.

DARROW: Did you hear any more?

SCHUKNECHT: I did not.

DARROW: Did you see any stones that night or the next day, in the yard?

SCHUKNECHT: I saw the two stones on the porch.

DARROW: Did you see any others?

SCHUKNECHT: Yes.

DARROW: Where?

SCHUKNECHT: I believe there was one or two on the roof and I saw two or three out on the front, on the lawn there.

DARROW: Do you know how many were on the lawn?

SCHUKNECHT: No, sir.

DARROW: Did you take them with you?

SCHUKNECHT: I did not. The detectives took charge of those.

DARROW: Do you know where they are?

SCHUKNECHT: I believe Lieutenant Johnson can tell you that.

DARROW: Well, do you know where they are?

SCHUKNECHT: No, I do not.

DARROW: Have you tried to see them since?

SCHUKNECHT: I have not.

DARROW: And you don't know how many?

SCHUKNECHT: Only what I seen.

DARROW: Do you know how many there were on the lawn?

SCHUKNECHT: I said there may have been two or three on the lawn.

DARROW: There might have been more, mightn't there?

SCHUKNECHT: I didn't see them.

DARROW: I say, there might have been, for all you saw?

SCHUKNECHT: *[No answer.]* . . .

DARROW: You do not know where all of the shots that you heard came from, do you?

SCHUKNECHT: Do I know where they came from?

DARROW: Yes.

SCHUKNECHT: I only know where the one came from that I seen fired.

DARROW: You saw the light from some of them? You saw the light of the powder from some of them, as it came out?

SCHUKNECHT: Out of the front and side windows, yes, sir.

DARROW: But you do not know how many shots that meant, do you?

SCHUKNECHT: I had judged there had been fifteen.

DARROW: No, I would rather you would not say that. You have told us that you judged there were fifteen or twenty shots. You have told us that. But you do not know how many of those shots were from guns from which you saw the light?

SCHUKNECHT: No, I couldn't say as to how many were.

DARROW: And you don't know whether anybody else shot back or front excepting just as you have told us?

SCHUKNECHT: That is all I had seen.

DARROW: All of these officers were armed?

SCHUKNECHT: Our officers?

DARROW: Yes.

SCHUKNECHT: Yes, sir.

DARROW: Do you know what kind of guns they carried?

SCHUKNECHT: Well, some of them carry Colt 32's and others carry Colt 38's.

DARROW: There was one stationed in the back, wasn't there?

SCHUKNECHT: There was.

DARROW: Who was that?

SCHUKNECHT: Mr. Gill, I believe that is his name.

DARROW: I think that is his name. I think I have read it in the testimony.

SCHUKNECHT: Mr. Gill was in the alley.

DARROW: Do you know what kind of a gun he carried? If you don't know, say so.

SCHUKNECHT: I don't know the caliber.

DARROW: We will probably get that from him. How long was it in your opinion from the time you heard the first shot until the time you heard the last?

SCHUKNECHT: Oh, my judgment was they were fired anywhere from about fifteen to thirty seconds.

DARROW: I suppose, in your twenty odd years of police service, you have heard a number of volleys fired, and you probably could guess pretty closely, couldn't you—closer than a man who had not; you would naturally expect to; you have been through things where there was shooting before this?

SCHUKNECHT: I would not say that, because some of my officers told me they thought there was fifty shots fired.

DARROW: I am not talking about the number now. I am talking about the time.

SCHUKNECHT: Which?

DARROW: The time in which it occurred?

TOMS: The time in which what occurred?

DARROW: Between the first and last.

SCHUKNECHT: They were all fired practically at one time. There was no let-up at any time.

DARROW: But you think from fifteen to thirty seconds would probably cover it?

SCHUKNECHT: I think so. It may have been in less time than that.

DARROW: It is pretty hard to be sure about those things?

SCHUKNECHT: That is my own personal judgment.

DARROW: You went in there then alone,—the first time you had been in Dr. Sweet's house, or spoken to him, wasn't it?

SCHUKNECHT: It was.

DARROW: And you did not know who was in there?

SCHUKNECHT: I did not.

DARROW: You assumed Dr. Sweet was there?

SCHUKNECHT: Yes, sir.

DARROW: And you asked him, with some words that I will admit— not because I am unfamiliar with them, I do not want you to think, but it is not necessary to repeat them;—

SCHUKNECHT: All right.

DARROW: *[Continuing]*—what he meant by shooting?

SCHUKNECHT: I did.

DARROW: And he told you, as you recall it, that they were destroying his property?

SCHUKNECHT: That is what he said.

DARROW: *[Reading from Schuknecht's prior testimony]* "[Sweet said,] 'They are ruining my property.' I said, 'What has been done?' I said, 'I haven't seen a man throw a stone. I haven't heard any commotion or anything else. I haven't heard of anyone throwing a stone.' " Is that correct?

SCHUKNECHT: Yes, sir.

DARROW: You were the first one who mentioned the question of stoning, between you and Dr. Sweet, is that right?

SCHUKNECHT: I didn't get that question.

DARROW: You were the first one, as between you and Dr. Sweet, who mentioned stoning?

SCHUKNECHT: No, he was the first one who mentioned that his property was being destroyed.

DARROW: But he did not say "by stones," did he?

SCHUKNECHT: I believe he did.

DARROW: You have not said so, either in your testimony this morning, or in the preliminary hearing, did you?

SCHUKNECHT: That may be.

DARROW: Do you think it must have been that he said it, or you would not have thought of stones yourself?

SCHUKNECHT: No.

DARROW: Well, now, Officer, in the preliminary hearing—I will show you this after I ask you the question, so that you will be sure I am fair with you. You had previously answered: "Do you want me to say just what I said to him?" Then the question was: "State as near as possible, and what he said to you." This was your answer, the way you answered: "All right, sir. I went in there, and I said, for Christ's sake, what the hell are you fellows shooting about." "Why," he said, "they are ruining my property." I said, "What has been done?" I said, "I haven't seen a man throwing stones, and I haven't heard any commotion or anything else. I haven't heard of anyone throwing a stone."... Now, that is the transcript; or, will you take my word for it *[handing transcript of testimony to witness]*.

SCHUKNECHT: Yes.

DARROW: I would not try to fool you?

SCHUKNECHT: I am not afraid....

SUPPLEMENTARY SELECTION

FROM *THE STATE OF TENNESSEE V. JOHN THOMAS SCOPES*, CIRCUIT COURT OF RHEA COUNTY, DAYTON, TENNESSEE, JULY 15, 1925
Cross-examination of Howard Morgan

In making its case against John Scopes for violating Tennessee's controversial new antievolution law, the prosecution presented testimony from two school students and one school administrator. Each of these witnesses testified that in April 1925—after the new law took effect—Scopes taught his students that humans evolved from lower forms of animals, which the law proscribed. The defense, led by Darrow, did not dispute this testimony. Indeed, it readily admitted that Scopes taught evolution. Instead, the defense sought to discredit the law itself, as in the following courtroom exchanges between prosecutor Tom Stewart, Judge John Raulston, Darrow, and state's witness Howard Morgan—a fourteen-year-old school student.

Direct examination by prosecutor Tom Stewart

STEWART: Your name is Howard Morgan?

MORGAN: Yes, sir....

STEWART: How old are you?

MORGAN: Fourteen years.

STEWART: Did you attend school here at Dayton last year?

MORGAN: Yes, sir.

STEWART: What school?

MORGAN: High school.

STEWART: Central High School.

MORGAN: Yes, sir.

STEWART: Did you study anything under Professor Scopes?

MORGAN: Yes, sir.

STEWART: Did you study this book, "General Science"?

MORGAN: Yes, sir.

STEWART: *[To defense counsel Clarence Darrow]* Do you want to see it?

DARROW: Will you mark the number?

THE COURT: Let the stenographer mark it....

STEWART: Did he ever undertake to teach you anything about evolution?

MORGAN: Yes, sir.

STEWART: Did he undertake to teach you anything about any theory—

DARROW: I think, your honor, I will object to that. Ask him what it is.

STEWART: What did he teach you in reference to?

THE COURT: What is the difference?

DARROW: Why—

THE COURT: All right.

STEWART: About any evolutionary theory as to where man came from. *[Laughter in courtroom.]*

STEWART: Just state in your own words, Howard, what he taught you and when it was.

MORGAN: It was along about the second of April.

STEWART: Of this year?

MORGAN: Yes, sir; of this year. He said that the earth was once a hot molten mass, too hot for plant or animal life to exist upon it; in the sea the earth cooled off; there was a little germ of one cell organism formed, and this organism kept evolving until it got to be a pretty good-sized animal, and then came on to be a land animal, and it kept on evolving, and from this was man.

STEWART: Let me repeat that; perhaps a little stronger than you. If I don't get it right, you correct me.

DEFENSE CO-COUNSEL ARTHUR GARFIELD HAYES: *[To Morgan]* Go to the head of the class.

STEWART: He said that in the beginning, the earth was a crystalline mass, too hot for any life to exist upon it; that it cooled off and finally the soil formed and the sea formed, plant life was on the earth, and that in the sea animal life began with a little one-celled animal.

MORGAN: Yes, sir.

STEWART: Which evolved and evolved and finally got bigger and became a land animal?

MORGAN: Yes, sir.

STEWART: And the culmination of which was man?

MORGAN: Yes, sir....

STEWART: I ask you further, Howard, how did he classify man with reference to other animals; what did he say about them?

MORGAN: Well, the book and he both classified man along with cats and dogs, cows, horses, monkeys, lions, horses and all that.

STEWART: What did he say they were?

MORGAN: Mammals.

STEWART: Classified them along with dogs, cats, horses, monkeys and cows?

MORGAN: Yes, sir.

STEWART: You say this was along about the second or third of April of this year?

MORGAN: Yes, sir.

STEWART: In high school of Rhea County.

MORGAN: Yes, sir.

STEWART: At Dayton?

MORGAN: Yes, sir.

STEWART: Cross-examine.

Cross-examination by lead defense counsel Clarence Darrow

DARROW: Let's see, your name is what?

MORGAN: Howard Morgan.

DARROW: Now, Howard, what do you mean by classify?

MORGAN: Well, it means classify these animals we mentioned, that men were just the same as them, in other words—

DARROW: He didn't say a cat was the same as a man?

MORGAN: No, sir; he said man had a reasoning power; that these animals did not.

DARROW: There is some doubt about that, but that is what he said, is it? *[Laughter in the courtroom.]*

THE COURT: Order.

STEWART: With some men.

DARROW: A great many.

DARROW: Now, Howard, he said they were all mammals, didn't he?

MORGAN: Yes, sir.

DARROW: Did he tell you what a mammal was, or don't you remember?

MORGAN: Well, he just said these animals were mammals and man was a mammal.

DARROW: No; but did he tell you what distinguished mammals from other animals?

MORGAN: I don't remember.

DARROW: If he did, you have forgotten it? Didn't he say that mammals were those beings which suckled their young?

MORGAN: I don't remember about that.

DARROW: You don't remember?

MORGAN: No.

DARROW: Do you remember what he said that made any animal a mammal, what it was, or don't you remember?

MORGAN: I don't remember.

DARROW: But he said that all of them were mammals?

MORGAN: All what?

DARROW: Dogs and horses, monkeys, cows, man, whales, I cannot state all of them, but he said all of those were mammals?

MORGAN: Yes, sir; but I don't know about the whales; he said all of these other ones. *[Laughter in the courtroom.]*

THE COURT: Order.

DARROW: You might never have seen a whale suckling its young?

MORGAN: I did not.

DARROW: But the others were all mammals?

MORGAN: Yes, sir.

DARROW: You don't know whether he told you why they were mammals or not, did you?

MORGAN: No, sir.

DARROW: And you don't know whether they were mammals or not, only what he told you?

MORGAN: I just know what he said; he said they were mammals.

DARROW: And you didn't know that the definition of a mammal was a species that suckled its young, did you?

MORGAN: No, sir.

DARROW: Well, did he tell you anything else that was wicked?

MORGAN: No, not that I remember of.

DARROW: Will you please step down here; I cannot come down there or I would.

[Witness steps down to counsel's table.]

DARROW: Is this one of the books he taught you from? *[Handing book to witness.]*

MORGAN: Yes, sir.

DARROW: Now, read that and see whether you remember that after you read it.

MORGAN: Examples of mammals, lions, monkey, lion, cat, dog, horse, cow, monkey and man.

DARROW: Isn't there some more that you remember when you look it over?

MORGAN: I don't remember.

DARROW: And I will read over this, and then see whether you can remember. Heading is Mammals. *[Reading.]* "Mammals compose a group of animals which are the most highly developed of all; the egg produced by the female is microscopic in size and fertilized within the body of the mother." Do you remember that? Anyway, you studied it, didn't you?

MORGAN: Yes, sir.

DARROW: And you are like the rest of us, you don't remember all you study, I suppose. Well, we are all that way. *[Reading.]* "And there grows into the young animal all the parts of an adult." That is the grown being, adult, I suppose. I don't suppose I dare read this. *[Reading.]* "After birth the young are nourished for a time by milk secreted by the mammary glands of the mother." Do you remember this is in the book?

MORGAN: It is in the book, but I don't remember him saying anything about it.

DARROW: Well, you read this anyhow?

MORGAN: Yes, sir.

DARROW: Examples of mammals are the elephant, lion, mink, cat, dog, horse, cow, monkey and man.

MORGAN: Yes, sir.

DARROW: Now, he said the earth was once a molten mass of liquid, didn't he?

MORGAN: Yes, sir.

DARROW: By molten, you understand melted?

MORGAN: Yes, sir.

DARROW: Running molten mass of liquid, and that it slowly cooled until a crust was formed on it?

MORGAN: Yes, sir.

DARROW: After that, after it got cooled enough, and the soil came, that plants grew; is that right?

MORGAN: Yes, sir; yes, sir.

DARROW: And that the first life was in the sea. And that it developed into life on the land?

MORGAN: Yes, sir.

DARROW: And finally into the highest organism, which is known as man?

MORGAN: Yes, sir.

DARROW: Now, that is about what he taught you? It has not hurt you any, has it?

MORGAN: No, sir.

DARROW: That's all.

SUPPLEMENTARY SELECTION

FROM *STATE OF IDAHO V. WILLIAM D. HAYWOOD*, ADA COUNTY
COURTHOUSE, BOISE, IDAHO, JUNE 26, 1907
Excerpts from the jury voir dire

The process of voir dire, in which opposing counsel in a jury trial select jurors based on their demeanor, background, and answers to carefully crafted questions, was a Darrow specialty. He knew he was choosing his audience for the coming weeks of the trial, and regarded the process as critical to his success.

Excerpt from the voir dire of John E. Tourtellotte

Tourtellotte was a local architect who had designed, among other local buildings, the bank owned by Frank Steunenberg, the murder victim, and the home of the prosecution team member William Borah, soon to be a United States senator. Tourtellotte's statement that he was opposed to the death penalty except in wartime and "in the case of an organization against society" seemed to guarantee that he would be challenged by the state, but Borah, who handled the prosecution team's voir dire, pronounced him acceptable.

DARROW: You pass this man for cause?

BORAH: He is up to you!...

DARROW: Have you thought in your mind that this defendant may belong to such an organization as you have said comes under your exceptions—an organization which has menaced society, as you described?

TOURTELLOTTE: I hadn't thought of it, until you spoke of it, but now I see how it might be ... a bunch of anarchists, for instance.

DARROW: But you would vote to hang an anarchist?

TOURTELLOTTE: Yes, if I understand what an anarchist is, I would hang him on sight. I regard it as a matter of self-defense. It is the right of society to protect itself.

DARROW: Then if you vote to take this defendant's life, then it would be on the theory that he is an enemy of society.

TOURTELLOTTE: That would be the only ground on which I would do it.

Darrow, to the surprise of Borah, the court, and Tourtellotte, accepted the architect as a juror. He already knew that his closing argument to the jury would ultimately rely heavily on his contention that Big Bill Haywood, far from being "an enemy of society," was in fact a heroic figure working for the betterment of society through justice for workingmen. This had been Darrow's strategy when he defended other labor leaders and it had worked well. Tourtellotte later managed to get himself dismissed by the judge.

Excerpt from the voir dire of Allen Pride

DARROW: Imagine yourself in the defendant's shoes. Would you want a man on the jury whose mind is in the same condition as your own?

PRIDE: I'd hate to be in such a predicament.

DARROW: You'd want a fair jury?

PRIDE: Yes.

DARROW: And you think you could be fair?

PRIDE: He might do worse.

DARROW: And he might do better, isn't that so?

PRIDE: Perhaps, but I think not.

Excerpt from the voir dire of Harmon Cox

Darrow presumed that Cox was unsympathetic to organized labor (and therefore biased against labor organizer Haywood) because his daughter worked as a "scab" operator during a strike at the Boise, Idaho, telephone company.

DARROW: Have you ever formed an opinion regarding the guilt or innocence of the accused?

COX: No, sir!

DARROW: Is that right?

COX: That's what I said.

DARROW: How much evidence would it take you to change the opinion you have?

BORAH: *[Objecting]* That's an improper question. The juror has not said he had an opinion to be changed.

DARROW: Are you stuck on this juror?

BORAH: I am stuck on you, sir! . . .

DARROW: I challenge this juror for incompetency. He is ignorant and no man should be tried for his life by such a man!

BORAH: State your challenge and cut out your stump speeches!

DARROW: You don't want to force this juror on us, do you? You wouldn't want a client of yours tried by a juror like that, would you?

Cox was empanelled by the court over Darrow's objections.

SUPPLEMENTARY SELECTION

FROM *TERRITORY OF HAWAII v. FORTESCUE ET AL.*, HONOLULU, HAWAII (1932)
Examination of expert witnesses

Lieutenant Thomas Massie, a U.S. naval officer stationed in Hawaii, fatally shot Joseph Kahahawai when he allegedly confessed to Massie (after the lieutenant and others kidnapped and beat him) that he was one of four assailants who had raped Massie's wife. Darrow, who had been a pioneer in the use of psychiatrists to mount an insanity defense, argued that Kahahawai's coerced confession triggered a "mental bomb" in Massey that rendered him temporarily insane, moved him to sudden violence, and left him with amnesia regarding the actual murder. The trial became a battle of expert witnesses.

Direct examination of defense expert Dr. J. Orbeson, Los Angeles psychiatrist

DARROW: Have you met Thomas Massie, the defendant?

DR. ORBESON: Yes.

DARROW: Have you examined him?

DR. ORBESON: Yes, I have examined him at your request for this trial, and at his request for his own condition and also Mrs. Massie's. I saw him for four or five hours at his home.

DARROW: Hear his testimony?

DR. ORBESON: Yes, all of it....

DARROW: How did they compare?

DR. ORBESON: His story told to me was exactly the same as on the stand.

DARROW: What do you say about the condition of his mind when the bullet was fired?

DR. ORBESON: He showed a very typical condition that is defined by law as insanity. He was in such a condition that he did not know what he was doing. He was mentally deranged. He was insane.

DARROW: Is such a case rare?

DR. ORBESON: No. I have seen any number of these cases in private practice, in the army.

DARROW: Is the case of one losing his mind, losing his grip on himself, and then recovering rare?

DR. ORBESON: No. Some last for a few minutes, a few hours, a few days....

DARROW: Could a great sorrow or shock induce such a condition?

DR. ORBESON: Yes, that is very common. A great majority of the cases do not even require such a shock or sorrow.

DARROW: You heard the trouble of Mrs. Massie, his wife. What do you think was the cause of his condition?

DR. ORBESON: I know: the ravaging of his wife. All the evidence points to that.

DARROW: Did anything add to that?

DR. ORBESON: Yes, the stories and rumors he heard, seeing people on the street, the things he was hearing all the time, the reflections on his character....

DARROW: Do you call this temporary insanity?

DR. ORBESON: Yes, all insanity is temporary, as I have said....

DARROW: What part of the body do the best students think is the origin of conduct?

DR. ORBESON: We don't know, but we do know that one of the motivating elements is the internal glandular apparatus.

DARROW: From what you have heard, from listening to the evidence and from his examination, you said Lt. Massie was insane.

DR. ORBESON: Yes, certainly. In my opinion he became insane the moment he heard the last words of Kahahawai. That man was under a terrific strain he'd never been subjected to before. As he went along it became a prey on his mind. It came to such a condition that he didn't know what he was doing....

DARROW: What did you derive from his conversation? ...

DR. ORBESON: He said the last thing he was conscious of was the last thing that came to his mind when he heard Kahahawai say "Yes, we done it." ...

DARROW: What opinion did you form from what he said?

DR. ORBESON: That he didn't know what he was doing.

DARROW: From what you have heard, and what you have seen, and what you were told by Lieutenant Massie, was he sane or insane at the moment of the shooting?

DR. ORBESON: He was insane for the reason that he did not know what he was doing....

DARROW: As far as you can discover about Massie, he's perfectly sane at this time?

DR. ORBESON: Yes.

DARROW: If a man picks up a man from whom he expects to get a confession, and just because he tells what he is expected to tell, that is of sufficient surprise to explode this "mental bomb" that you referred to?

DR. ORBESON: That's entirely different. This man carried with him a "mental bomb" and at the same time the idea that "I must not do anything to interfere with getting the confession." And he did it.

Cross-examination of prosecution expert Dr. Joseph Catton of Stanford University

In his cross-examination of the opposing side's expert, Darrow's objective was to use the doctor's opinions in other cases to support the defense experts' explanations for Massie's actions.

DARROW: How often have you testified in cases like this?

DR. CATTON: About once or twice a month for the past two years—about fifty times in that period.

DARROW: How old are you?

DR. CATTON: Forty-two on August 10.

DARROW: You know of cases of amnesia?

DR. CATTON: Yes.

DARROW: Can you give a definition of insanity?

DR. CATTON: A condition in which, because of disturbed functions of portions of the brain, the individual is prevented from continuing action and behavior which allows him to fit in and adjust himself to persons, places and things about him.

DARROW: All those people are insane?

DR. CATTON: That is as clearly as can be stated. . . .

DARROW: Are you especially interested in this case?

DR. CATTON: I am only interested in telling you the medical aspects of this case.

DARROW: You remember a case where you testified in a case of a man named Harlow who had killed his wife?

DR. CATTON: Yes.

DARROW: You testified he was insane?

DR. CATTON: Yes.

DARROW: How long ago was that?

DR. CATTON: Eight or nine years ago.

DARROW: And they found Harlow sane?

DR. CATTON: I thought they convicted him of manslaughter.

DARROW: You believed that Guiteau, who shot President Garfield, was insane?

DR. CATTON: I still think so.

DARROW: Harlow or his attorneys paid you?

DR. CATTON: Harlow's attorneys paid me....

DARROW: What is this "fight" business?

DR. CATTON: Anger-fight mechanism.

DARROW: Then everything is the result of those mechanisms?

DR. CATTON: Yes, everything.

Darrow then withdrew his earlier objection to Dr. Catton's entire testimony.

CHAPTER 6

FICTION

AUTOBIOGRAPHICAL INTRODUCTION

FROM CLARENCE DARROW, "REALISM IN LITERATURE AND ART,"
ARENA, VOL. 9 (1893)

The old novel which we used to read, and to which the world so fondly clings, had no idea of relation or perspective. It had a hero and a heroine, and sometimes more than one. The revolutions of the planets were less important than their love. War, shipwreck, and conflagration all conspired to produce the climax of the scene, and the whole world stood still until the lovers' hearts and hands were joined....

In real life the affections have played an important part, and sometimes great things have been done and suffered in the name of love, but most of the affairs of the human heart have been as natural as the other events of life.... The realist paints the passions and affections as they are. Both man and woman can see their beauty and their terror, their true position, and the relation that they bear to all the rest of life. He would not beguile the girl into the belief that her identity should be destroyed and merged for the sake of this feeling, which not once in ten thousand times could realize the promises the novel made; but he would not leave her as an individual to make the most she can, and all she can, of life, with all the hope and chance of conquest, which men have taken for themselves. Neither would the realist cry out blindly against these deep passions which have moved men and women in the past, and which must continue fierce and strong as long as life exists. He is taught by the scientist that the fiercest heat may be transformed to light, and is taught by life that from the strongest passions are sometimes born the sweetest and the purest souls.

In these days of creeds and theories, of preachers in the pulpit and preachers out, we are told that all novels should have a moral and be written to serve some end. So we have novels on religion, war, marriage, divorce, socialism, theosophy, woman's rights, and other topics without end. It is not enough that the preachers and lecturers shall tell us how to think and act; the novelist must try his hand at preaching too. He starts out with a theory, and every scene and incident must be bent to make it plain that the author believes certain things. The doings of the men and women in the book are secondary to the views the author holds. The theories may be true, but the poor characters that must adjust their lives to these ideal states are sadly warped and twisted out of shape.

The realist would teach a lesson, too, but he would not violate a single fact for all the theories in the world—for a theory could not be true if it did violence to life. He paints his picture so true and perfect that all men who look upon it know it is a likeness of the world that they have seen; they know that these are men and women and little children that they meet upon the streets; they see the conditions of their lives, and the moral of the picture sinks deep into their minds.

There are so-called scientists that make a theory and then gather facts to prove their theory true; the real scientist patiently and impartially gathers facts, and then forms a theory to explain and harmonize these facts. All life bears a moral, and the true artist must teach a lesson with his every fact. Some contend that the moral teacher must not tell the truth; the realist holds that there can be no moral teaching like the truth. The world has grown tired of preachers and sermons; today it asks for facts. It has grown tired of fairies and angels, and asks for flesh and blood. It looks on life as it exists, both its beauty and its horror, its joy and its sorrow; it wishes to see it all; not the prince and the millionaire alone, but the laborer and the beggar, the master and the slave. We see the beautiful and the ugly, and with it know what the world is and what it ought to be; and the true picture, which the author saw and painted, stirs the heart to holier feelings and grander thoughts....

The true realist cannot worship at the shrine of power, nor prostitute his gifts for gold. With an artist's eye he sees the world exactly as it is, and tells the story faithful unto life. He feels for every heart that beats, else he could not paint them as he does. It takes the soul to warm a statue into life and make living flesh and coursing blood; and each true picture that he paints or draws makes the world a better place in which to live.

The artists of the realistic school have a sense so fine that they cannot help catching the inspiration that is filling all the world's best minds with the hope of greater justice and more equal social life. With the vision of the seer they feel the coming dawn when true equality shall reign upon the earth; the time when democracy shall no more be confined to constitutions and to laws, but will be a part of human life. The greatest artists of the world today are telling facts and painting scenes that cause humanity to stop, and think, and ask why one should be a master and another be a serf; why a portion of the world should toil and spin, should wear away its strength and life, that the rest should live in idleness and ease....

Not all the world is beautiful, and not all of life is good. The true artist has no right to choose the lovely spots alone and make us think that this is life. He must bring the world before our eyes and make us read and learn. As he loves the true and noble, he must show the false and bad. As he yearns for true equality, he must paint the master and the slave. He must tell the truth, and tell it all, must tell it o'er and o'er again, till the deafest ear will listen and the dullest mind will think. He must not swerve to please the world by painting only lovely tales. He must think, and paint, and write, and work, until the world shall learn so much and grow so good, that the true will all be beautiful and all the real be ideal.

MAIN SELECTION

CLARENCE DARROW, "THE BREAKER BOY," *CHICAGO EVENING AMERICAN* (1902)

Johnny McGaffery was eleven years old when he became a man.

Five years before this his father and mother with their four children and steerage tickets sailed out of the Queenstown Harbor, bound for the United States. They had heard of America—all Irishmen had—they knew that America had no English landlords, no rack-rented tenants, no hopeless men and ragged women and hungry boys and girls. So, as they stood on the steerage deck and looked through the wire netting at the fading white houses and green fields of their native land, Owen and Bridget were light of heart. Beyond the great turbulent oceans were contentment, equality and wealth; a home for themselves and a brilliant future for the four children who, half in fear and half in wonder, were looking out at the white gulls and the white-crested waves.

Two weeks later they landed in New York, were rushed through Castle Garden and hurried to the railway train, where they set out for Scranton, Pennsylvania.

Within a few days Owen had found a job in the mines and had opened an account with a "company" store, and rented a "company" house, with a kitchen and parlor below and two little bedrooms above. Down under the kitchen floor was a hole in the ground which was called a cellar, and some rough wooden steps led down to the bottom from the side of the house. The hut was closed with boards which ran up and down, and the inside was without paper or even plaster, while here and there the cracks let in the daylight and, through the winter, the wind and sifting snow.

Owen and Bridget were a little disappointed at their home. In their little stone hut in their far-off island they had never dreamed that a house like this could be found in a land so rich and free. But they were starting life in a strange new world, and with strong hopes and brave hearts they set to work to make the best of what they had, never doubting but what the looked-for mansion would soon be theirs.

Owen went to work in the coal mines—down five hundred feet beneath the ground. Every morning he stepped on board a car, holding his dinner pail in one hand while he grasped the iron rail in his other hand, and held his breath until it dropped him to the bottom; and then at night he went back to the foot of the pit and boarded the car to be taken again to the top of the earth.

But this story is about Johnny, so we have no time to tell more of Owen, except that one day a great piece of rock broke off from the roof of the chamber where he worked and fell squarely upon him, crushing him to death.

The miners took him to the top of the shaft and back to the little hut, and consoled the helpless widow and children the best they could, and then followed him to the grave. The story of his hopes and struggles was told.

Johnny was almost eleven when they laid his father in the little consecrated ground and put the white wooden cross above his head. He was at school the day the rock came down, and had done so well that he was already in the third reader and had reached division in the arithmetic.

Johnny's older brother was already tending a door in the mine, and his sisters were in school with him. Luckily, some years before, a wise, good man, seeing how scant was the miner's income, had built a lace mill so that his girls could earn something to help the family along. So one night when the older sister left the school she carefully packed up her books and slate and took them home, and the next day went to the mill.

Bridget planned and saved the best she could. She had great hopes for little Johnny. He would surely be a scholar and make famous the McCaffery name. But all her hopes and struggles went for naught. Owen's funeral had left them hopelessly in debt, and the earnings of the boy and girl could not keep the family alive. There was really nothing left to do but send Johnny to the breaker. The law had humanely said that a child should be spared from the mine until he was twelve years old, but Bridget soon saw that this law was no protection against poverty and want; so she went to a justice of the peace and swore that Johnny's age was twelve, and sent him to the breaker. She somehow did not think much about this oath. In fact, she almost felt that Johnny was twelve years old. She knew of other boys of the same age who were at work.

Well, Johnny went to the breaker. He was halfway pleased to be released from school. If there is any place for a boy more cruel and hopeless than the breaker it is the ordinary public school.

Johnny lived about half a mile from the breaker where he went to work. Over and over again he had seen the huge rough black building standing up against the sky, and just beyond, the great pile of refuse which they called "culm" that loomed up higher still; especially at night, they rose up somber and black like the mountains just behind. The front of the building was a hundred feet high. It sloped slowly and evenly down to about twenty-five feet in height at the rear. Its great sides were dotted with windows, little gray spots in the vast surface of black weatherbeaten boards. Johnny had never seen a cathedral, but from the stories his teacher told at school he thought this building was about the size of one of those medieval temples—but it was a temple built not to God but to mammon.

Along the side of the great building ran the zigzag stairs, and in the early morning light, sometimes before the gloom had been fairly driven away, little boys tugged up the hundred steps to the breaker's top. Here the cars of coal were raised in an elevator and then dumped into a chute; the coal went sliding and scattering down through a myriad of sieves and chutes and turning wheels and the jaws of the great iron rolls which crushed the large lumps into little blocks, on, down, down, down from the place where it started a hundred feet above, until it landed in the huge iron pocket at the back of the breaker, twenty feet from the ground and just above the railroad track, ready for a gate to be opened to be let into the waiting car.

All the way down these long slanting chutes the lumps of coal tumbled and slid and fell. The clatter and shuffle of the endless rushing black stone over the sheet-iron lining of the long trough drowned even the sound of the whirling machinery and the crunching of the mighty iron teeth as they ground the large blocks into little bits, while above all an overhanging black cloud of dust from the sliding coal covered the black building and the black young children with an everlasting pall.

Over the top of the slanting chutes were nailed a row of little planks like wide steps upon a mighty ladder. Johnny was told to sit upon one of these little planks and put a foot on each side of the chute, and then as the lumps of coal ran swiftly down between his legs to snatch at the pieces of slate as fast as his hands and arms could move, and throw them into another pitching trough at his side. From the top of the great breaker down almost to the bottom sat this stairway of little boys, each grabbing at a chunk of slate as the coal rushed madly by, until it passed the last boy and tumbled clean and free from slate into the iron pockets above the tracks.

It took Johnny but a little time to become a breaker boy. He only had to learn the difference between slate and coal, and he had known this from a child. True, it took some skill to snatch the stone from the madly rushing black flood covered with its dense black cloud of dust; but little eyes are sharp and little fingers are nimble, and it was really remarkable to see how this long line of little hands would unerringly grasp the slate and let the coal pass by. The rich man who owned the breaker, whose name was Fox, used sometimes to stand and watch these little hands, lost in admiration of their dexterity and skill— their rapid movements and machine-like precision seemed to him the beauty and rhythm of a poem.

Mr. Fox had a daughter whom he dearly loved. He fancied that she had musical talent, and he got her the most skillful teacher that money could procure. Sometimes he stood by the piano and watched the girl take lessons in finger development, and he marveled at her dexterity and skill; but when he paused for a few moments beside the great long chutes and saw the black diamonds rushing down into his great iron pockets, and watched the little deft hands of the breaker boys, he could not help thinking that the piano was not the only place to develop finger movement. Still, that was about all he thought. Mr. Fox was not a bad man. He was really good. He loved his daughter, and he intended to send her to Paris and Vienna to complete her studies when she was old enough. Really, every lump of coal that rolled down the chutes proved how fondly he loved the girl.

In a few weeks Johnny was a full-fledged breaker boy. His mother woke him at six in the morning. He put on his oldest clothes, ate his breakfast and went to the breaker. Morning after morning he climbed the long flight of stairs to the top of the breaker. Morning after morning he went down the ladder until he found his little flat seat, nailed across the chute. Then he sat down on the rough board, placed one foot on each side of the trough and waited for the flood of coal to come rattling down. In front of him and behind him and at the side of him were other little boys covered with the same black pall that ever hung above his head. No one spoke or looked up in the gloom. They simply picked, picked, picked, while the black flood moved down. The constant stooping made his back very lame and sore. And often in the night his mother was awakened with his crying and left her bed to rub his little back.

Then, too, in the winter when the frost was in the air and on the black lumps his hands grew cold and numb, and he felt that he picked the coal with wooden prongs instead of flesh and blood. The nails of his fingers were worn, often he bound them with rags to protect them from the cold, or to save some bleeding wound made by the quickly rushing coal. His face was always as black as the coal that tumbled down the chute, and the dust filled his nose and lungs, and the flakes and splinters sometimes flew into his eyes, but still he worked away. Of course, he did not know why he worked. There was no more reason why he sat on the chute day after day than why Mr. Fox's daughter took "finger practice" on the piano in her luxurious home.

Not much happened to Johnny while he sat upon the hard, rough board. Not much can happen to a boy of this sort; and if it did, why should it matter? One day his little companion who always sat beside him leaned too far over as he picked the slate. He lost his balance and fell into the trough where the lumps of coal ran down. He plunged madly along with the rushing flood into the iron teeth of the remorseless breaker. Johnny shouted, but no one heard him in the din. Then he ran up the ladder and gave the signal to stop the great engine below, but of course it was too late. It took a long while to stop the mighty machine, and then it was almost an hour before the boy could be put together into one pile. Several days thereafter a man in a little town in Massachusetts thought that he saw blood on some lumps of coal that he was pouring into the top of his fine nickel-plated stove—but still there is blood on all our coal—and for that matter on almost everything we use, but a man is a fool if he looks for other people's blood.

It will not do to imagine that Johnny had no fun. He learned to chew plug tobacco and often went to the saloon at night. Of course he was pretty young for this—still, a boy who is old enough to go to a breaker is old enough to go to a saloon. When one is old enough to do manly work he is old enough to have manly sport. He used to go home at night so black that his closest friends could not have told his name. Then he washed himself in a tub of water in the parlor, changed all his clothes, got his supper and went out with the rest of the boys to play. There were the ordinary games for boys; there were cats to stone; there was a great cave where a house had gone down into an old worked-out mine and where the boys gathered at night and built a fire from old rubbish. One boy who had gone as far as the fourth grade read to the rest, wonderful stories from the nickel novels that they managed somehow to get. Then there was the night school kept up for miners' boys and girls—of course they could not be expected to study much after the day's work at the mill. Sometimes Johnny went to the night school, but he often fell asleep when he tried to study, and he never got past the third reader after all.

So Johnny went on until his fourteenth year. There was really nothing to tell after that time, and very little before it. In fact, it is rather absurd to write a story about a breaker boy. There must be some dramatic situation to make a story, and there is nothing dramatic in a life of endless toil. Strange as it may seem, Johnny never had an unknown uncle who died and left him a fortune. Mr. Fox never looked down at his swiftly moving fingers and took a fancy to him and invited him to his home and married him to his daughter. In fact, Mr. Fox never even saw him in the dust and gloom.

Almost all his life must be skipped because it is so dull. In writing biography you cannot dwell long on the parts that are very dull, and you must entirely omit the parts that are very interesting—and so biography is not biography after all. Anyhow, Johnny left the breaker when he was fourteen and was promoted to the place of door-keeper in the mine.

Somehow I forgot to state that all of this was forty years ago.

Forty years makes a great change in anyone who lives upon the earth—but it makes a greater change in the miner than in most other men. Fifty-four is not very old, so at least most of us think who cling tenaciously to the forties, and still more those who watch anxiously while the fifties are checked off. But at fifty-four the man who has money and can have leisure still feels that he is young. He can eat and drink; he can laugh and dance and play; he can marry and travel and write; in fact, can still chase all the phantasies and bubbles that make us forget the waiting open grave.

Forty years entirely transformed Johnny. Even his name was changed: he was now John; generally Uncle John. He had been a door boy, a driver, a helper, a miner, and he had now come up out of the earth to spend his last few years above the ground. His face was scarred and one ear was missing. This came not from war, but from powder all the same. A belated fuse exploded when he thought it had gone out. But still he counted this as luck, for his life was saved. One arm was crippled from a fallen rock and his right hip was never free from pain, but this was only the rheumatism that he caught while working in the ground. Except for the asthma he could still have stayed a number of years inside the earth before the last time that he should be lowered, to come up no more. But his old valves were growing more and more rusty every year. He wheezed instead of breathing, and he could walk but a very little way and could stand upon his feet only a few minutes at a time. His strength was almost gone. Some doctors would have advised rest and travel and a higher altitude, but his did not. In fact, he had no doctor. Everyone in the mine knew all about asthma, the black shadow that hangs ever above a miner's life.

John did not live in the same house where his father first placed him when he came from Ireland so long ago, but he lived very near the spot, still in a "company" house. The miners, and the mules, and machinery, had changed from time to time, but the breaker, the black culm pile, and the "company" houses still remained.

In forty years John had buried his mother, had married, raised a family, and traveled back and forth along the short path from his hut to the open mouth of the mine day after day; and this was all. As the years passed his one ambition had been to go back to Ireland, even for a short time, as his father's had been to come to the United States, but this ambition he had buried in the mines long years ago. He had left the valley once in forty years. He had gone to Philadelphia to the Centennial, and his ticket had cost him $5.40. This was a quarter of a century ago, but he remembered the exact money that he gave in exchange for the little pasteboard at the station window.

John really had earned the right to rest, but then, he and his family must live—at least he thought they must, and so they must, else the coal could never be dug up. The mine boss was really not unkind, so when John told him that he could not go down the shaft again, he promised him an easier job. The boss took him to the breaker, up the long flight of stairs, down the ladder of little boards nailed across the chute, and sat him down on the old board that he had left forty years ago.

John was not a poet or a dreamer. In fact, he never had a great deal of imagination, and what he had was buried long ago in the deep, black mine. He did not seem to think of the strange fate that sat him down on the narrow board after the circle of his life was done. He thought no more about it than do the rest of us of the everlasting turning of the wheel to which all of us are strapped.

This is about all of John's story. It is really up to date. The other morning he walked up the slope to the great black mill. As he went up the hill his wheezing could be heard a hundred feet away. Every few rods he stopped to rest. In his right hand he carried the everlasting dinner pail. In his mouth was a black briar pipe. Thank God, he could smoke. He reached the breaker and started up the steps. At the first landing he stopped to rest. The boys rushed past, calling out, "Hello, Uncle John!" At the second landing he stopped again, and so on at each landing to the top. Then he took a good long wait until he finally got his breath before he started down the ladder to his seat. Slowly and deliberately he sat down upon the rough, hard board. Mechanically he took his tobacco pouch from his pocket, knocked the ashes from his pipe, filled it full of fresh tobacco, put it in his mouth, struck a match upon the sheet-iron lining of the chute, drew in his wheezy breath and commenced to smoke. Then he took his rheumatic leg in his hand, raised his foot until it rested on the right side of the chute; then he raised his left foot to the other side, bent over and looked down at the black, iron trough, and waited for the coal to tumble down.

SUPPLEMENTARY SELECTION

CLARENCE DARROW, "LITTLE LOUIS EPSTINE,"
PILGRIM, VOL. 9 (1903)

This story is about little Louis Epstine, aged nine years. As might be guessed, Louis was a Jew. But there are different kinds of Jews. There are Jews who live on Grand Boulevard, and Jews who live on Maxwell Street. For the most part, the Jews on Grand Boulevard own wholesale clothing stores, and, for the most part, the Jews on Maxwell Street work in the stores. Louis Epstine lived on Maxwell Street. When this tale began, he had only one hand. How he lost the other is a matter quite outside of this story. It seems as if he was run over by a beer wagon when he was a baby. His nurse—or, no, it was an older sister, just past five—left him for a moment alone on the street, and the wagon came along. But he had long since forgotten all about this, if indeed he ever knew.

When Louis Epstine was nine years old, he went to a Jewish charity school. This was kept up by the wealthy Jews, who wished to do something for the poor. The fathers and mothers and brothers and sisters of the little fellows worked for the men who paid for the charity school. The patrons of the school never asked why their employees had to use the charity school. People do not get rich by asking foolish questions of this sort.

Louis was not the only child in the family. His mother had five more besides him, and they all lived together in two large rooms back of a bakery. They had lived a whole year without moving. The rent was five dollars a month. Louis had plenty of playmates when he was a child, for Maxwell Street is full of houses and shops and flats, and even then there is not room for all the children. Some of them live in the basements. Over on Grand Boulevard there are great houses and big yards, and the people fancy it is a good place for children, but Maxwell Street is a much better place. Either poverty makes large families, or large families make poverty; at least there are a hundred children on Maxwell Street to every one on Grand Boulevard.

When Louis was nine years old, he helped the family by selling papers. He got up at five o'clock in the morning and went over to Newspaper Alley and bought his papers, and then stood on the corner until about eleven o'clock, and sold them; then he went to school in the afternoon. In this way he managed to make three or four dollars a week, sometimes even five. Once in a while a good man would come along and give him a nickel for a paper, and now and then some kind-hearted fellow would give him a paper which he had read, and then Louis would sell it again. He never took a nickel from a customer and then ran to a corner to get it changed and forget to come back, although he knew some boys who did. Louis' mother had told him that this was not honest and that he would never get rich if he got money that way, although the boys who did it always seemed to get along as well as the others, sometimes better. But Louis' mother had taught him to be honest, and he had heard of a man who once sold papers and who always gave the change, and he was now a floor walker in a department store. Louis had seen the man himself. Louis' mother was a good woman and she loved her child and he loved her, although he never said anything about it to anyone. She kept him and the other children as clean as she possibly could, and they almost always had something to eat. It is not necessary here to tell how she managed to get it, indeed, perhaps we could not tell. Really, the mother hardly knew herself, but if anyone doubts the fact, let them visit Maxwell Street. No one can tell how all the children are fed, but all the same they live. True, some of them do not grow to be very old, but there are always plenty of new ones to take their places if they die.

Well, Louis got along fairly well up to his ninth year. Nothing serious happened to him, barring the loss of his hand, and this never bothered him a great deal; in fact, he never thought anything about it. If boys had three hands, they would doubtless use them, but one is really quite enough. Louis could do almost anything that the other boys could do. Of course, he could run as fast, he could play all sorts of games, he could throw stones at cats, he never had any trouble to eat everything his mother gave him, and even his stub of a left arm was quite useful; he could hold papers under it and fix his hat on his head and use this stub in connection with his right hand to do almost anything he wished to do. He really felt quite lucky to think that only his hand was gone. He knew a boy who had lost his whole arm, and it was his right one, too.

One day, Louis' mother had been better to him than usual. She had bought him a nice warm cap that pulled down over his ears, and cost twenty-five cents at the department store. He had never seemed to know how good she was before, and then suddenly in his boyish mind he commenced to think how hard she worked, what poor clothes she had, how she never went to a circus or killed a rat in the gutter, or had any kind of fun; how she got up every morning and fixed his breakfast before he was out of bed; and how she washed the dishes after he had gone to sleep. He felt very tenderly toward her. It was really more pity than love. And then he remembered a string of great red glass beads that he had seen hanging in the department store on the corner where he sold his papers, and which were marked forty-eight cents, and he thought how happy his mother would be if he could buy this string of beads. He was only a boy, and did not know why the beads were not as valuable as a string of pearls, and perhaps they were. So in his foolish, boyish mind he conceived the thought of saving enough money to buy the beads and giving them to his mother at Christmas time. He kept out a penny or two each day and carefully hid it away until he had thirty-five cents that no one but himself knew anything about. Every morning when he took his stand before the great store he looked in through the polished window to see that the beads were still hanging in their place. As Christmas time drew on, he always looked with quaking heart, for he felt almost sure that some rich lady would buy them before he had saved enough.

The eighteenth of December came around. The day can easily be remembered, because it was so very cold. This morning was far the coldest of the winter, and all through the night Louis had kept waking up because there were not enough quilts on the bed. In the morning he was ready to get up and go after his papers before the usual time. He mother urged him not to go, telling him it was too cold, but Louis would not hear to this; it was only a week till Christmas time, and besides, if it was cold he could sell more papers, for some of the other boys would stay away. So his mother got him a cup of coffee and a big slice of black bread with some yellow stock yards' butter—not a bad breakfast for a poor child in the Ghetto. In fact, somehow he had been getting pretty well fed this fall and winter. He still had the memory of a nice turkey that the alderman had sent them on Thanksgiving, and there was a rumor in the ward that this year another one would be sent on Christmas. Some of the boys said that the alderman wanted to be assessor in the spring. Louis did not know what this was. He had never even seen an assessor, but then he had never seen a king.

Well, on this morning, after breakfast, Louis' mother bundled him up the best she could. His shoes were not very good. He had bought them "second hand," or whatever it is with shoes. And they were really not mates, but neither were his feet exactly, for that matter. One shoe had a hole on the side and was ripped down the back, but otherwise was pretty good. The other was worn through in one place on the bottom and his old stocking stuck out at the toe. Both of them were pretty large, but his mother had always told him that large shoes wore the best and would wear the longest and would not make corns. As he understood it, only rich people wore shoes that were too small, and then mostly ladies. His pants had most likely been made from gray cloth, and certainly for someone else. These, too, were quite large, and had a number of patches scattered around in various places like sores. There was one on each leg about the knee and quite a large one in the back, and a few more besides. Then there were several places where there was no patch. The cloth did not seem to hold the thread very well, and anyhow Louis expected a new pair—or, rather, another pair—this winter. He could have had them long ago only for the beads. His pants were held up by a black strap, just like the swells that he had seen on State Street, well not just like them, but still with a black strap. His coat was really a prize affair. It was the best garment he had except a woolen comforter which we have not yet reached. This coat had been given him two years before by a charity society. It is not sure where it came from, but it must have been from some rich people on the North Side. There was not much wrong with the coat. The lining, of course, was torn, and when Louis put his hand into the sleeve he had to grasp hold of the wristband of his shirt, and hold it until his hand came out at the bottom of the sleeve, but this was partly because the buttonhole of the shirt was broken out. This was his right hand. He always put his left stub down through the arm very carefully, as a navigator would steer a ship through the shoals. He put this arm through first. Then his mother wound a wool comforter around his neck. This was really a grand affair, or had been once. Now so many threads had been broken that it was getting pretty ragged, and it seemed to be about the same color all the way through, although it would be hard to tell what that was. His mother often told Louis how it looked years ago. It had been given to her by a rich uncle in Russia who was a peddler, but it really was very warm. Then on top of his head, best of all, was the new cap, the cause of all his trouble. This he pulled clear down over his face so that only his eyes could be seen. There is no use to describe his shirt and things like that. Even poor boys ought to have some privacy, and besides you could only see his shirt in one place, down below his coat, and not then unless his back was turned. Of course, he had no overcoat. None of the boys had these, except some of the little dudes that he had seen their mothers leading into the department stores on State Street.

When Louis went to get his papers, he was in the habit of going down Van Buren Street and then along Franklin Street. The buildings on these streets were so big that they kept the wind away. When he could go down on the cold mornings, he would meet men and boys with great stacks of overcoats on their heads and in their arms. They were carrying them in and out of the great stores; none of the men and boys wore overcoats, except now and then one that was very old and poor; and then he would pass great rows of clothing stores—miles and miles of these kind of stores, and he looked in through the great square windows and saw endless heaps of overcoats, and other nice new coats and pants, too, piled up in great high heaps and long rows as far as he could see. There was not much else the whole line of Franklin Street, except these clothes, and now and then a great building full of shoes, and Louis used to think that there were more coats than all the boys on the whole West Side could wear, more than all the boys he ever heard of could possibly use; and then in his foolish way he wondered why these were locked up all the cold winter when none of the little boys had coats; but Louis was not a statesman or a political economist, he was only a poor little Jew boy, nine years old.

On this morning, Louis' mother opened the door and started him out. She did not kiss him goodbye. This is no use when a mother has any other way of showing her love. She just opened the door and let him out. She told him to be sure and keep his coat buttoned up. He sang out, "Gee, ain't this cold!" And that was all that was said as he went away. He walked down the street to Jackson Boulevard, and then crossed over to the South Side. He always liked to cross on the Boulevard. The buildings were so grand, and the walk so smooth. He went on down to Franklin Street, and turned north past the great clothing stores. The coats and pants and vests seemed to be piled up higher than ever. He looked at them and said, "Gee, I wish I had one o'dem." But he never thought of going in and getting it; poor people never do. In this way he got down to Newspaper Alley, where the boys were trying hard to trade their pennies for papers. There were fewer there this morning than before. He got his bundle of papers, thrust them under his stub arm and started off. Besides the cold, there was a cutting wind, and as he came north it was all he could do to walk, but when he turned south with his papers it was easier, though the drifting snow bothered him quite a bit. He darted along one or two alleys and in one place walked through an arcade. These made him a little warmer than before. Finally, he got down to the department store and took his stand just in front of the great red beads and began to call off something that they had told him was in the papers, something about some grand affair, a charity ball, or an inaugural, or something of the sort. Anyhow, he didn't know what it was. On the corner he missed the man who usually sold lead pencils and the boy without any legs, who always sat with his cap in his hand and raked out the pennies as fast as the people put them in.

Louis did not stand there very long until he began to get cold, so he commenced walking up and down the block and calling his papers whenever anyone passed. There were not many people out on the street that morning and they all hurried pretty fast, most of them not stopping long enough to buy a paper. Along toward eight o'clock his hand had begun to get very cold. He couldn't put it in his pocket, and use the other one. He was obliged to make all the change with this one, and could only use his stub to hold the papers. Two or three times he stepped into the outside doorway of the store for a minute, but he could not sell papers there, and then the last time the floor walker drove him out. The floor walker had once sold papers, but this was long ago. He was now a self-made man. Louis had not yet learned never to expect anything from a self-made man. He did not know that the man who is born in poverty and misfortune almost always grows very hard, unless he keeps his poverty and misfortune. Indeed, he is obliged to grow hard to get over his poverty and misfortune.

Two or three times in the morning Louis thought he would give it up and go home, but then there were the glass beads and besides he had the papers and could not afford to get "stuck" with them on his hands; so he stayed at his post. It is possible he might have gone away anyhow, except that along about nine o'clock or half-past, his hand began to get warmer, and although his feet and body were pretty cold, he could move around and manage to stand this. So he stayed and sold out his papers and went back home about the usual time. Soon after he got into the house his hand commenced to feel queer—it was all prickly and numb, and seemed to burn. He told his mother, and she had him put it in cold water; still it ached so bad that she finally sent over to the corner for a doctor. He looked the hand over carefully and then shook his head. The doctor finally said that the hand was badly frozen, and he did not know whether Louis could ever use it again or not. But he put some stuff on it and wound it up in a cloth and went away. In a few hours he came back. The hand did not pain as much as before, but it felt numb and queer. The doctor took off the bandage and shook his head again. It was red and purple clear up to the wrist. The doctor told Louis and his mother that he must go to the hospital, and he was afraid they must cut off the hand, but they would ask the doctor at the hospital first. Louis and his mother had no time to cry,—they had to start at once. They went in to the great big building. Louis thought it smelled pretty badly, although he was used to all kinds of smells in the Ghetto. They found the big doctor, and he looked at Louis' hand and said it must be amputated at once. Louis did not know exactly what that was, but of course he made no objection and his mother made none. It had all come so suddenly that neither of them fully realized what it meant, and then poor people never do object to anything that the rich say must be done. The doctor told Louis that it would not hurt, and this was the main thing at the time. They took him into a great long bedroom, where there were dozens of little white cots all the same size, and most of them with a child lying on top. They told him that they would give him something which would put him to sleep, but that he would wake up all right, and it would be all over without his knowing it.

There is no need to tell about the operation. If anyone really has a taste for that sort of thing he can visit a hospital any day in the week. Most people stay away as long as they possibly can, and of course they would not like to read about it—for that matter, they do not like to see how poor people live.

Well, Louis went to sleep, and the next thing he knew he was lying in one of the little cots, and his mother, the doctor and a girl with a striped blue and white dress were standing by the bed. His hand was tied up in a cloth and was aching pretty bad. It took him some time to remember where he was, and then he asked them about his hand, why it was hurting so much. Then his mother told him all about it, although it was almost as hard for her as for Louis. But the little fellow was rather dazed at first, and did not seem to think much about his hand. Then Louis lay still for quite awhile. He was looking at the ceiling and the walls, and following the zigzag pattern of the paper up and down. Finally, he turned away from his mother, and pretty soon they heard a sob. The poor woman went around to the other side of the cot, and stroked Louis' face and hair gently, and asked him not to cry. She told him that he would be well again before long, and that she and his brothers and sisters would always be good to him and take care of him as long as he lived. Louis told her that he knew this, but it was so near Christmas and he couldn't get the rest of the money. She asked him what he meant, and then between his sobs he told her all about the beads.

Supplementary Selection

From Clarence Darrow, *Farmington*, Chapter 16, "Rules of Conduct" (1904)

Farmington *was Darrow's first novel. It is a semiautobiographical account of a middle-aged man's return to his hometown.*

I was very young when I first began to wonder why the world was so unreasonable; and now I am growing old, and it is not a whit more sensible than it used to be. Still, as a child I was in full accord with the other boys and girls about the stupidity of the world. Of course most of this perversity on the part of older people came from their constant interference with our desires and plans. None of them seemed to remember that they once were young and had looked out at the great wide world through the wondering eyes of the little child.

It seemed to us as if our elders were in a universal conspiracy against us children; and we in turn combined to defeat their plans.

I wonder where my little playmates have strayed on the great round world, and if they have grown as unreasonable as our fathers and mothers used to be! Reasonable or unreasonable, it is certain that our parents never knew what was best for us to do. Anyhow, I thought so then; and although the wisdom, or at least the experience, of many years has been added to my childish stock, I am bound to say that I think so still. Even a boy might sometimes be trusted to know what he ought to do; and the instinct and teachings of Nature, as they speak directly to the child, should have some weight.

But with our parents and teachers all this counted not the least. The very fact that we wanted to do things seemed ample reason why we could not. I venture to say that nine-tenths of our requests were denied; and when consent was granted, it was given in the most grudging way. The one great word that always stood straight across our path was "No," and I am sure that the first instinct of our elders on hearing of our desires was to refuse. I wondered then, and I wonder still, what would happen if our elders and the world at large should take the other tack and persuade themselves to say "Yes" as often as they could!

Every child was told exactly what he ought to do. If I could only get a printed list of the rules given for my conduct day by day, I am sure they would fill this book....

I could not eat a single meal without the use of rules, and most of these were violated when I had the chance. I distinctly remember that we generally had pie for supper in our youthful days. Now we have dessert for dinner, but then it was only pie for supper. Of course we never had all the pie we wanted, and we used to nibble it slowly around the edges and carefully eat toward the middle of the piece to make it last as long as possible and still keep the pie-taste in our mouths.

I never could see why we should not have all the pie that we could eat. It was not because of its cost, for my mother made it herself, just the same as bread. The only reason we could see was that we liked pie so well. Of course we were told that the pie was not good for us; but I have always been told this about everything that I liked to eat or do. Then, too, my mother insisted that I should eat the pie after the rest of the meal was done. Now, as a boy, I liked pie better than anything else that I could get to eat; and I have not yet grown so old but that I still like pie. I could see no reason why I should not eat my pie when I was hungry for it and when it looked so good. My mother said I must first eat potatoes and meat, and bread and butter; and when I had enough of these, I could eat the pie. Now, of course, after eating all these things even pie did not seem quite the same; my real appetite was gone before the pie was reached. Then, too, if a boy ate everything else first, he might never get to pie; he might be taken ill, or drop dead, or be sent from the table, or one of the other boys might come along and he be forced to choose between going swimming and eating pie,—whereas, if he began the meal according to his taste and made sure of the pie, if anything else should be missed it would not matter much.

Our whole lives were fashioned on the rules for eating pie. We were told that youth was the time for work and study, so that we might rest when we got old. Now, no boy ever cared to rest,—it is the very thing a boy does not want to do; but still, by all the rules we ever heard, this was the right way. Since I was a child I have never changed my mind. I do not think the pie should be put off to the end of the meal. I always think of my poor Aunt Mary, who saved her pie all through her life, and died without eating it at last. And, besides all this, it is quite possible that as we grow old our appetites will change, and we may not care for pie at all; at least, the coarser fare that the hard and cruel world is soon to serve up generously to us all is likely to make us lose our taste for pie. For my part, I am sure that when my last hours come I shall be glad that I ate all the pie that I could get, and if any part of the meal is left untasted it shall be the bread and butter and potatoes, and not the pie....

CHAPTER 7

BIOGRAPHICAL WRITINGS AND SPEECHES

AUTOBIOGRAPHICAL INTRODUCTION

FROM CLARENCE DARROW'S REFLECTIONS ON HIS SIXTY-FIRST
BIRTHDAY AT A PRIVATE DINNER GIVEN IN HIS HONOR IN CHICAGO,
ILLINOIS, ON APRIL 18, 1918

I have always yearned for peace, but have lived a life of war. I do not know why, excepting that it is the law of my being. I have lived a life in front trenches, looking for trouble....

Perhaps in some respects my life has not been quite the same as others. I have always had a feeling that I was doing what I wished to do, but a certain knowledge that I never did anything I chose to do. I have always had an ambition for freedom, but I know that I never had the slightest influence over myself. I am sure that I have everlastingly been controlled by the influences before me and the infinite influences around me, and that I have never known what freedom is. I keep on working for it and hoping for it and wanting it, but I know that I never shall have it. In this, no doubt, my life has been like the life of every being that ever lived. Even while I have fought for freedom, the freedom of others and the freedom of myself, I have always had a consciousness that I was doing it to amuse myself, to keep myself occupied so I might forget myself; which after all is the best thing that any of us can do as we go along. I remember reading a while ago a statement of Anatole France. He said that the chief business of life is "killing time." And so it is....

The one thing that gets me, perhaps more than anything else, is the terrible cruelty of man. Someone here said that I loved my fellow-man. I don't know whether I do or not. It depends on whether you are speaking intellectually or chemically. Intellectually, I think human beings are a pretty poor lot. Here and there no doubt is nobility of character, but the human race is not a proper subject for worship. It has always taken itself too seriously. It amounts to little. If it should die, it would doubtless be as well or better for the rest of creation. The thing I see everywhere present is the cruelty of man. Men torturing animals, regardless of the suffering of the weak. Men torturing each other, simply for the joy of doing it. Man is cruel, one of the cruelest animals of the brute creation. I remember the great naturalist, Fabre, said that there is no other species that devours and enslaves members of its own species; this is left for man alone. We seem to get pleasure in torturing our fellow-men....

Most of life is hard for those who think. No doubt there are those who believe that "God's in his heaven and all's right with the world." If one can live on this delusion, he would be foolish to awaken from his dream. But if we really think and feel, life is serious and hard. All who live a full and long life without illusions, at times involuntarily look with almost longing eyes to the last release. The plaintive, wistful, mournful words of Swinburne are not unwelcome music to his ears:

> *From too much love of living,*
> *From hope and fear set free,*
> *We thank with brief thanksgiving*
> *Whatever Gods may be;*
>
> *That no life lives forever,*
> *That dead men rise up never;*
> *That even the weariest river*
> *Winds somewhere safe to sea.*[1]

---

[1]From "The Garden of Proserpine" (Verses 10–11), by Algernon Charles Swinburne (1837–1909).

Main Selection

Voltaire

From *Infidels and Heretics: An Agnostic's Anthology* by Clarence Darrow
and Wallace Rice, published by the Stratford Company, Boston,
Massachusetts (1929)

Voltaire was born in Paris in 1694.

At that time, Louis XIV was on the throne in France. Through long years of profligacy and dissipation, the lords and rulers of France had reduced the country to poverty and the people to slavery and superstition.... Noblemen, priests and women of easy virtue were the rulers, and people lived only to furnish them amusement and dissipation. Everyone believed in miracles, witchcraft and revealed religion. They not only believed in old miracles but in new ones. (A person may be intellectual and believe in miracles, but the miracles must be very old.)

Doctors plied their trade through sorcery, and sacred charms. Lawyers helped keep the poor in subjection: the criminal code was long, cruel and deadly. The priest, the doctor and the lawyer lived for the rich and helped make slaves of the poor. Doctors still believe in sorcery, but they administer their faith cures through a bottle instead of vulgar witchcraft. Lawyers still keep the poor in their place by jails and barbarous laws, but the criminal code is shorter and less severe.

When Voltaire was born there was really but one church, which, of course, was ignorant, tyrannical and barbarous in the extreme. All creeds are alike ... whenever there is but one, and the rulers honestly believe in that one, [it is] bound to be ignorant, barbarous and cruel. All sorts of heresies were punishable by death. If anyone dared to write a pamphlet or book that questioned any part of the accepted faith, the book was at once consigned to flames and the author was lucky if he did not meet the same fate. Religion was not maintained by the precepts of the priest, but by the prison, the torture chamber and the fagot. Everyone believed; no one questioned....

It was in this state and at that time that Voltaire was born. He was a puny child, whom no one thought would live. The priest was called in immediately that he might be baptized so his soul would be saved.

Voltaire's father was a notary of mediocre talents and some property, but his name would have been lost excepting for his brilliant son. [Voltaire's] mother was his mother, and that was all.... No one can find in any of his ancestors or kin any justification for the genius of Voltaire. Had the modern professors of eugenics had power in France in 1694, they probably would not have permitted such a child to have been born. Their scientific knowledge would have shown conclusively that no person of value could have come from the union of his father and mother. [But] in those days, nature had not been instructed by the professors of eugenics, and so Voltaire was born....

Before he was ten years old, it was plain that the young Voltaire had a clever mind, [and] he was sent to a boys' school in France. His body was lean and thin and his mind was keen and active, and neither his body nor his mind changed these characteristics until the day of his death. At the school, he said, he learned "Latin and nonsense," and nothing else. In two hundred years, the schools are still teaching Latin and nonsense. The course of Latin is the same, but the kinds of nonsense have somewhat changed.

... On Voltaire's return from school, [at] about fifteen, his father decided to make him an advocate. He had picked out the profession for his son, as most fathers do, because it was his own; but Voltaire's early efforts at poetry had given him the ambition to write and he insisted that he should not follow his father's footsteps, but devote his life to literature. This his father would not consent to....

But even Voltaire's father could not make a lawyer out of a genius. To be a good lawyer, one must have a mind and a disposition to venerate the past; a respect for precedents; and a belief in the wisdom and the sanctity of the dead. Voltaire had genius, imagination, feeling, and poetry, and these gifts always have been, and always will be, incompatible with the practice of law.

While studying law, Voltaire was writing verses, verses that were wicked, sacrilegious, and sometimes malicious.... On account of some boyish scrape, he was sent by his father to Caen and . . . at once captured the society and intellect of the town. His father, seeing something of the boy's brilliancy, sent him word that if he would come back home he would buy him a good post in the government. "Tell my father," was the answer, "I do not want any place that can be bought. I will make one for myself that will cost nothing."

Later in his life, in writing the story of the great dramatist Molière, he said, "All who have made a name for themselves in the fine arts, have done so in spite of their relations. Nature has always been much stronger with them than education." . . . The usual is always mediocre. When nature takes it into her head to make a man, she fits him with her own equipment and educates him in her own school.

Voltaire's father got him a post in Holland, where he wrote more verses [and] fell in love (or at least thought he did, which comes to the same thing). He was forbidden to see his mistress; after various difficulties in meeting, she wisely concluded that the chances were so uncertain she had better take someone else. Naturally, this serious matter made a deep impression on the boy. He concluded there was nothing to live for and turned more deliberately to literature for consolation. He went seriously to work and never stopped until he died at eighty-four. Had he been able to marry the girl . . . but what's the use in speculating upon that?

Louis XIV died in 1715. . . . Voltaire by this time was known for his epigrams, his rhymes and his audacity. . . . Whatever else he was during his life, he was never dull, and the world forgives almost anything but stupidity. Commencing early in his life, most of the epigrams and brilliant satires in France were charged to Voltaire. On account of a particularly odious epigram, he was exiled to Sully. His keepers found him a most agreeable guest, and he was at once a favorite in the society of the place. "It would be delightful to stay at Sully," he wrote, "If I were only allowed to go away from it." He spent his time hunting, flirting and writing verses. In his verses and his epigrams he could flatter when he thought flattery would accomplish his end, and by this means his exile was brought to a close.

He returned to Paris after an absence of about a year. No

sooner was he back, than a violent attack on the government appeared. This was at once charged to Voltaire, who had in fact not written it...but on account of the anonymous verses which he did not write he was sent to the Bastille....

It was some time before he was given a pen and ink, which all his life he needed more than anything else; but [even] without these, he began to compose a new play. He was able to carry in his mind whole cantos of the play and, as Frederick the Great said, "His prison became his Parnassus." Voltaire was not the first or last man to convert a prison into a hall of fame. A prison is confining to the body, but whether it affects the mind, depends entirely upon the mind.

It was while in prison that he changed his name from the one his father gave him—Arouet—to the one he has made famous throughout all time—Voltaire. He said, "I was very unlucky under my first name. I want to see if this one will succeed any better."...In a year he was released, but whether in prison or surrounded by the gayest court in Europe, he was always forging his keen, witty, malicious darts against the enemies of truth and liberty.

When Voltaire was twenty-four, his first play, *Oedipe,* was produced in Paris....This play, together with his earlier works, got him a pension, but the pension did not succeed in keeping his mouth closed....Pensions are the favors of the powerful, and dangerous to any great intellect. It is only here and there down throughout the ages that a Voltaire is born who does not fall a victim to their blandishments. Not only pensions, but what the world calls good society, was always open to Voltaire. He needed but to obey the mandates of the rules to live as the pampered child of luxury and ease, but this Voltaire always refused to do....

Voltaire, with all his other talents, was a businessman. For this he was criticized by biographers and enemies. While he was ever generous to his friends and ready to give his time and money for an unpopular cause, he constantly haggled and dickered over business matters and seldom got the worst of any trade. No iconoclast can possibly escape the severest criticism. If he is poor, he is against existing things because he cannot succeed. If he is rich, he is not faithful to his ideals. The world always demands of a prophet a double standard. He must live a life consistent with his dreams, and at the same time must obey the conventions of the world.... In trying to live up to both standards, one invariably misses both....

Voltaire loved the good things of life. He loved society; he loved the witty and intelligent; he loved fame; and he was singularly vain. He loved the society of the courts of France, adapting himself the best he could, but at the same time seeing through [that society's] shams, despising its vanities, its cruelties and its injustice to the poor. But he [had to] do his work, and to do his work in France two hundred years ago, he [had to] have the patronage of princes, of priests, of kings and influential courtesans.

...For another of his brilliant sayings he was thrown into the Bastille for a short time in 1726. He was pardoned on the condition that he go to England. No sooner had he reached that island than he was at once received by [its] poets, philosophers and statesmen.... Swift, Pope, Young, Gray and Walpole were then shedding their luster on the British isle. Newton was dying and Locke, though dead, had just begun to speak.

Voltaire at once threw himself into the life of England. Here he found a land where one could write and speak and publish his honest thoughts. Here he felt that he had reached the "promised land." He was everywhere received by the intellectual spirits of England, and within six months he was master of the English tongue....

Voltaire's residence in England made a great impression on his future life. He seemed to dedicate himself anew to the great cause of human liberty, [and] felt that it was for him to destroy oppression, superstition and tyranny....

After three years in England, Voltaire managed to get permission to return to Paris. He set to work to write another play and to organize a company to act it. During all his life he was passionately fond of the stage, writing plays on every subject, ancient and modern, plays which always held keen thrusts against the injustice of the world. He was busy organizing companies to produce his plays, constantly associated with actors; in his later years he built a theater of his own at Ferney and frequently took parts in his own plays.

In those days the business of an actor was more despised than it is today. Actors were servants of the rich, men and women who contributed to their pleasure for the purpose of satisfying their idle hours. Everybody went to the theater, but no one had any regard for those who performed.... While the king might sit in a box, the dead player could not be buried in consecrated ground.

Soon after his return to Paris, Adrienne Lecouvreur died at the age of thirty-eight. She was the greatest actress of her time ... taken with a fatal illness while playing one of Voltaire's plays. Voltaire hastened to her bedside. She died in his arms, in agony for which the doctors of that day could furnish no relief.... In her death she could have neither priest nor absolution, was denied Christian burial, taken out of the city at night and "thrown in the kennel" like a dog....

Voltaire ... was touched to the soul by the injustice of the French law, French society and French religion. He had been, he said, "her admirer, her friend, and her lover." "Shall I ever cease to see," he wrote, "the light-minded Frenchman sleeping under the rule of superstition? Is it only in England that mortals dare to think? Men deprived of burial here to whom Greece would have raised altars! In London she would have had a tomb among geniuses, kings and heroes. Ye gods, why is my country no longer the fatherland of glory and talent?"

During the rest of his life Voltaire worked tirelessly to improve the condition of the actors of his day.... "Actors are paid by the king," he said, "and excommunicated by the church. They are commanded by the king to play every evening and by the church forbidden to do so at all. If they do not play, they are put in prison. If they do, they are spurned into a kennel. We delight to live with them and object to be buried with them. We admit them to our tables and exclude them from our cemeteries." Even in old age ... his greatest dread was that he might be thrown in the gutter after his death.

There was no field of literature that was not open to Voltaire. A poet, an essayist, a writer of plays, a historian, a novelist, a scientist, [and] a philosopher, he tried them all, and excelled in all. His histories were as brilliant as his plays. He understood as well as any man who ever lived the difficulty that besets the author who would write history. "Who so writes a history of his own times," he said, "must be expected to be blamed for everything he has said, and everything he has not said."

His *English Letters* had been prepared in England and after his return to France: these, he knew, were too dangerous to be published in Paris. He was saving them until it might be safe. Somehow they were stolen and were published in 1737. These letters contained studies of the great English philosophers and comments on life, which were modern then and are still modern. The truth is always modern and there never comes a time when it is safe to give it voice.

The publisher of Voltaire's *English Letters* was thrown into the Bastille. The book was denounced and publicly burned in Paris by the hangman as "scandalously contrary to religion, morals and society," but still, Paris was not so old-fashioned. Men are constantly thrown into prisons today in America for publications which are "scandalous" and "contrary to morals and authority"—publications which tell the truth. Voltaire's house was searched, but he got the news in time and once more fled to save his liberty and his life....

Voltaire could not keep out of trouble. Almost every person of importance was his enemy at some period of his life, but...he never turned the other cheek. When he was attacked, he replied with pamphlets and epigrams more poisonous than those any other author ever penned. Whenever he was at peace, he was uneasy.... If his critics and traducers let him alone for a time, he was busy writing some pamphlet, poem or play to get himself into trouble once more.

He seldom signed his own name.... More than one hundred names were used by Voltaire in the course of his long literary career, but whatever the name ... if [a pamphlet was] especially bitter, mocking, rebellious or ungodly, it was always laid to Voltaire; and whatever the utterance that made the trouble ... Voltaire was ready to deny that he was the author.... He sometimes condemned his own books and was present in the crowd to see them burned, but no doubt most men would have preferred to deny the pamphlets than to have been burned with them....

Voltaire fled from Paris when the *English Letters* were published. He fled to a distant part of France. From there he went to live on an old estate with Madame du Chatelet and her husband. The husband was an army officer and seldom at home, and of very little consequence when he was. Madame du Chatelet was one of the most remarkable women of her age, or any other.... Voltaire was forty years of age when he fled from Paris to the estate of Madame du Chatelet and his life and fortunes were bound up with her for sixteen years. The estate was old and dilapidated and in a barren and dreary part of France, but with his industry and his money, he made it a place of beauty sought by the greatest people of Europe.

Madame du Chatelet was not a housekeeper.... She was intellectual, and no woman ought to expect to be intellectual and a housekeeper too. She was difficult, irascible, and voluble. Voltaire was impressionable, sensitive, quick-tempered. They kept each other very much entertained. Sometimes they loved, often they fought, but still they seemed to find each other necessary for their work.... Together they visited nobles, princes, and courts, perhaps "the most brilliant pair in France" of that day. No doubt after some years, the tie between them grew galling ... but it had grown to be a habit. Had they been married, they would probably have gotten a divorce; but as they were not married, they could not be divorced and stayed together.

Voltaire was particularly blessed by two women, Madame du Chatelet, at whose estate he lived for sixteen years, and Madame Denis, his niece, who kept his house near Geneva for more than twenty-five years. Neither of them gave him a moment's peace, and forced him to flee [to] his study for consolation and rest.

If either of these women had made his life comfortable, his great work would probably never have been done. There are two things that kill a genius—a fatal disease and contentment. When a man is contented he goes to sleep. Voltaire had no chance to be contented, and so he wrote eternally and unceasingly, more than any other man in the history of the world....

[A vacancy in the French Academy] occurred...and Voltaire, at the age of fifty-two, was admitted, long after he had been admitted to almost every other great society in Europe. It was the custom of the new members to read a paper, so Voltaire read one to the Academy.... The paper was witty, audacious and sacrilegious. It offended all the august personages who heard and read it. They regretted that he was a member of the Academy, but it was too late. They should have known before that such a leopard could not change its spots. Again he was chased from the court....

All his life he could joke and with him there was no subject too serious for a comedy. Voltaire said, "It is because one can be frivolous that the majority of people do not hang themselves." He has often been criticized because he could joke. The ordinary mind cannot understand that a serious purpose and a sense of humor can go together. It is only the sense of humor that can keep a man alive for the serious purpose. The world has never been able to distinguish between stupidity and seriousness. If the stupidly serious really had any humor, they would die from laughing at themselves.

Voltaire spent a short time traveling through various parts of France, fearing to go back to Paris, and then turned to Geneva. Geneva was then an independent state, afterward annexed to France and later to Switzerland.... He was sixty years old when he reached this little state. He had been sobered by age and experience. He had learned much of the follies and frivolities of the world. He knew that after all, his was a serious life and his work the greatest ever undertaken by man in any age. He seemed to take new vows to the service of the great cause which was really the greatest of his life, the cause of liberty. From that time on, he was tireless, unremitting, and brilliant in that cause. Whenever he found superstition, injustice, tyranny, and cruelty, Voltaire placed himself in the arena ready for the fray. Whether his work was history, poetry, drama, novels or pamphlets, it was the same....

When Voltaire went to Geneva, that state was still held in the mental paralysis of the doctrines of John Calvin.... Geneva was obsessed by a strange idea, an idea as common now as then ... the doctrine that men can be changed and made perfect by human laws.

The Geneva laws fixed the time at which people should go to bed and get up in the morning, and of course both hours were early; fixed the kind of drink and food and the amount and quality that was proper for a man to take. It regulated the religious creeds and social customs. No matter what one wished to do, he could find out whether it was right or wrong by consulting the statutes of Geneva.

The same obsession rules the human race today. We have changed the diet, the religious and moral code, the social code, the social customs, but not the fundamental idea that the state should tell us what to do and especially what not to do, and that to disobey is to be a criminal, punished, outlawed, and reviled....

[Voltaire] soon purchased two estates about three miles from Geneva, in the territory of France. He was near enough to Geneva so he could build a theater of his own and the people could come across the border to see his plays and the barbarous laws of Calvin could not forbid. He was near enough to the French border so he could flee to Switzerland or Geneva whenever the king of France should determine to send him to the Bastille. The estate where he spent the great portion of his remaining life, he called Ferney, almost on the shores of the beautiful Lake Geneva, with Mount Blanc and the other Alpine peaks in full view, the clear sky and the snow-capped mountains almost above him, the green fields of France and Switzerland around him—an ideal spot in which to live and work and dream. It was not for the beauty that he chose this spot. The love of natural beauty never entered the soul of Voltaire....

These estates were old and dilapidated and Voltaire set to work to improve them. He commenced cultivating the soil, planting trees, building a house. He hired gardeners, farmers and servants without end.... While many literary men have been farmers, very few of them have made it pay, but Voltaire made it pay. Had he been more religious and less versatile, he could have been the J. Pierpont Morgan of his age. Later at Ferney he developed other industries. He imported the silkworm and manufactured silk. He had a large watch factory and the town became a prosperous industrial place.... But still neither farming nor manufacturing was his real work. His pen was never idle....

On November 1, 1755, Lisbon was destroyed by an earthquake. The news reached Voltaire and stirred him to the soul. Thirty thousand people were destroyed almost in the twinkling of an eye. The earthquake was on All Saints Day and the greatest loss of life was in the cathedrals and churches of the place. For months, all his letters contained allusions to this catastrophe, which took possession of his mind. "The best of all possible worlds!" [Voltaire wrote.] "If [Alexander] Pope had been there, would he have said, 'Whatever is is right?' 'All is well,' seems to me absurd, when evil is on land and sea."

Voltaire wrote a searching poem on the problems of life, entitled "The Disaster of Lisbon." At the same time was published his poem on "Natural Law" covering the eternal questions as to the meaning, plan, scheme, and end of all. Voltaire answered these questions as all other thinkers have ... that upon these subjects man has no guide and no light. But the churches and the authorities read, or at least heard of, these two poems. They were promptly burned in Paris and pious Genevans held up their hands in horror at the theology, or rather lack of theology, which they taught. But the Lisbon earthquake shocked the world. Even the king of France had serious thoughts....

About this time, an unfortunate lunatic named Damins made a weak attempt on the life of Louis XV. The orthodox in church and state said that plainly the act was inspired by the "New Thought" of that day. It was perfectly easy to trace the act of a crazy man to the writings of Voltaire, which the man had never read. True, when the man was captured, he had in his hand a copy of the New Testament. Voltaire was delighted when he got this news. "A testament? I told you so. All assassins have a Bible in their daggers, but have you ever heard of one who had a Cicero, a Plato, or a Virgil?"

The assault on the king threw politicians and statesmen into panic all over Europe and at once they began to make the penal code more barbarous, the prohibitory laws stricter, and the censorship of the press more complete. There was but one way to deal with the act of a crazy man and that was to persecute and torture thousands of innocent ones. This was two hundred years ago, but every penal code in the United States has been made more savage and barbarous and the people, if possible, more brutal and unreasoning, because an insane man killed the President of the United States. How the world does change!

... In his house in Ferney, he installed his niece, Madame Denis, or rather she installed herself. She was uncouth, talkative, and fond of pleasure. She loved to consort with the great, but bored everyone she met.... A constant stream of visitors poured into Ferney through all these years. He had some sixty servants, besides the other employees of the place, but these were kept busy looking after travelers and friends. No one was denied admission, whether rich or poor, whether priest or pagan. All were housed and fed.... Voltaire said that for fourteen years he was the innkeeper of Europe. Here he built his theater and brought the greatest actors and actresses of the day, played himself, entertained his company and his friends and the constant stream of visitors who came from Geneva to see his plays. Even Madame Denis was kept from boredom by the life of Ferney.

In Geneva lived Jean-Jacques Rousseau. He too was a rebel, mighty in war. Voltaire was keener, wittier, deeper, greater. Rousseau was more fiery, emotional, passionate. Both were really warriors in the same great cause. From their different places, three miles apart, both sent forth their thunderbolts to wake a sleeping world. When the world awakened and shook itself, churches, thrones, institutions, laws, and customs were buried in the wreck. Some charged the wreck to Voltaire, some to Rousseau.

These two men, engaged in the same cause, fighting the same foes, could not agree. Rousseau joined with the clergy of Geneva in defaming Voltaire's theater and his plays. Voltaire fought back with weapons keener than any Rousseau knew how to use. Two geniuses cannot possibly live so close together. In fact, the world itself is hardly big enough for two at the same time. As Wendell Phillips once said: "No one hates a reformer as much as another reformer," and the war of these two men was long and bitter. It ended only with death, when both were brought to Paris and placed in the Pantheon, side by side....

In making improvements and overhauling the estate at Ferney,

Voltaire built a new church.... He dedicated his church to "God alone" and was fond of saying that it was the only church in the universe that was dedicated to "God alone" and not to a saint. "For my part," he said, "I would rather build for the Master than for the servants."

Then he designed for [himself] a tomb attached to the church and jutting out from the wall. "The wicked will say," he remarked, "that I am neither inside nor out." Later he shocked the holy people by going into the pulpit himself to preach....

While he was toying with his own church, consorting with the priests, corresponding with the Pope and attending mass, he was always forging his thunderbolts against the Church. For the last twenty-five years of his life, the superstition, the ignorance, and above all, the cruelty of the Church, was constantly in his mind. He scarcely wrote a letter, a tract or a book, that he did not revert to these over and over again, and in spite of all his contortions and somersaults, there probably cannot be found a line in Voltaire which defended superstition, gave countenance to cruelty or barbarism, and did not plead for the enlightenment and freedom of man.

His life at Ferney was one of constant work. All day he was busy with his books, his writings and his farm.... Here he wrote volume after volume of his *Philosophical Dictionary,* every page filled with subtle and deadly stabs at the Church. Here he poured forth his pamphlets without number, sowing seeds of revolution and revolt. "What harm can a book do that costs a hundred crowns?" wrote Voltaire, "Twenty volumes folio will never make a revolution. It is the little pocket pamphlets of thirty sous that are to be feared." Here too he wrote his letters; letters to all kinds of people, especially scholars and rulers—letters more voluminous than ever came from the pen of any other correspondent in the world. Seven thousand of these have been preserved and printed and no one knows how many more were lost forever. These letters, like his pamphlets and his books, were urging tolerance, enlightenment, and the freedom of the mind....

On one occasion two of [Voltaire's] house servants robbed their master. The police discovered it and were hot on their trail. Voltaire bade his secretary to see the servants and urge them to flee. "For if they are arrested," he said, "I shall not be able to save them from hanging." He gave them money for their journey and helped them in every way he could.

His many acts of humanity could not be recorded. His fight for Jean Calas is one of the most heroic of this or any other age. Calas was an old resident of Toulouse. Toulouse, like the rest of France, was an intensely religious town; the priests and the state religion held full sway. Calas was a Protestant and a respectful merchant of the place; all his family were Protestants, except one son, who had joined the Catholic Church. Another son, who like his father was a Protestant, decided to study law, but he could not be admitted to practice unless he joined the established church. He grew despondent and ... was discovered in a room of the house, dead, and hanging by the neck.

His family and friends sought to conceal the act, as suicide in those days, as now, was a mortal crime: one should have nothing to say either about coming into the world or going out. A suicide's soul would go to hell, but [first] his body would be drawn and quartered and thrown to the dogs. Someone of the people, (which means the mob), started the cry that the son was about to become a Catholic and the father had murdered him. This was taken up until the whole city was worked into a frenzy against the helpless old man and his family.

The body of the dead [son] was taken from the home and buried in state from the cathedral with all the rites and ceremonies of the Catholic Church. Calas was arrested, tried, and of course condemned. He was old and feeble and could not have committed the deed even had there been any motive or desire. Of course there was no substantial evidence. Someone testified that a neighbor had told them that another neighbor had said that a peddler had seen Calas coming from the room where the son was hanged. Of course the peddler was not found, neither the one to whom he had talked. In those days, hearsay evidence was a favorite....

[Calas'] wrists were bound to an iron ring fastened to a stone post; his feet to another ring in the floor. They then turned the wheel until every joint in his arms and legs was dislocated. He was brought back to life, asked to confess, but he still refused. They contrived further tortures which still failed to bring a confession. The executioner then bound him to a wooden cross, broke his legs and arms with an iron bar and strangled him. They then took his body, chained it to a stake and he was burned. His property was confiscated, his sons and daughters placed in Catholic institutions and the widow left to wander....

This revolting affair was brought to the attention of Voltaire at Ferney. Calas was dead, but the system still lived. He took one of the sons into his home, learned the facts, corresponded with all the notable people of Europe, industriously prepared the case, hired a lawyer and presented [it] for review to the parliament of Paris. In this case he enlisted Frederick the Great, Catherine of Russia, and many other illustrious people throughout Europe.... After six years of constant battle, the parliament of Paris, by unanimous opinion, decided that Calas was innocent of any crime. The estate was given back to the family and the children to their mother. Voltaire raised a large amount of money to take care of the family during the trial and to give them an estate after the vindication was complete....

Many other cases almost as revolting were brought to Voltaire's attention and received his help. Of course in these cases the victim was dead, and it was easier to clear a dead victim than a live one. The most barbarous and ferocious of men and women begin to think and feel remorseful [after a] deed is done. But the great battle of Voltaire for the memory of those tortured dead no doubt saved many other innocent men from the same cruel fate and went a long way toward ridding the world of the cruelty and barbarism of his age.

Voltaire no doubt realized that his long years of work were probably responsible for the charges of heresy lodged against many of the victims.... The world today, in court and out, acts upon the same reasoning as the judges in France at the time of Voltaire. Those who speak are often held responsible, in court and out, for the revolutionary acts of men whom they never saw or of whom they never heard. It is cruel to charge men criminally with the result of their words and thoughts. No doubt there is much immature talking and hasty writing and will always be where liberty of speech and press prevails. The political, religious, and social views of any age and even of the most radical members of society, were born, long before their time. Those who invented the alphabet and the printing press are indirectly responsible for much of the violence of a changing social state; but in the same way, they are responsible for the progress of the world, for the enlightenment, for the civilization, and for all that makes the present better than the past. Great changes never did and never can come unless accompanied by violence, by cruelty, by suffering and by pain. These are incident to the progress of the race; they are the labor pains that herald the birth of a new civilization and a better social life. . . .

Voltaire clearly saw the effects of the new intellectual life that was coming to the world. He knew what his years of toil would mean to France. . . . Not only what he had done, but what had been done by Rousseau and Diderot and the other writers and thinkers of his age, was bound at last permanently to affect the world. Then, too, the earth had grown tired of kings and princes who lived upon the unpaid labor of the poor. It had grown tired of the priests and superstitions which covered the land with a pall of night. France was awakening. The day was dawning.

Only a few years before the thunderbolt of the French Revolution burst with fire and sword upon the earth, he wrote: "Everything I see shows the signs of a revolution which must infallibly come. I shall not have the pleasure of beholding it. The French reach everything late, but they do reach it at last. Young people are lucky. They will see great things. I shall not cease to preach tolerance upon the housetops until persecution is no more. The progress of the right is slow. The roots of prejudice are deep. I shall never see the fruits of my efforts, but their seeds must one day germinate."

At Ferney, at the age of eighty-three, Voltaire wrote his last play, *Irene*. This play was to be produced in the National Theater at

Paris. With this thought strongly in mind, a longing to see Paris once more began to overwhelm him. Madame Denis was anxious to go back; although she was growing old, she yet longed for the chatter of the crowd. She urged Voltaire to go. All his friends urged him to go. "Paris," said Voltaire, "do you not know that there are forty thousand fanatics who would bring forty thousand fagots to burn me? That would be my bed of honor."

Louis XVI was then on the throne.... He hated Voltaire. He knew what the works of Voltaire and Rousseau meant to the world. "These two men have lost France," said the king. Still Voltaire wanted to go [back to Paris] ... to put *Irene* on the stage himself, to be present at its rehearsal, to see to every detail of its production; so in February 1778, he set out for Paris....

His journey to Paris took five days.... Men, women, and children turned out at every town to do him honor. This man who had been in prison, repeatedly exiled and forbidden his city, was returning after twenty-eight years to the home of his birth.

He was the intellectual king of France, if not the world.... The philosophers, dramatists, members of the Academy, and above all, the people stood around in crowds to worship at his shrine. Nobles and churchmen stood by sullen, insolent and ominous. He was denounced from the pulpit and called "Anti-Christ"; gladly would they have sent him once more to the Bastille, but they did not dare. Full well they knew that it needed but a match to start a conflagration which would forever destroy the old regime.

His rooms at the Hotel Villette were crowded with the intellectuals of the capital day after day. Here came Dr. Franklin presenting his grandson, a boy of seventeen. Voltaire raised his hand above the boy's head and blessed him with the words "God" and "Liberty." Literary men, actors, ambassadors were to do him honor....

All this was too much for old Voltaire. He fell ill and his friends feared for his life. The priest came to get a confession from Voltaire. His confession would be fame enough for any priest. On February twenty-eighth, when he believed his last hour had come, in the presence of his secretary he wrote down his Confession of Faith: "I die adoring God, loving my friends, not hating my enemies, and detesting superstition." This was dated and signed, and is preserved in the National Library at Paris.

For a few days he seemed to recover from his illness.... Through tumultuous crowds he drove to the Academy where he was received with wild acclamation, the Academy which had repeatedly refused to make him a member, but which now worshiped his genius and popularity. He spoke to the members, outlined a project for making a dictionary which is today the foundation of all the dictionaries of Europe.

He went to the theater to see his play. The building was crowded by a tumultuous, suffocating mob, representing all members of French society. Voltaire was hailed as a king. His bust was placed upon the stage; again and again they called for the old man to speak from the box. A laurel wreath was placed upon his head.... When he left the theater the crowds went with him, following his carriage with shouts, and praise, and tears, until the old man reached his room. Voltaire himself wept like a child: "If I had known the people would have committed such follies I would never have gone to the theater."

For a few days, he seemed to regain his strength. He bought a house in Paris and determined to stay, but in May another attack seized him. The priest came to see him. Some say he made a confession, some say he refused it. Whether he did or not is of small importance. What he did in his dying hours has nothing to do with the life he lived. One must be judged by his life and not by the agonies of death.... All his life he had feared that he would be thrown in the gutter when dead. That was doubtless present in the old man's mind to the last....

On account of the testimony of the priest who said he had received absolution, and Voltaire's written confession of faith, he was accorded an honorable burial in consecrated ground at Romilly-on-Seine, 100 miles from Paris, the burial which all his life he desired. The next day a mandate was sent from the Church forbidding that he be laid in consecrated ground, but he was already there.

Thirteen years later, by order of the National Assembly, which was then taking the first steps to overthrow the old regime and usher in the Revolution, he was brought back to Paris.... In the Pantheon, [Voltaire] reposed in peace until 1814. After the Revolution was over and the Bourbons returned to power, the tombs of both Voltaire and Rousseau were broken open. [The bodies] were removed in a sack at night, taken to a place outside the city, emptied into a pit and consumed with quicklime. His ashes met the fate that he had dreaded all his life.

It is hardly necessary to sum up Voltaire. Born in a day of gross superstition, brutal barbarism, the densest bigotry and faith, he wrote his first play at the age of eighteen, and finished his last just before his death at eighty-four. During all this sixty-six years he worked unceasingly, dealing telling, deadly blows at the superstitions which held the minds of men. He died on the morning of the French Revolution, a revolution which more than any other man Voltaire inspired. Had he lived a few years longer most likely Voltaire would have died on the guillotine with many other victims of that delirious spasm of liberty that burned through France, and prepared the soil for a civilization and tolerance far greater than the world had ever known.

Voltaire was small in stature, lean and spare of figure, and active in body. His nimble mind was ever ablaze during all his life. Valiantly he fought on every intellectual battlefield.... Voltaire marks the closing of an epoch. His life and his work stand between the old and the new. When he was old, superstition had not yet died, but had received its mortal wound. Never again can savagery control the minds and thoughts of men. Never again can the prison thumbscrews and the rack be instruments to save men's souls. Among the illustrious heroes who have banished this sort of cruelty from the Western world no other name will stand so high and shine so bright as the illustrious name.

SUPPLEMENTARY SELECTION

JOHN BROWN (1800–1859)

Clarence Darrow had good reason to be thinking about whether the ends justify the means when he was invited to give a lecture to the Radical Club Forum in December 1912. He had just narrowly averted a career-ending catastrophe when two juries failed to convict him, despite strong evidence, of attempting to bribe jurors during the sensational McNamara trial in Los Angeles. Apparently Darrow had concluded that a rigged hung jury was morally preferable to his other options: wounding the labor movement by pleading his union leader clients guilty of the fatal bombing they had in fact engineered, or pleading them innocent only to have them convicted and executed because of the overwhelming evidence against them. For his lecture, he decided to deliver a eulogy to a Darrow family hero who had also been willing to break the law for what he considered a greater good, John Brown. Darrow's father, Amirus, had been a vocal supporter of the abolitionist, who led a murderous raid on Harpers Ferry in 1859 and organized it just a few miles from the Darrow home in Kinsman, Ohio. The speech became one of Darrow's most requested, and is one of his most revealing.

John Brown was born in Connecticut in 1800. His parents were farmers, and like all who really work, were poor. His natural instincts were never warped or smothered or numbed by learning. His mind was so strong, his sense of justice so keen, and his sympathies so deep, that he might have been able even to withstand an education.

He believed in Destiny and in God. He was narrow, fanatical, and self-willed, like all men who deeply impress the generation in which they live. Had he been broad and profound, he would have asked himself the question, "What is the use?" and the answer would have brought an easier life and a peaceful death. He was a man of one idea, which is all that the brain of any man of action can ever hold. He was not a philosopher, and therefore believed he had a mission in the world, and that he must early get at his Master's work, and never rest by day or night, lest that work should not be done. He was of the type of Cromwell, or Calvin, or Mahomet: not a good type for the peace of the world, but a type that here and there down through the ages, has been needful to kindle a flame that should burn the decaying institutions and ancient wrongs in the fierce crucible of a world's awakening wrath.

His life was one of toil and hardship and poverty. In his earlier years, he was a farmer, a wool grower, a merchant, a tanner, in all a fairly successful man. Up to his middle life, the demands of business and the claims of a large family took nearly all his time and strength. But more and more the crime of slavery obsessed his mind.... He turned to the helpless and the poor, and waving aside his kin, he said, "These are my brethren and sisters." Ever the same eternal voice has called to the devoted souls—"Unless you desert father and mother, brethren and kindred, you cannot be my disciple." His own slender means, with all that he could beg and borrow, was from that time devoted to the cause for which he gave his life, and while he lay in the poor Virginia jail waiting for the end, he could not spare the money to bring his family to his side to give their kind ministrations before he mounted the gallows that choked out his life and immortalized his name. His work was so important that he had no time to get money, and no thought of its value. Unlike many other reformers, he went about his Master's work in such great haste that he did not even wait to accumulate enough money before he began his task.

Most of John Brown's biographers tell us when and why he became the champion of the black, but they do not tell us right. His love of the slave was a part of the fire that, although it seems to slumber still now and then, through the long and dreary night kindles a divine spark in the minds of earth's strong souls which lights the dark and devious pathways of the human race to nobler heights.

Lucky are the sons of men when these prophets are born upon the earth. Above their neglected cradles sing the morning stars, and around their humble homes, hushed and expectant, awaits the early breeze that shall drive away the fog and mist before the rising sun.

John Brown found the power of slavery thoroughly entrenched

in the United States; no other institution in the land seemed more secure. True, here and there voices were raised to denounce the curse, but for the most part these came only from the weak, the poor and the despised. The pulpit, the press, the courts, the wealthy and respectable gave it their sanction, and more powerful still was the fact that slavery was hopelessly interwoven with the commercial and financial institutions of the land, and any attack on these was an attack on the sacred rights of property—the sin of sins!

Even in his business life, he talked and worked against slavery. He was one of the chief conductors of that underground railroad which sent so many helpless captives, by devious ways, across the continent beneath the Stars and Stripes, until they were landed as free men in Canada, under the protection of the British flag. But to John Brown this was like bailing out the ocean with a dipper. This might free a slave, but it would not abolish slavery.

The system must be destroyed.

When the slave power, reaching out its arm to perpetuate itself, turned to Kansas to fasten its shackles on a new state, John Brown sent forth four devoted sons and two others of his kinsmen to help fight the battle of freedom in this new land. In the meantime, he was busy in the East raising money and men to help the cause.

Kansas was then in the throes of civil war. It is idle to ask or answer the question as to where the blame should be placed for any special act through these long bloody days and nights. The war was not between men, but between two systems old as the human race—freedom and slavery. Then, as ever, officials and power and wealth were with slavery, and the dreamer and idealist with liberty. Then as ever, the power of slavery was united, and the forces of freedom divided. Fighting for liberty were the Garrisons, who believed in nonresistance; the Beechers, who believed in appealing to the heart—the heart of a system that had no heart; the Sewards and Sumners, who believed [in] the ballot; and John Brown, who believed that all of this meant war and could be settled by no other method.

John Brown could not long resist the lure of Kansas. With a slender purse, a few trusted men, a small number of guns, a large family and a devoted soul, he made his way to that historic land. He found the enemy militant, triumphant and insolent, [and] the friends of freedom peaceable, discouraged, and submissive. He gathered a small devoted band and prepared to fight.

"Where will you get your supplies?" asked one of the peaceful and the meek. "From the enemy," came back the reply.

Guerrilla warfare was the order of the day. Guerrilla warfare is murder because the killed are so very few. In this warfare, the name of Brown was a terror to the other side. He was silent, active, resolute and unyielding. Next to his belief in abolition, he believed in God: none of his band drank, smoked, told doubtful stories, jested on sacred things or indulged in levity of any kind. They had daily prayers, stern visages, frequent Bible readings... and they knew how to shoot. The commander, like all fanatics, believed he was called of God to do His work, and so he was. Every man is called of God, if he but believes it strong enough. When an army goes to battle singing psalms and muttering prayers with a leader called of God to perform his task, let the world beware: such an army cannot lose, no matter what its size. Even though vanquished and destroyed, from the bones and ashes of the dead will spring a multitude that will prevail against all the powers of hell.

At first, victory seemed with the slaveholder in the guerrilla war, [for] the village of Lawrence, a free-soil town, was sacked and burned without a struggle in its defense. John Brown, chagrined that a town should be given up without a fight, called together his four sons, two kinsmen and two other trusted men, armed them with knives and pistols, [and] bade them mount their horses and follow him. He did not need to tell the party the specific errand for which they rode; whatever the details might chance to be, the cause was freedom, and with them the method did not count. Across the prairies and swamps and through the night they kept their way, until they reached a little settlement where slept the leaders of the Lawrence raid. Five of these they dragged from their homes, took to the woods, cut them to pieces, and then rode away.

At once Kansas was aflame. The Free Soilers with whom Brown had fought were the ones who most loudly condemned the act...

they hastened to deny either sympathy or complicity with the deed. A silence profound and deadly fell over all the leaders of the state. A price was put on John Brown's head, but no one seemed overanxious to win the prize. The pendulum swung back, as pendulums always have and always will. Even the nonresistants took up their guns, and the battle for freedom in Kansas was won.

Then John Brown turned East. He did not wait even to run for office, and claim the reward of his labor. There still was work to do, and he was growing old. For a time he busied himself gathering bands of slaves and taking them across the United States to the hospitable northern land. Long since he had exhausted his own funds and collected all he could for the great cause. Long since he had given up all other business except "his Master's work": at Harpers Ferry he said, "For twenty years I have never made any business arrangements that would prevent me answering to the call of the Lord."

Perhaps no one knew the exact plan of his last great fight. For years he had given up all hope of a peaceful solution of the cause; he did not believe in moral suasion or political action. To the nonresistant, he answered in the language of the Hebrew prophet: "Without the shedding of blood there can be no remission of sins." As near as can be known, Brown had a plan of forcibly taking possession of various points in the Allegheny and the Blue Ridge Mountains, of fortifying them and collecting forces of men, black and white, to engage in the wholesale business of deporting the black from the South. He had long lived in these mountains and looked upon their rising peaks and deep ravines with reverence and awe. He believed that God had raised the Alleghenies as a bulwark for freedom and for the liberation of the slaves.

Harpers Ferry was the place to strike the blow. Harpers Ferry was a natural outlet of the great Black Way to the north. This great Black Way lay east of the mountains, running from Harpers Ferry south through the Virginias and Carolinas, reaching three out of the four million blacks in the United States. Along this way with weary feet had fled most of the poor fugitives in their escape from the land of darkness to the land of light. Harpers Ferry, too, had the government arsenal packed with arms, used by the nation in defense of slavery. These he would capture and place in the hands of the blacks and his comrades to fight for freedom. Immediately surrounding this town was a country where the blacks were more numerous than the whites, and where he might expect to get recruits when the blow was struck.

When Brown had formed his plan, he visited all the abolitionists that he knew and could trust to enlist their help. He received some contributions of money, given for vague, indefinite purposes, but no man of influence would either join the expedition or give sanction to the plan. Frederick Douglass, the leading colored man of his time, counseled him not to undertake the task. He pointed out that it would surely fail, and he believed that failure would seriously harm the cause. But all argument was of no avail; win or lose, [John Brown] had no choice. Whether he had many followers or few, a voice had spoken to his soul, and that voice he must obey. How could he fail? His cause was the greatest cause for which any martyr ever lived and died—the liberty of man. No sordid motive ever moved his life; his Commander was the great Jehovah, and the outcome had been determined since the morning stars sang together and the world was new.

With scarcely a score of men he reached Harpers Ferry, rented a farmhouse, and began to collect arms and make his plans. It was a strange and motley band that hid for weeks in an old farmhouse, awaiting the fatal day. John Brown ... tall, gaunt and gray, with serious face and stooping frame ... [was] taking upon his devoted head the crime and sorrows of the world. Around him were five sons and kindred whom he loved with a tender devotion, next to the Negro and his God; seven obscure blacks, fresh from the bonds of slavery; and nine more unknown whites. [These] made up the army that with bowed heads and consecrated souls challenged the strongest institution of the land [and] made war upon the United States with force and arms. And strange to say, this poor and motley band of humble, unknown men were triumphant in the cause for which they fought and died.

On the seventeenth of October, 1859 ... the little army left the farmhouse for Harpers Ferry, five miles away. They quickly captured the arsenal and took possession of the town. Then their plans began to go awry: the citizens rallied, [and] the regular troops were brought upon the scene. Brown and his followers were penned in the engine house, and made a last desperate stand against overwhelming odds. John Brown was seriously wounded, [and] two of his sons were shot down by his side. Six [of his band] escaped; all the rest were either shot or hanged.

Brown was indicted [and] immediately placed on trial while still suffering from his wounds. [He] was brought in and out of the courthouse on a cot. Of course, [he was] convicted, and within six weeks after the raid, [John Brown] was hanged. He was convicted and hanged, for though one of the purest and bravest and highest-minded patriots of any age he was tried by the law, which makes no account of the motives of men, but decides upon their deeds alone.

The news of John Brown's raid sent an electric shock around the world. The slave power was aghast at the audacity of the act, and knew not where to turn. The leading abolitionists of the North were stunned and terrified at the manhunt coming on. The great William Lloyd Garrison promptly and fiercely denounced Brown's mad act; Beecher and Seward cried out against the man who had so criminally and recklessly hazarded his friends and the cause. Bold and wrathful were all these old abolitionists when there was no risk to run, but here was a maniac who transformed their words to deeds.

In the first mad days but one man stood fearless and unmoved while the universe was falling around his head, and this man was John Brown. When faint voices cried out for his rescue, Brown promptly made reply, [saying] "I do not know that I ought to encourage any attempt to save my life. I think I cannot now better serve the cause I love than to die for it, and in my death, I may do more than in my life."

... But when the scaffold bore its fruit, and the dead hero's heart was cold, the pulse of humanity once more began to beat. The timid, the coward, the time server, the helpless and the weak looked on the brave, cold clay, and from a million throats a cry for vengeance was lifted to the stars. Men cried from the hustings to wake a sleeping world. Newspapers condemned the act, [and] ministers who still were Christians appealed from the judgment of the court to the judgment of their God. Church bells with sad tones tolled out the tidings of Brown's passing soul, and men and angels wept above his bier. And still the tide rolled on, until, in less than two short years, the land resounded with the call to arms, and millions of men were hurrying to the field of strife to complete the work John Brown began.

Once more at Harpers Ferry was gathered a band pledged to the same great cause, "the Liberty of Man," a band that under the leadership of Grant swept down the great Black Way with fire and sword, and in a sea of blood washed the crime of slavery away.

But while the victorious hosts were destroying the infamous system that had cursed the earth so long, John Brown was sleeping in a felon's grave, and around his decaying neck was the black mark of the hangman's noose, the reward of a Christian world for the devoted soul that had made the supreme sacrifice for his loyalty and love. More than any other man, his mad raid broke the bondsman's chain. True, the details of his plan had failed, where the plans of prophets always fail; the men who worked with him and the poor for whom he fought left him to die alone. John Brown offered his life and the lives of those he loved for the despised and weak; and while he fought and died, these idle and nerveless and stupid looked blindly on as their masters strangled him to death. But this story too is old, [as] old as the human race. Ever and ever hangs the devoted Christ upon the cross, and ever with faint heart and dumb mouths and palsied hands, the poor for whom he toiled, stand helpless and watch their savior die.

The world has long since accepted the results of John Brown's work. Great as the cost was, all men know that it was worth the price. But even now the idle, carping, and foolish still ask, "Did Brown do right, and would it not better have been done some other way?" Of all the foolish questions asked by idle tongues, the most childish is to ask if a great work should not have been done some other way. Nothing in the universe that was ever done, could have been done in any other way. He who accepts results must accept with them every act that leads to the result. And all who think must accept all results. High above the hand of man is the hand of destiny, all potent in the world. To deny destiny is to deny God and all the forces that move the universe of which man is so small a part. To condemn an act as wrong assumes that the laws of justice laid down by the weak minds of man are the same as the laws of the universe, which stretch over infinite matter, infinite time and space, and regards nothing less than all....

John Brown was right; he was an instrument in the hands of a higher power. He acted as that power had given him the grain to see, and the will to do. In answering his inquisitors in Virginia, he said, "True, I went against the laws of man, but whether it be right to obey God or man, judge ye."

Long ago it was said, "By their fruits ye shall know them." The fruits of John Brown's life are plain for all to see; while time shall last, men and women, sons and daughters of bondsmen and slaves, will live by the light of freedom, be inspired by the hope of liberty.

The earth needs and will always need its Browns; these poor, sensitive, prophetic souls, feeling the suffering of the world, and taking its sorrows on their burdened backs.... The radical of today is the conservative of tomorrow, and other martyrs take up the work through other nights, and the dumb and stupid world plants its weary feet upon the slippery sand, soaked by their blood, and the world moves on.

CHAPTER 8

CLOSING ARGUMENTS

AUTOBIOGRAPHICAL INTRODUCTION

FROM CLARENCE DARROW, *THE STORY OF MY LIFE*, CHAPTER 37, "THE CAMPAIGN AGAINST CRIME" (1932)

The open violence, the crowded prisons, the state of anarchy that prohibition has brought about led to a mad and senseless crusade against crime. New penal statutes were passed, prison terms were lengthened, courts and juries, in obedience to the mania, convicted defendants almost indiscriminately. Many innocent persons were sent to prison and executed in this carnival of hate.

... To be sure, in this madness, mistakes were made. Men and women who were guilty of no crime often suffered the severest penalties. Judges meted out the most outrageous sentences. New statutes created new crimes, increased the penalties, and destroyed age-long safeguards for freedom. Boards of parole and pardon ceased to function. The unfortunates in prisons felt that there was no chance for regaining liberty once the prison doors closed upon them. This hopelessness kindled prison revolts, which led to fearful slaughter, to the destruction of all that the years of earnest work had done to modify conditions by building up humane prisons, caring for juvenile offenders, and giving even the condemned hope or opportunity once more to be free.

For myself, I always worked against capital punishment, and all severe penalties. I had always believed in clemency to first offenders, and believed, as do most men of science, that every kind of human conduct comes from causes, and in order to change conduct the causes that bring it about must be altered or removed.

… In the olden times, the criminal and the insane were tortured and chained indiscriminately, and, for that matter, they are today. There is no way of determining who is sane or who is insane, or who is good or who is bad, but one thing is certain: In the treatment of criminals a great change has come over the world in a hundred and fifty years. This change has been toward humanity, tolerance, and understanding. Most of this important work has been brought about in the last fifty years, for it is only a short time since scientists have even tried to find out the causes of human conduct…. But ideas are very slow in affecting the mass of mankind. They are held back by prejudice, by ignorance, by common conception until long after the intelligent specialist has thoroughly proved conditions and discovered remedies.

MAIN SELECTION

FROM *THE PEOPLE OF MICHIGAN V. HENRY SWEET,* DETROIT,
MICHIGAN, MAY 18, 1926
Closing argument

In 1926, the NAACP hired Clarence Darrow to defend Dr. Ossian Sweet, his brother Henry, his wife, and eight other blacks, who were accused of murder. Eight Detroit police officers had testified that a deadly gunshot had come from one of the windows of the Sweets' house without provocation and killed Leon Breiner, who was peacefully smoking his pipe. The first trial of the eleven had ended in a hung jury and a mistrial. The defense requested that the defendants be tried individually, and Henry Sweet, Dr. Sweet's younger brother, who was accused of firing the bullet that killed Breiner, was the first to be tried. Darrow then achieved one of his most remarkable acquittals, following a seven-hour closing argument, excerpted here. After the verdict, prosecutors dropped all charges against the Sweets and their family members.

I shall begin about where my friend Mr. Moll [Assistant Wayne County Prosecutor Lester Moll] began yesterday. He says lightly, gentlemen, that this isn't a race question. "This is a murder case. We don't want any prejudice; we don't want the other side to have any. Race and color have nothing to do with this case. This is a case of murder."

... I insist that there is nothing *but* prejudice in this case; that if it was reversed and eleven white men had shot and killed a black while protecting their home and their lives against a mob of blacks, nobody would have dreamed of having them indicted. I know what I am talking about, and so do you. They would have been given medals instead.

Eleven colored men and one woman are in this indictment, tried by twelve jurors, gentlemen. Every one of you are white, aren't you? At least you all think so. We haven't one colored man on this jury. We couldn't get one. One was called and he was disqualified. You twelve white men are trying a colored man on race prejudice.... I want to put this square to you, gentlemen. I haven't any doubt but that every one of you are prejudiced against colored people. I want you to guard against it. I want you to do all you can to be fair in this case, and I believe you will.

A number of you people have answered the question that you are acquainted with colored people.... Some of the rest of you said that you had employed colored people to work for you, are even employing them now. All right.... How many of you jurors, gentlemen, have ever had a colored person visit you in your home? How many of you have ever visited in their homes? How many of you have invited them to dinner at your house? Probably not one of you.

Now, why, gentlemen? There isn't one of you men but that know just from the witnesses you have seen in this case that there are colored people who are intellectually the equal of all of you. Am I right? Colored people living right here in the City of Detroit are intellectually the equals and some of them superior to most of us. Is that true? Some of them are people of more character and learning than most of us. I have a picture in my mind of the first witness we put on the stand—Mrs. Spalding: modest, intelligent, beautiful. The beauty in her face doesn't come from powder or paint, or any artificial means, but has to come from within; kindly, human feeling. You couldn't forget her. I couldn't forget her. You seldom have seen anybody of her beauty and her appearance. She has some colored blood in her veins. Compare her with the teacher who for ten years has taught high school on what she called the corner of Garland and "Gote" Street [The street's name was "Goethe Street"]. Compare the two.

Now, why don't you individually, and why don't I and why doesn't every white person whose chances have been greater and whose wealth is larger, associate with them? There is only one reason, and that is prejudice. Can you give any other reason for it? They would be intellectual companions. They have good manners. They are clean; they are all of them clean enough to wait on us. But not clean enough to associate with! Is there any reason in the world why we don't associate with them excepting prejudice? Still, none of us want to be prejudiced. I think not one man of this jury wants to be prejudiced. It is forced into us almost from our youth until somehow or other we feel we are superior to these people who have black faces.

Now, gentlemen, I say you are prejudiced.... You will overcome it, I believe, in the trial of this case. But they tell me there is no race prejudice, and it is plain nonsense, and nothing else. Who are we, anyway? A child is born into this world without any knowledge of any sort. He has a brain which is a piece of putty; he inherits nothing in the way of knowledge or of ideas. If he is white, he knows nothing about color. He has no antipathy to the black.

The black and the white both will live together and play together, but as soon as the baby is born we begin giving him ideas. We begin planting seeds in his mind. We begin telling him he must do this and he must not do that. We tell him about race and social equality and the thousands of things that men talk about until he grows up. It has been trained into us, and you, gentlemen, bring that feeling into this jury box, and that feeling which is a part of your lifelong training.

You need not tell me you are not prejudiced. I know better. We are not very much but a bundle of prejudices anyhow. We are prejudiced against other peoples' color. Prejudiced against other men's religion; prejudiced against other peoples' politics. Prejudiced against peoples' looks. Prejudiced about the way they dress. We are full of prejudices. You can teach a man anything beginning with the child; you can make anything out of him, and we are not responsible for it. Here and there some of us haven't any prejudices on some questions, but if you look deep enough you will find them; and we all know it.

All I hope for, gentlemen of the jury, is this: That you are strong enough, and honest enough, and decent enough to lay it aside in this case and decide it as you ought to. And I say, there is no man in Detroit that doesn't know that these defendants, every one of them, did right. There isn't a man in Detroit who doesn't know that the defendant did his duty, and that this case is an attempt to send him and his companions to prison because they defended their constitutional rights. It is a wicked attempt, and you are asked to be a party to it. You know it. I don't need to talk to this jury about the facts in this case. There is no man who can read or can understand that does not know the facts. Is there prejudice in it?

Now, let's see. I don't want to lean very much on your intelligence. I don't need much. I just need a little. Would this case be in this court if these defendants were not black? Would we be standing in front of you if these defendants were not black? Would anybody be asking you to send a boy to prison for life for defending his brother's home and protecting his own life, if his face wasn't black?...

Gentlemen, it is a reflection upon anybody's intelligence to say that everyone did not know why this mob was there. You know! Every one of you knows why.

...Gentlemen, that mob was bent not only on making an assault upon the rights of the owners of that house, not only making an assault upon their persons and their property, but they were making an assault on the Constitution and the laws of the nation, and the state under which they live. They were like Samson in the temple, seeking to tear down the pillars of the structure, so that blind prejudices and their bitter hate would rule supreme in the City of Detroit. Now, that was the case.

Gentlemen, does anybody need to argue to you as to why those people were there? Was my friend Moll even intelligent when he told you that this was a "neighborly" crowd? I wonder if he knows you better than I do. I hope not. A neighborly crowd? A man who comes to your home and puts a razor across your windpipe, or who meets you on the street and puts a dagger through your heart is as much a neighbor as these conspirators and rioters were who drove these black people from their home.

... Gentlemen,—neighbors? They were neighbors in the same sense that a nest of rattlesnakes are neighbors when you accidentally put your foot upon them. They are neighbors in the sense that a viper is a neighbor when you warm it in your bosom and it bites you. And every man who knows anything about this case knows it. You know what the purpose was....

There isn't one of you who does not know that they tried to drive those people out and now are trying to send them to the penitentiary so that they can't move back; all in violation of the law, and are trying to get you to do the job. Are they worse than other people? I don't know as they are. How much do you know about prejudice? Race prejudice. Religious prejudice. These feelings that have divided men and caused them to do the most terrible things. Prejudices have burned men at the stake, broken them on the rack, torn every joint apart, destroyed people by the million. Men have done this on account of some terrible prejudice which even now is reaching out to undermine this republic of ours and to destroy the freedom that has been the most cherished part of our institutions.

[The prosecution's] witnesses honestly believe that they are better than blacks. I do not. They honestly believe that it is their duty to keep colored people out. They honestly believe that the blacks are an inferior race and yet [when] they look at themselves, I don't know how they can. If they had one colored family up there, some of the neighbors might learn how to pronounce "Goethe." It would be too bad to spread a little culture in that vicinity. They might die. They are possessed with that idea and that fanaticism, and when people are possessed with that they are terribly cruel. They don't stand alone. Others have done the same thing. Others will do the same thing so long as this weary old world shall last. They may do it again, but, gentlemen, they ought not to ask you to do it for them. That is a pretty dirty job to turn over to a jury, and they ought not to expect you to do it....

I want to talk to you a little more about who was around that house, and why, and what they were doing, and how many there were. You may remember a man named Miller. This man Miller expressed it pretty well. I suppose I prodded him quite a bit. I asked—what was the organization for? "Oh, we want to protect the place." Against what? "Oh, well, generally." You can't make it more definite? "Yes, against undesirables." Who do you mean by "undesirables?" "Oh, people we don't want," and so on and so forth. Finally, he said, "against Negroes." I said: Anybody else? He thought awhile, and he said: "Well, against Eyetalians." He didn't say "Italians." He hadn't got that far along yet, but he said "Eye-talians."

... Well, now, gentlemen, just by the way of passing, words are great things, you know. You hear some fellow who wants more money than you want, and he calls himself a one-hundred-percent American. Probably he doesn't know what the word American means. But he knows what he wants. You hear some fellow who wants something else talking about Americanism. I don't know where Miller came from; about how early or how late an arrival he is in America. The only real Americans that I know about are the Indians, and we killed most of them and pensioned the rest.

I guess that the ancestors of my clients got here long before Miller's did. They have been here for more than three hundred years; before the Pilgrims landed, the slave ships landed, gentlemen. They are Americans and have given life and blood on a thousand different kinds of fields for America and have given their labor for nothing, for America. They are Americans. Mr. Miller doesn't know it. He thinks he is the only kind of American. The Negroes and Eye-talians don't count. Of course, he doesn't like them. Mr. Miller doesn't know that it was an Eye-talian that discovered this land of ours. Christopher Columbus was an "Eye-talian," but he isn't good enough to associate with Miller....

Gentlemen, lawyers are very intemperate in their statements. My friend Moll said that my client here was a coward....

Who are the cowards in this case? Cowards, gentlemen! Eleven people with black skins, eleven people, gentlemen, whose ancestors did not come to America because they wanted to, but were brought here in slave ships, to toil for nothing, for the whites—whose lives have been taken in nearly every state in the Union—they have been victims of riots all over this land of the free. They have had to take what is left after everybody else has grabbed what he wanted. The only place where he has been put in front is on the battle field. When we are fighting we give him a chance to die, and the best chance. But, everywhere else, he has been food for the flames, and the ropes, and the knives, and the guns and hate of the white, regardless of law and liberty, and the common sentiments of justice that should move men. Were they cowards? No, gentlemen.... They may have tried to murder, but they were not cowards.

Eleven people, knowing what it meant, with the history of the race behind them... with the knowledge of shootings and killings and insult and injury without end, eleven of them go into a house, gentlemen, with no police protection, in the face of a mob, and the hatred of a community, and take guns and ammunition and fight for their rights, and for your rights and for mine, and for the rights of every being that lives. They went in and faced a mob seeking to tear them to bits....

And then my clients are called cowards. All right, gentlemen, call them something else. These blacks have been called many names along down through the ages, but there have been those through the sad years who believed in justice and mercy and charity and love and kindliness, and there have been those who believed that a black man should have some rights, even in a country where he was brought in chains. There are those even crazy enough to hope and to dream that sometime he will come from under this cloud and take his place amongst the people of the world. If he does, it will be through his courage and his culture. It will be by his intelligence and his scholarship and his effort, and I say, gentlemen of the jury, no honest, right feeling man, whether on a jury, or any-where else, would place anything in his way in this great struggle behind him and before him.

No, perhaps some of you gentlemen do not believe in colored men moving into white neighborhoods. Let me talk about that a minute, gentlemen. I don't want to leave any question untouched that might be important in this case, and I fancy that some of you do not believe as I believe on this question.

Let us be honest about it. There are people who buy themselves a little home and think the value of it would go down if colored people come. Perhaps it would . . . I don't know. Suppose it does? What of it? I am sorry for anybody whose home depreciates in value. Still, you can not keep up a government for the purpose of making people's homes valuable. Noise will depreciate the value of a house, and sometimes a streetcar line will do it. A public school will do it. People do not like a lot of children around their house; that is one reason why they send them to school. You can not get as much for your property. Livery stables used to do it; garages do it now. Any kind of noise will do it. No man can buy a house and be sure that somebody will not depreciate its value. Something may enhance its value, of course. We are always willing to take the profit, but not willing to take the loss. Those are incidents of civilization. We get that because we refuse to live with our fellow-man, that's all.

. . . What are you, gentlemen? And what am I? I don't know. I can only go a little way toward the source of my own being. I know my father and I know my mother. I knew my grandmothers and my grandfathers on both sides, but I didn't know my great-grandfathers and great-grandmothers on either side, and I don't know who they were. All that a man can do in this direction is but little. He can only slightly raise the veil that hangs over all the past. He can peer into the darkness just a little way and that is all. I know that somewhere around 1600, as the record goes, some of my ancestors came from England. Some of them. I don't know where all of them came from, and I don't think any human being knows where all his ancestors came from. But back of that, I can say nothing. What do you know of yours?

I will tell you what I know, or what I think I know, gentlemen. I will try to speak as modestly as I can; knowing the uncertainty of human knowledge, because it is uncertain. The best I can do is to go a little way back. I know that in back of us all and each of us is the blood of all the world. I know that it courses in your veins and in mine. It has all come out of the infinite past, and I can't pick out mine and you can't pick out yours, and it is only the ignorant who know, and I believe that in back of that—in back of that—is what we call the lower order of life; in back of that there lurks the instinct of the distant serpent, of the carnivorous tiger. All the elements have been gathered together to make the mixture that is you and I and all the race, and nobody knows anything about his own.

Gentlemen, I wonder who we are anyhow, to be so proud about our ancestry? We had better try to do something to be proud of ourselves; we had better try to do something kindly, something humane, to some human being, than to brag about our ancestry, of which none of us know anything.

… The Police Department went up there on the morning of the eighth, in the City of Detroit, in the State of Michigan, U.S.A., to see that a family [was] permitted to move into a home that they owned without getting their throats cut by the noble Nordics who inhabit that jungle. Fine, isn't it? No race question in this? Oh, no, this is a murder case, and yet, in the forenoon of the eighth, they sent four policemen there, to protect a man and his wife with two little truckloads of household furniture who were moving into that place.

Pretty tough, isn't it? Aren't you glad you are not black? You deserve a lot of credit for it, don't you, because you didn't choose black ancestry. People ought to be killed who chose black ancestry. The policemen went there to protect the lives and the small belongings of these humble folk who moved into their home. What are these black people to do?

… We are willing to have them in our houses to take care of the children and do the rough work that we shun ourselves. They are not offensive, either. We invited them; pretty nearly all the colored population has come to Detroit in the last fifteen years; most of them, anyhow. They have always had a corner on the meanest jobs. The city must grow, or you couldn't brag about it.

The colored people must live somewhere. Everybody is willing to have them live somewhere else.... Are you going to kill them? Are you going to say that they can work, but they can't get a place to sleep? They can toil in the mill, but can't eat their dinner at home? We want them to build automobiles for us, don't we? We even let them become our chauffeurs. Oh, gentlemen, what is the use! You know it is wrong. Every one of you knows it is wrong! You know that no man in conscience could blame a Negro for almost anything. Can you think of these people without shouldering your own responsibility? Don't make it harder for them, I beg you.

... Gentlemen, nature works in a queer way. I don't know how this question of color will ever be solved, or whether it will be solved. Nature has a way of doing things.... She makes a man. She tries endless experiments before the man is done. She wants to make a race and it takes an infinite mixture to make it. She wants to give us some conception of human rights, and some kindness and charity and she makes pain and suffering and sorrow and death. It all counts. That is a rough way, but it is the only way. It all counts in the great, long broad scheme of things.

I look on a trial like this with a feeling of disgust and shame. I can't help it now. It will be after we have learned in the terrible and expensive school of human experience that we will be willing to find each other and understand each other....

Now, let us get to the bare facts in this case.... There was a mob assembled there. The Court will tell you what a mob is. I don't need to tell you. He will tell you that three or more people gathered together with a hostile intent is a mob; there were five hundred; they were plotting against the persons of these people and their lives, perhaps, as well. Did any policeman try to disperse it? Did they raise their hands or their voices, or do one single thing? Did they step up to any man and say: "Why are you here?" Never! They stood around there or sat around there like bumps on a log, while the mob was violating the constitution and the laws of the state, and offending every instinct of justice and mercy and humanity....

Suppose a crowd gathers around your house; a crowd which doesn't want you there; a hostile crowd, for a part of two days and two nights, until the police force of the city is called in to protect you. How long, tell me, are you going to live in that condition with a mob surrounding your house and the police force standing in front of it? How long should these men have waited? I can imagine why they waited as long as they did. You wouldn't have waited. Counsel says they had just as good reason to shoot on the eighth as on the ninth. [I] concede it. They did not shoot. They waited and hoped and prayed that in some way this crowd would pass them by and grant them the right to live.

The mob came back the next night and the colored people waited while they were gathering; they waited while they [the mob] were coming from every street and every corner, and while the officers were supine and helpless and doing nothing. And they waited until dozens of stones were thrown against the house on the roof, probably—don't know how many. Nobody knows how many. They waited until the windows were broken before they shot.

Why did they wait so long? I think I know. How much chance had these people for their life after they shot, surrounded by a crowd as they were? They would never take a chance unless they thought it was necessary to take the chance. Eleven black people penned up in the face of a mob. What chance did they have?

Dr. Sweet scraped together his small earnings by his industry and put himself through college, and he scraped together his small earnings of three thousand dollars to buy that home—because he wanted to kill somebody? It is silly to talk about it; he bought that home just as you buy yours, because he wanted a home to live in, to take his wife and to raise his family. There is no difference between the love of a black man for his offspring and the love of a white. He and his wife had the same feeling of fatherly and motherly affection for their child that you gentlemen have for yours, and that your father and mother had for you. They bought that home for that purpose; not to kill somebody.

They might have feared trouble, as they probably did, and as the evidence shows that every man with a black face fears it, when he moved into a home that is fit for a dog to live in. It is part of the curse that, for some inscrutable reason, has followed the race—if you call it a race—and which curse, let us hope, sometime the world will be wise enough and decent enough and human enough to wipe out.

They went there to live. They knew the dangers. Why do you suppose they took these guns and this ammunition and these men there? Because they wanted to kill somebody? It is utterly absurd and crazy! They took them there because they thought it might be necessary to defend their home with their lives, and they were determined to do it. They took guns there that in case of need they might fight, fight even to death for their home, and for each other, for their people, for their race, for their rights under the Constitution and the laws under which all of us live; and unless men and women will do that, we will soon be a race of slaves, whether we are black or white. "Eternal vigilance is the price of liberty," and it has always been so and always will be. Do you suppose they were in there for any other purpose? Gentlemen, there isn't a chance that they took arms there for anything else.

. . . Instead of being here under indictment, for murder, they should be honored for the brave stand they made, for their rights and ours. Some day, both white and black, irrespective of color, will honor the memory of these men, whether they are inside prison walls or outside, and will recognize that they fought not only for themselves, but for every man who wishes to be free.

Did they shoot too quick? Tell me, just how long a man needs wait for a mob? The Court, I know, will instruct you on that. . . . How long do you suppose ten white men would be waiting? Would they have waited as long? I will tell you how long they needed to wait. I will tell you what the law is, and the Court will confirm me, I am sure. Every man may act upon appearances as they seem to him. Every man may protect his own life. Every man has the right to protect his own property. Every man is bound under the law to disperse a mob even to the extent of taking life.

…Now, let me tell you when a man has the right to shoot in self-defense, and in defense of his home: not when these vital things in life are in danger, but when he thinks they are. These despised blacks did not need to wait until the house was beaten down above their heads. They didn't need to wait until every window was broken. They didn't need to wait longer for that mob to grow more inflamed. There is nothing so dangerous as ignorance and bigotry when it is unleashed, as it was here. The Court will tell you that these inmates of this house had the right to decide upon appearances, and if they did, even though they were mistaken, they are not guilty. I don't know but they could safely have stayed a little longer. I don't know but it would have been well enough to let this mob break a few more window-panes. I don't know but it would have been better and been safe to have let them batter down the house before they shot. I don't know.

…The first instinct a man has is to save his life. He doesn't need to experiment. He hasn't time to experiment. When he thinks it is time to save his life, he has the right to act. There isn't any question about it. It has been the law of every English speaking country so long as we have had law. Every man's home is his castle, which even the King may not enter. Every man has a right to kill to defend himself or his family, or others, either in the defense of the home or in the defense of themselves….

Now, let us look at these fellows. Here were eleven colored men, penned up in the house. Put yourselves in their place. Make yourselves colored for a little while. It won't hurt, you can wash it off. They can't, but you can; just make yourself black men for a little while; long enough, gentlemen, to judge them, and before any of you would want to be judged, you would want your juror to put himself in your place. That is all I ask in this case, gentlemen. They were black, and they knew the history of the black.

…I should imagine that the only thing that two or three colored people talk of when they get together is race. I imagine that they can't rub color off their face or rub it out of their minds. I imagine that it is with them always. I imagine that the stories of lynchings, the stories of murders, the stories of oppression are a topic of constant conversation. I imagine that everything that appears in the newspapers on this subject is carried from one to another until every man knows what others know, upon the topic which is the most important of all to their lives.

What do you think about it? Suppose you were black. Do you think you would forget it, even in your dreams? Or would you have black dreams? Suppose you had to watch every point of contact with your neighbor and remember your color, and you knew your children were growing up under this handicap. Do you suppose you would think of anything else?

... The jury isn't supposed to be entirely ignorant. They are supposed to know something. These black people were in the house with the black man's psychology, and with the black man's fear, based on what they had heard and what they had read and what they knew. I don't need to go far. I don't need to travel to Florida. I don't even need to talk about the Chicago riots. The testimony showed that in Chicago a colored boy on a raft had been washed to a white bathing beach, and men and boys of my race stoned him to death. A riot began, and some hundred and twenty were killed.

I don't need to go to Washington or to St. Louis. ... I don't need to go far either in space or time. Let us take this city. Now, gentlemen, I am not saying that the white people of Detroit are different from the white people of any other city. I know what has been done in Chicago. I know what prejudice growing out of race and religion has done the world over, and all through time. I am not blaming Detroit. I am stating what has happened, that is all. And I appeal to you, gentlemen, to do your part to save the honor of this city, to save its reputation, to save yours, to save its name, and to save the poor colored people who can not save themselves.

... Gentlemen, it is only right to consider Dr. Sweet and his family. He has a little child. He has a wife. They must live somewhere. If they could not, it would be better to take them out and kill them, and kill them decently and quickly. Had he any right to be free?

... I shall not talk to you much longer. I am sorry I have talked so long. But this case is close to my heart.

... Gentlemen, these black men shot. Whether any bullets from their guns hit Breiner, I do not care. I will not discuss it.... There are bigger issues in this case than that. The right to defend your home, the right to defend your person, is as sacred a right as any human being could fight for, and as sacred a cause as any jury could sustain. That issue not only involves the defendants in this case, but it involves every man who wants to live, every man who wants freedom to work and to breathe; it is an issue worth fighting for, and worth dying for, it is an issue worth the attention of this jury, who have a chance that is given to few juries to pass upon a real case that will mean something in the history of a race....

We come now and lay this man's case in the hands of a jury of our peers—the first defense and the last defense is the protection of home and life as provided by our law. We are willing to leave it here. I feel, as I look at you, that we will be treated fairly and decently, even understandingly and kindly. You know what this case is. You know why it is. You know that if white men had been fighting their way against colored men, nobody would ever have dreamed of a prosecution. And you know that, from the beginning of this case to the end, up to the time you write your verdict, the prosecution is based on race prejudice and nothing else.

Gentlemen, I feel deeply on this subject; I cannot help it. Let us take a little glance at the history of the Negro race. It only needs a minute. It seems to me that the story would melt hearts of stone.

... Some other men, reading about this land of freedom that we brag about on the 4th of July, came voluntarily to America. These men, the defendants, are here because they could not help it. Their ancestors were captured in the jungles and on the plains of Africa, captured as you capture wild beasts, torn from their homes and their kindred; loaded into slave ships, packed like sardines in a box, half of them dying on the ocean passage; some jumping into the sea in their frenzy, when they had a chance to choose death in place of slavery. They were captured and brought here. They could not help it. They were bought and sold as slaves, to work without pay, because they were black.

They were subjected to all of this for generations, until finally they were given their liberty, so far as the law goes—and that is only a little way, because, after all, every human being's life in this world is inevitably mixed with every other life and, no matter what laws we pass, no matter what precautions we take, unless the people we meet are kindly and decent and human and liberty-loving, then there is no liberty. Freedom comes from human beings, rather than from laws and institutions.

Now, that is their history. These people are the children of slavery. If the race that we belong to owes anything to any human being, or to any power in this universe, they owe it to these black men. Above all other men, they owe an obligation and a duty to these black men which can never be repaid. I never see one of them, that I do not feel I ought to pay part of the debt of my race, and if you gentlemen feel as you should feel in this case, your emotions will be like mine.

... It is not often that a case is submitted to twelve men where the decision may mean a milestone in the progress of the human race. But this case does. And, I hope and I trust that you have a feeling of responsibility that will make you take it and do your duty as citizens of a great nation, and, as members of the human family, which is better still.

Now, gentlemen, just one more word, and I am through with this case.... I am the last one to come here to stir up race hatred, or any other hatred. I do not believe in the law of hate. I may not be true to my ideals always, but I believe in the law of love, and I believe you can do nothing with hatred. I would like to see a time when man loves his fellow-man, and forgets his color or his creed. We will never be civilized until that time comes.

I know the Negro race has a long road to go. I believe the life of the Negro race has been a life of tragedy, of injustice, of oppression. The law has made him equal, but man has not. And, after all, the last analysis is "What has man done?" and not "What has the law done?" I know there is a long road ahead of him before he can take the place which I believe he should take. I know that before him there is suffering, sorrow, tribulation and death among the blacks, and perhaps the whites. I am sorry. I would do what I could to avert it. I would advise patience. I would advise toleration. I would advise understanding. I would advise all of those things which are necessary for men who live together.

Gentlemen, what do you think is your duty in this case? I have watched, day after day, these black, tense faces that have crowded this court. These black faces that now are looking to you twelve whites, feeling that the hopes and fears of a race are in your keeping.

This case is about to end, gentlemen. To them, it is life. Not one of their color sits on this jury. Their fate is in the hands of twelve whites. Their eyes are fixed on you, their hearts go out to you, and their hopes hang on your verdict.

This is all. I ask you, on behalf of this defendant, on behalf of these helpless ones who turn to you, and more than that on behalf of this great state, and this great city which must face this problem, and face it fairly—I ask you, in the name of progress and of the human race, to return a verdict of not guilty in this case!

SUPPLEMENTARY SELECTION

FROM *STATE OF IDAHO V. WILLIAM D. HAYWOOD*, ADA COUNTY
COURTHOUSE, BOISE, IDAHO, JULY 24–25, 1907
Closing argument

Bill Haywood was the president of the Federated Mine Workers, and when former Idaho governor and union foe Frank Steunenberg was blown up by a booby-trapped gate at his Caldwell, Idaho, home on December 20, 1905, the trail quickly led to "Big Bill" and other union officials. The bomber was a serial criminal and occasional union employee named Harry Orchard, who, after initially proclaiming his innocence, testified that Haywood and his associates had planned and directed the assassination. Darrow's closing argument in Haywood's murder trial took eleven hours spread over two days (July 24 and 25, 1907) to deliver, achieving an acquittal and saving the life of Darrow's client but nearly killing Darrow himself. Exhausted, he came down with a dangerous infection that required hospitalization and surgery.

… This murder was cold, deliberate, cowardly in the extreme, and if this man sitting in his office in Denver fifteen hundred miles away employed this miserable assassin to come here and do this cowardly work, then for God's sake, hang him by the neck until dead. Don't compromise in this case, whatever you do. If he is guilty—if, under your conscience and before your God, you can say that you believe this man's story and believe it beyond a reasonable doubt, then take him! Take him and hang him.... If he is to die, he will die as he has lived, with his face to the foe.

... But sometimes I think I am dreaming in this case. I sometimes wonder whether here in Idaho, or anywhere in the country, a man can be placed on trial and lawyers seriously ask to take the life of a human being upon the testimony of Harry Orchard.... For God's sake, what sort of community exists up here that sane men should ask it? Need I come here from Chicago to defend the honor of your state?

If a man may commit every crime known to man; if he may be a perjurer, a thief, a bigamist, a burglar, a murderer; if he may kill man after man, and then when he is caught, with the blood dripping from his fingers, he can turn to you and say, "Here now, you told me to do it" ... then if twelve jurors can turn from that assassin, with his hands dripping with blood, and swear it upon you, and take your life ... then, gentlemen, no other criminal need suffer in Idaho.

... Has any other voice been raised to accuse him? Oh no! You have been asked to take his life because he has been organizing the weak, the poor, the toilers; has been welding together in one great brotherhood those men; has been calling them to fight under one banner for a common cause—for that reason ... you are asked to kill Bill Haywood.

To kill him, gentlemen! I want to speak to you plainly. Mr. Haywood is not my greatest concern. Other men have died before him; other men have been martyrs to a holy cause since the world began. Wherever men have looked upward and onward, forgotten their selfishness, struggled for humanity, worked for the poor and the weak, they have been sacrificed. They have been sacrificed in the prison, on the scaffold, in the flame. They have met their death, and he can meet his if you twelve men say he must. Gentlemen, you short-sighted men of the prosecution, you men of the Mine Owners' Association, you people who would cure hatred with hate—

you who think you can crush out the feelings and the hopes and the aspirations of men by tying a noose around his neck, you who are seeking to kill him not because it is Haywood but because he represents a class, don't be so blind, don't be so foolish as to believe you can strangle the Western Federation of Miners when you tie a rope around his neck. Don't be so blind in your madness as to believe that if you make three fresh new graves you will kill the labor movement of the world.

... I don't mean to tell this jury that labor organizations do no wrong. I know them too well for that. They do wrong often, and sometimes brutally; they are sometimes cruel; they are often unjust; they are frequently corrupt.... But I am here to say that in a great cause these labor organizations, despised and weak and outlawed as they generally are, have stood for the poor, they have stood for the weak, they have stood for every human law that was ever placed upon the statute books.

... I don't care how many wrongs they committed, I don't care how many crimes these weak, rough, rugged, unlettered men who often know no other power but the brute force of their strong right arm, who find themselves bound and confined and impaired whichever way they turn, who look up and worship the god of might as the only god that they know—I don't care how often they fail, how many brutalities they are guilty of. I know their cause is just.... And I want to say to you, gentlemen of the jury, you Idaho farmers removed from the trade unions, removed from the men who work in industrial affairs, I want to say that if it had not been for the trade unions of the world, for the trade unions of England, for the trade unions of Europe, the trade unions of America, you today would be serfs of Europe, instead of free men sitting upon a jury to try one of your peers. The cause of these men is right.

... I am not an unprejudiced witness in this case.... For thirty years I have been working to the best of my ability in the cause in which these men have given their toil and risked their lives.... I have given my time, my reputation, my chances—all this to the cause which is the cause of the poor. I may have been unwise, I may have been extravagant in my statements, but this cause has been the strongest devotion of my life, and I want to say to you that never in my life did I feel about a case as I feel about this. Never in my life did I wish anything as I wish the verdict of this jury, and if I live to be a hundred years old, never again in my life will I feel that I am pleading a case like this.

...I have known Haywood. I have known him well and I believe in him. I do believe in him. God knows it would be a sore day to me if he should ascend the scaffold; the sun would not shine or the birds would not sing on that day for me. It would be a sad day indeed if any calamity should befall him. I would think of him, I would think of his mother, I would think of his babes, I would think of the great cause that he represents. It would be a sore day for me.

But, gentlemen, he and his mother, his wife and his children are not my chief concern in this case. If you should decree that he must die, ten thousand men will work down in the mines to send a portion of the proceeds of their labor to take care of that widow and those orphan children, and a million people throughout the length and the breadth of the civilized world will send their messages of kindness and good cheer to comfort them in their bereavement. It is not for them I plead.

Other men have died... in the same cause in which Bill Haywood has risked his life: men strong with devotion, men who love liberty, men who love their fellow-men. They have raised their voices in defense of the poor, in defense of justice, have made their good fight and have met death on the scaffold, on the rack, in the flame; and they will meet it again until the world grows old and gray. Bill Haywood is no better than the rest. He can die... if this jury decrees it; but, oh, gentlemen, don't think for a moment that if you hang him you will crucify the labor movement of the world!

...Are you so blind as to believe that liberty will die when he is dead? Do you think there are no brave hearts and no other strong arms, no other devoted souls who will risk their life in that great cause which has demanded martyrs in every age of this world? There are others, and these others will come to take his place, will come to carry the banner where he could not carry it.

Gentlemen, it is not for him alone that I speak. I speak for the poor, for the weak, for the weary, for that long line of men who in darkness and despair have borne the labors of the human race. The eyes of the world are upon you, upon you twelve men of Idaho tonight. Wherever the English language is spoken, or wherever any foreign tongue known to the civilized world is spoken, men are talking and wondering and dreaming about the verdict of these twelve men that I see before me now.

If you kill him your act will be applauded by many. If you should decree Bill Haywood's death, in the great railroad offices of our great cities men will applaud your names. If you decree his death, amongst the spiders of Wall Street will go up paeans of praise for those twelve good men and true who killed Bill Haywood. In every bank in the world, where men hate Haywood because he fights for the poor and against the accursed system upon which the favored live and grow rich and fat—from all those you will receive blessings and unstinted praise.

But if your verdict should be "Not Guilty," there are still those who will reverently bow their heads and thank these twelve men for the life and the character they have saved. Out on the broad prairies where men toil with their hands, out on the wide ocean where men are tossed and buffeted on the waves, through our mills and factories, and down deep under the earth, thousands of men and of women and children, men who labor, men who suffer, women and children weary with care and toil, these men and these women and these children will kneel tonight and ask their God to guide your hearts. These men and these women and these little children, the poor, the weak, and the suffering of the world, are stretching out their hands to this jury in mute appeal for Bill Haywood's life.

SUPPLEMENTARY SELECTION

FROM *STATE OF ILLINOIS V. LEOPOLD AND LOEB*,
CHICAGO, ILLINOIS, AUGUST 22, 1924
Closing argument

Teenagers Nathan Leopold and Richard Loeb were charged with the murder of fourteen-year-old Bobby Franks. Both defendants were brilliant students (Leopold was the youngest graduate in the history of the University of Chicago; Loeb the youngest graduate of the University of Michigan), Jewish, and the sons of wealthy and successful Chicago businessmen. Neither showed any remorse for their act, which had been coldly undertaken as a demonstration of their superior intellects. The Leopold and Loeb families hired Darrow to keep their sons from dying on the gallows, and he decided to plead their cases directly to the judge. His summation remains the most persuasive and eloquent argument against capital punishment ever made in court or anywhere else. And it worked: Judge John Caverly spared Leopold and Loeb, and they were sentenced to life imprisonment.

Your Honor, it has been almost three months since the great responsibility of this case was assumed by my associates and myself. It has been three months of great anxiety....

I have heard in the last six weeks nothing but the cry for blood. I have heard from the office of the state's attorney only ugly hate. I have heard precedents quoted which would be a disgrace to a savage race. I have seen a court urged almost to the point of threats to hang two boys, in the face of science, in the face of philosophy, in the face of humanity, in the face of experience, in the face of all the better and more humane thought of the age....

Your Honor, it may be hardly fair to the court, I am aware that I have helped to place a serious burden upon your shoulders. And at that, I have always meant to be your friend, but this was not an act of friendship. I know perfectly well that where responsibility is divided by twelve, it is easy to say: "Away with him." But, Your Honor, if these boys hang, you must do it. There can be no division of responsibility here. You can never explain that the rest overpowered you. It must be by your deliberate, cool, premeditated act, without a chance to shift responsibility. It was not a kindness to you. We placed this responsibility on your shoulders because we were mindful of the rights of our clients, and we were mindful of the unhappy families who have done no wrong....

Why did they kill little Bobby Franks? Not for money, not for spite, not for hate. They killed him as they might kill a spider or a fly, for the experience. They killed him because they were made that way. Because somewhere in the infinite processes that go to the making up of the boy or the man something slipped, and those unfortunate lads sit here hated, despised, outcasts, with the community shouting for their blood. Mr. Savage [the prosecutor], with the immaturity of youth and inexperience, says that if we hang them there will be no more killing. This world has been one long slaughterhouse from the beginning until today, and killing goes on and on and on, and will forever.... Kill them. Will that prevent other senseless boys or other vicious men or vicious women from killing? No!

...I know that every step in the progress of humanity has been met and opposed by prosecutors, and many times by courts. I know that when poaching and petty larceny was punishable by death in England, juries refused to convict. They were too humane to obey the law; and judges refused to sentence. I know that when the delusion of witchcraft was spreading over Europe, claiming its victims by the millions, many a judge so shaped his cases that no crime of witchcraft could be punished in his court. I know that these trials were stopped in America because juries would no longer convict.

...Do I need to argue to Your Honor that cruelty only breeds cruelty? That hatred only causes hatred; that if there is any way to soften this human heart which is hard enough at its best, if there is any way to kill evil and hatred and all that goes with it, it is not through evil and hatred and cruelty; it is through charity, and love, and understanding?

I am not pleading so much for these boys as I am for the infinite number of others to follow, those who perhaps cannot be as well defended as these have been, those who may go down in the storm, and the tempest, without aid. It is of them I am thinking, and for them I am begging of this court not to turn backward toward the barbarous and cruel past.

...As a rule, lawyers are not scientists. They have learned the doctrine of hate and fear, and they think that there is only one way to make men good, and that is to put them in such terror that they do not dare to be bad. They act unmindful of history, and science, and all the experience of the past.

Still, we are making some progress. Courts give attention to some things that they did not give attention to before.

Once in England they hanged children seven years of age.... If somebody committed a crime, he would be hanged by the head or the heels, it didn't matter much which, at the four crossroads, so that everybody could look at him until his bones were bare, and so that people would be good because they had seen the gruesome result of crime and hate.

Hanging was not necessarily meant for punishment. The culprit might be killed in any other way, and then hanged. Hanging was an exhibition. They were hanged on the highest hill, and hanged at the crossways, and hanged in public places, so that all men could see. If there is any virtue in hanging, that was the logical way, because you cannot awe men into goodness unless they know about the hanging. We have not grown better than the ancients. We have grown more squeamish; we do not like to look at it, that is all....

We have raised the age of hanging. We have raised it by the humanity of courts, by the understanding of courts, by the progress in science which at last is reaching the law....

Your Honor, if in this court a boy of eighteen and a boy of nineteen should be hanged on a plea of guilty, in violation of every precedent of the past, in violation of the policy of the law to take care of the young, in violation of all the progress that has been made and of the humanity that has been shown in the care of the young; in violation of the law that places boys in reformatories instead of prisons, if Your Honor in violation of all that and in the face of all the past should stand here in Chicago alone to hang a boy on a plea of guilty, then we are turning our faces backward, toward the barbarism which once possessed the world. If Your Honor can hang a boy at eighteen, some other judge can hang him at seventeen, or sixteen, or fourteen. Someday, if there is any such thing as progress in the world, if there is any spirit of humanity that is working in the hearts of men, someday men would look back upon this as a barbarous age which deliberately set itself in the way of progress, humanity, and sympathy, and committed an unforgivable act.

I do not know how much salvage there is in these two boys, hate to say it in their presence, but what is there to look forward to? I do not know but what Your Honor would be merciful if you tied a rope around their necks and let them die; merciful to them, but not merciful to civilization, and not merciful to those who would be left behind....

Now, I must say a word more and then I will leave this with you where I should have left it long ago.... I have stood here for three months as one might stand at the ocean trying to sweep back the tide. I hope the seas are subsiding and the wind is falling, and I believe they are, but I wish to make no false pretense to this court. The easy thing and the popular thing to do is to hang my clients. I know it. Men and women who do not think will applaud. The cruel and the thoughtless will approve. It will be easy today; but in Chicago, and reaching out over the length and breadth of the land, more and more fathers and mothers, the humane, the kind, and the hopeful, who are gaining an understanding and asking questions not only about these poor boys but about their own, these will join in no acclaim at the death of my clients. But, Your Honor, what they shall ask may not count. I know the easy way. I know Your Honor stands between the future and the past. I know the future is with me, and what I stand for here; not merely for the lives of these two unfortunate lads, but for all boys and all girls; for all of the young, and as far as possible, for all of the old. I am pleading for life, understanding, charity, kindness, and the infinite mercy that considers all. I am pleading that we overcome cruelty with kindness and hatred with love. I know the future is on my side. Your Honor stands between the past and the future. You may hang these boys; you may hang them by the neck until they are dead. But in doing it you will turn your face toward the past. In doing it you are making it harder for every other boy who in ignorance and darkness must grope his way through the mazes which only childhood knows. In doing it you will make it harder for unborn children. You may save them and make it easier for every child that some time may stand where these boys stand. You will make it easier for every human being with an aspiration and a vision and a hope and a fate. I am pleading for the future; I am pleading for a time when hatred and cruelty will not control the hearts of men. When we can learn by reason and judgment and understanding and faith that all life is worth saving, and that mercy is the highest attribute of man.

I feel that I should apologize for the length of time I have taken. This case may not be as important as I think it is, and I am sure I do not need to tell this court, or to tell my friends, that I would fight just as hard for the poor as for the rich. If I should succeed in saving these boys' lives and do nothing for the progress of the law, I should feel sad, indeed. If I can succeed, my greatest reward and my greatest hope will be that I have done something for the tens of thousands of other boys, or the countless unfortunates who must tread the same road in blind childhood that these poor boys have trod, that I have done something to help human understanding, to temper justice with mercy, to overcome hate with love.

I was reading last night of the aspiration of the old Persian poet Omar Khayyam. It appealed to me as the highest that I can vision. I wish it was in my heart, and I wish it was in the hearts of all:

> *So I be written in the Book of Love,*
> *I do not care about that Book above.*
> *Erase my name or write it as you will,*
> *So I be written in the Book of Love.*

SUPPLEMENTARY SELECTION

FROM *TERRITORY OF HAWAII V. FORTESCUE ET AL.*,
HONOLULU, HAWAII (1932)
Closing argument

The highly publicized Massie case aroused strong emotions among Americans and Hawaii residents. Thalia Massie, the twenty-year-old wife of a Caucasian navy lieutenant stationed in Honolulu, accused five Hawaiian youths of beating and raping her outside a Waikiki nightclub on the evening of September 12, 1931. After a jury failed to convict the youths due to a lack of evidence, Thalia Massie's husband, Thomas Massie, her wealthy mother, Grace Fortescue of Washington, D.C., and two navy sailors kidnapped one of the youths, Joe Kahahawai, and killed him. Caught red-handed before they could dispose of the body, Thomas Massie admitted that he fired the fatal shot but claimed that he did so only as an instinctive reaction after Kehahawai confessed to raping his wife. Offered one more chance to participate in a sensational murder trial, Darrow came out of retirement to defend Massie, Fortescue, and the two sailors. They were convicted of manslaughter and sentenced to ten years of hard labor. The territorial governor, Lawrence Judd, commuted their sentences to one hour served in his office, adding fuel to an already racially charged atmosphere. Events surrounding the case and its outcome divided Hawaii along racial lines for years.

We are getting close to the end of this case and probably all of you will be glad when it is over. It has been a long, serious trial. You who have been kept together here during this work have had the worst of it. This case illustrates the mysterious workings of man and human destiny, illustrates the effect that grief and sorrow has upon human minds and upon human lives. It shows us how weak and powerless human beings can be in the hands of relentless circumstances.

Eight months ago Mrs. Fortescue lived in Washington, respected, known, moving along her way like any other woman. Eight months ago Thomas Massie, who worked himself up as a mere youth, was a lieutenant in the navy, respected by his friends, intelligent, courageous, belonging to the most dangerous branch of the service. Eight months ago his young wife, handsome, attractive, intelligent, was known, respected and admired by the whole community. What has befallen this family in this short space of time? They are here today in the criminal court. The jury is asked to send them to prison for life.

What has happened in the long series of events beginning plainly at a certain time, and ending—no one knows where! How much had they to do with it all? In this case you see the fate of the whole family, their life, their future, their name, bound up in a criminal act committed by some one else in which they had no part.

I want to call your attention to what happened. It was part of the condition of Massie's mind, how long it has been ailing, and whether there is a reason for it; and whether there is a reason for this entire calamity which has overwhelmed Tommy....

As to the early history of this case—the [Massies] went to a dance with their friends—a part of the official family. Along about half past eleven o'clock Mrs. Massie, who didn't especially care for these festivities, went out for a walk intending to go down the street and come back and join her husband again at the dance. It was only a few steps from safety to destruction. What did Massie learn from her a few hours later? An unbelievable story—almost—at least an unthinkable one which even my friend [the prosecutor] who opened this argument for the state said "it was a terrible story"—and that he pitied them. Still, he asks you to send these people to prison.

She had gone but a short way when four or five men drove up behind her in an automobile—you can't tell what may come in a short space of time—dragged her into an automobile, beaten, her jaw broken in two places by ruffians unknown to her. And then after that they dragged her into the bushes, and she was raped by four or five men. Can any of you imagine anything worse that could have happened or any greater calamity that could have fallen upon that family? They had nothing to do with it—not the slightest. She was going on her way as she had a right to go and in the twinkling of an eye her whole life, the life of the family, was changed and they are now here in this court for you, and you, and you, and you, to say whether they will go to prison—for life! Is there a more terrible story anywhere in literature!—I don't know whether it is, or who it was, or where I can find that sad tale but right here you and all the other people in this city and in this county—you have been chosen to take care of their fate kindly, and complete the work that I hope that you will—kindness and humanity and understanding—no one else but you can do this.

She was left on that lonely road in pain and agony, and suffering. In this Mrs. Massie suffered the greatest humiliation that a woman can suffer at the hands of a man. She had done nothing! Massie had done nothing! So far, suffering has been inflicted on them, suffering that few people encounter in their lives.

Massie dances until the dance is nearly over. He is ready to go home. He looks for his wife, she is not there. He goes to a friend's house. She is not there. He first calls on the telephone, and she isn't there. He looks wherever he can and he calls again and she sobs out a part of the story over the telephone, part of the story as terrible, as cruel, as any story I have ever heard: "Hurry home, something terrible has happened to me!" You would think, upon the presentation of a portion of this case and the efforts of the prosecution—these counsel, to send this family to prison, that she had done something, or that they had done something instead of being harmless and subject to the cruel fate which overhangs them.

Tommy rushes home! She meets him in the door and sobs, and tells him this terrible story—isn't that enough to unsettle any man's mind? Suppose you'd heard it!—then and there—what effect would it have had on your mind—what effect would it have had on anybody's mind!...

Tommy faced the boy and told him why he was there, and pointed the gun at him. He never intended to use it and that it went off is unfortunate. It's not a question of improbability or unreasonability that he went insane. It might happen. It wasn't the consequence of his act—but the happening. He told him all he wanted—that he wanted the truth and was going to get it. He had done all this lying in court and he was going to have the truth. He denied it—and finally Tommy seemed to catch him in what seemed to be a lie. He pressed that idea until this boy said: "Yes, I done it." …

Tommy says, and everyone else has said in this case, as far as there is any indication of the facts, that there was no intent to kill. He has told you what they tried to do and he believed he took all care and precaution, but added to his other burden, that man said, "I done it." There came up in the picture, in his mind, and we all of us have our dreams, our patterns of action, we have those pictures—"here is the man who had beaten his wife, who broke her jaw, who when she tried to pray to the God whom she believed, to save her, in the hands of five men"—here is a man, and here is a picture, and every mind is always weaving pictures, castles, dungeons, upon whatever subject it may dwell—and here is the man that destroyed her life and peace of mind—Everything was blotted out and he probably shot him.

Now gentlemen, I didn't see it. I am sorry, but how many men would have done the same? How many men who are real men would have done anything else? Would you have done anything but throw discretion to the winds?

You cannot think that right into the law books—that what a man should do and should not do—that is quite another thing. Being a living, breathing, pulsing human being moved by the instincts of life, to say what you would do with a horrible picture before you and the long months behind you and the hope— Gentlemen, I ask you to put yourselves where he was, and no man can judge another without it, if I am to judge I must use all the imagination I have, place myself where you are and then pronounce my verdict—so I ask you to put yourselves in his place and consider what you would have done.

If you know Tommy, if you can put yourself in his place, if you can think of his raped wife, if you can think of his long months of suffering—he was more or less deranged, if you can think of the cruel fate that unrolled for him—then you can judge him. Life doesn't come from harsh judgment and the people who do judge harshly could produce no children to carry on and that life would end, for it is the human emotions that have preserved the human race and that will preserve it as long as humans inhabit the earth.

Gentlemen, I want you to take my facts in this case, and understanding them—let me say again, while I think there was no malice connected with this shooting, while I think it was purely automatic, he had no intent to kill—he had in his hand a revolver—in it were eight bullets, seven of them inside and one—what do you call this thing—ah yes, of course—one in the clip. One there and the rest in the revolver. Let me ask you. I want you to put yourself in Tommy Massie's place—here is the man who destroyed the one you held dearest—suppose you had been there—do you know what you would have done? I don't know what all of you would have done, I don't know what you, or you, or you, or you, would have done, but I know what at least ten out of twelve would do. You would do what poor Tommy Massie did!

The thing they're asking you is to send him to prison for the rest of his life....

Now, gentlemen of the jury, I believe I have covered this case so far as I care to go. There are little things here and there. The broad facts are here before you. It was a hard, cruel and fateful episode in the lives of these poor people. Is it possible that any one should think of heaping more sorrows on their devoted heads? Is it possible that intelligent looking, kindly men would wish to make their burden greater and add to the terrible picture of their wrongs?

I can't understand it! There are many things in this world that I simply cannot understand. On top of all they have suffered, is it possible that anyone should say that the black gates of a prison should close upon them? Are they that type? Tell me. What have they done? Would they steal? Would they forge? Do they look like any sort of a criminal type?

They are here because of the circumstances of their lives, because of all the things that have happened to them, and I am asking you, gentlemen, to take these poor, pursued, suffering people kindly! Take them into your care. Take them and use them as you would wish to be done by under the circumstances of their case. Don't take them in anger but coolly, deliberately judge, with a heart of pity and understanding.

Let me say one last word. I would be sorry to leave this beautiful land, this fairy land, with the thought that I had made anybody's life harder; that I had compared any class against any other class, that I have all sympathy and understanding to make these Islands happier instead of more pain. I have loved your green mountains, your coral locked land, its waves that turn to every hue of the rainbow as they dash against the rocks. I love its flower-scented breath. I love the peace and calm and quiet which only man disturbs. I never knew that it was in my life to have any feeling of prejudice against any race on earth. I didn't learn it. It came to me from my parents before I left my mother's womb and I defy to have anybody find a single word of mine or line that I have written that would contradict what I say. To me nature forces and the circumstances of life make what we call race. To me these questions must be solved not by force, but by kindness and understanding....

I have no feeling against the four or five men who committed this crime upon Mrs. Massie. I have no feeling on account of their race. And my feelings were well understood by my clients before I took this case and I'll not say one thing when I think something else. There are people of every race and of every land who are not unlike the rest who either from environment or experiences in their early life take a course that is not approved by their fellows or others who must live with them.

I suppose I am a Caucasian. I knew my grandfather and grandmother but that is as far as I can go, but back further in the endless ages I presume we could find anything. If we went back far enough. I know there are Americans, Caucasians, with whom we can't live; the prisons are full of them, even in Chicago. There are Chinese and Japanese and Hawaiians who are different from the rest. I know all Japanese and Hawaiians are not alike. And I say that nobody can afford to stand by and condemn anybody on account of his race.

In every land on this sea, populated with every people on the earth, they must live with understanding, toleration, kindness and love if we produce a civilization that is worthy of this beautiful land. And nature will do it and she has plenty of them to do anything she chooses.

I put this case regardless of race, regardless of nationality or feelings of any individuals. To many they are alike. I ask everybody in this box for the sake of this case, at least, to forget this and pass upon it as a human case. As it affects the Massies so it affects you and it affects me. I know how it is. The forces that surround all of us. We are all human beings. Take this case—with its dire disaster written all over by the hands of Fate—take this case as you would take one of your own and ask what is right and I'll be content with your verdict.

Gentlemen, it isn't hard to see, it is not hard. Every life has been passed by Fate—what the individual has to do is probably very small. What we do is affected by things around us; we are made more than we make.

Take it that way. Take it broadly, kindly and humanly. Consider, gentlemen, as you should, the terrible mishaps of this family. I want you to help them. I want you to understand them and if you understand them, that is all that is needed.

I want to say that I have enjoyed my short stay, troubled though it has been. I would like to think that some time not too far away—it couldn't be too far away—I might come back with the consciousness that perhaps I had done something to make more understanding, something to make us more humane to each other—that I had done my small part in bringing peace and justice to an Island that today is wracked and worn by internal strife.

Take it—gentlemen. You have in your hands not only the fate but the life of these poor people. What is there for them if you pronounce a sentence of doom upon them? What have they done? You are in a position to heal; you are not a people to take and destroy—to bind up wounds, to bring love and happiness and understanding. This case is placed in your hands and I ask you to be kind, understanding, considerate, both to the living and to the dead.

ACKNOWLEDGMENTS

Clarence Darrow has been our companion for years as we have studied and presented his words and works. Our thanks go first to him as an inspiring speaker and writer. Like so many American lawyers, we have learned much from Darrow and are pleased to have this opportunity to share our selections from his spoken and written words with readers.

Many people and institutions have helped us in our efforts to bring Darrow's words to light. First, we would like to thank Nelson Smith for bringing us together on this project and assisting us along the way. Grace Marshall has been a continued inspiration, adviser, and organizer. This book simply would never have existed without either Nelson or Grace. Our deepest thanks go to both of them. We would also like to express our appreciation to the Clarence Darrow Estate for its assistance and cooperation.

Each of us has also been helped by many friends and associates in our separate work on this book. Jack would especially like to acknowledge the assistance of Jim Alexander, Ross Wolfarth, Leslie

Nielson, Eleanor Gomberg, Paul Morella, Professor Douglas Linder, and Jack Marshall, Sr. Ed would like to thank Sharon Bradley and James Donovan of the University of Georgia Law Library; Charles E. Campbell of the Richard B. Russell Foundation; Kay Kirk for her quick and accurate transcribing of documents; the reference librarians at the Pepperdine University Law Library; and the court archivists or clerks in Boise, Idaho; Detroit, Michigan; Los Angeles, California; Dayton, Tennessee; and Honolulu, Hawaii.

For many years, as lawyers, lecturers, and law teachers, we have engaged our colleagues, audiences, and students with Darrow's words. Their responses and reactions have shaped what we have written here. We thank them all—too many to name—and look forward to more years of sharing Darrow in public and private settings. Finally, we wish to recognize the support, counsel, and encouragement of our editors at the Modern Library, Will Murphy, Kate Hamill, and Dan Mallory.

Biographical Timeline

1857—Born, Farmdale, Ohio

1863—Moved to Kinsman, Ohio

1872—Mother died

1873–74—Attended Allegheny College, Meadville,
      Pennsylvania

1874–76—Taught school, Vernon, Ohio

1877–78—Attended University of Michigan Law School

1878–80—Read law as clerk in law office, Youngstown,
      Ohio

1880—Married Jessie Ohl

1880—Entered private practice of law in Ohio

1885—Birth of only child, Paul Edward Darrow

1887—Moved to Chicago and opened law office

1890–92—Served on legal staff for City of Chicago

1892–95—Served as corporation counsel for Chicago & North Western Railway

1895—Defended Eugene V. Debs in Pullman strike case, Chicago, Illinois

1896—Lost race for U.S. House of Representatives

1897—Divorced Jessie Ohl

1898—Defended Thomas I. Kidd in woodworkers' strike case, Oshkosh, Wisconsin

1899—Published *A Persian Pearl and Other Essays*

1902—Elected to Illinois state legislature

1903—Counsel for United Mine Workers in arbitration hearings, Scranton, Pennsylvania

1903—Married Ruby Hammerstrom

1904—Published *Farmington*

1907—Defended union leader William D. Haywood against murder charges, Boise, Idaho

1911—Defended the McNamara brothers in strike-related murder case, Los Angeles, California

1912–13—Tried twice for jury tampering, Los Angeles, California

1920—Defended twenty communists in "Red Scare" case, Chicago, Illinois

1920—Defended Benjamin Gitlow in "Red Scare" case, Chicago, Illinois

1924—Defended Nathan Leopold and Richard Loeb in murder case, Chicago, Illinois

1925—Defended John Scopes in Tennessee antievolution case, Dayton, Tennessee

1925—Defended Ossian and Henry Sweet in murder case, Detroit, Michigan

1926—Defended Henry Sweet in retrial of murder case, Detroit, Michigan

1927—Defended Calogero Greco and Donate Carillo in murder case, New York, New York

1927—Announced retirement from law practice

1932—Defended Thomas Massie and Grace Fortescue in murder case, Honolulu, Hawaii

1932—Published *The Story of My Life*

1934–35—Chaired National Recovery Administration Review Board

1938—Died, Chicago, Illinois

SUGGESTIONS FOR FURTHER READING

Over the years, Clarence Darrow has attracted the interest of lawyers, novelists, and historians. They have produced a number of fine books about him. Nevertheless, there is no better place to start reading further about Darrow than with his own autobiography, *The Story of My Life* (1932). We have extracted portions of it to introduce most of our chapters, but there is much more to read.

The most inspirational book about Darrow is by the novelist Irving Stone. *Clarence Darrow for the Defense: A Biography* (1941) is half novel, half history, and wholly delightful. *Clarence Darrow: A Sentimental Rebel* (1980), by Arthur and Lila Weinberg, is another fine choice for this sort of biography. We recommend both of them for enjoyable reading. Arthur Weinberg also edited two collections of Darrow's works, *Attorney for the Damned* (1957) and, with Lila Weinberg, *Verdicts out of Court* (1963). For a traditional biography, we recommend *Darrow: A Biography* (1979), by Kevin Tierney, though there are other fine choices.

No American lawyer has participated in more legendary trials than Clarence Darrow. Some of these trials have become the subject of books or plays; many of them are discussed in works of legal history. Our book contains excerpts from all of Darrow's most famous trials. To read further about one or more of them, we suggest the following books. *Big Trouble: A Murder in a Small Western Town Sets Off a Struggle for the Soul of America* (1997), by J. Anthony Lukas, is an extraordinarily detailed and broadly conceived history of the 1906 Haywood trial. *The People v. Clarence Darrow* (1993), by Geoffrey Cowan, examines the 1912–13 prosecutions of Darrow for jury tampering in the McNamara brothers' trial. *Summer for the Gods: The Scopes Trial and America's Continuing Debate over Science and Religion* (1997) is Edward Larson's Pulitzer Prize–winning history of the famous trial. Two 2004 books about the 1926 Sweet brothers' trial are *Arc of Justice: A Saga of Race, Civil Rights, and Murder in the Jazz Age,* by Kevin Boyle, and *One Man's Castle: Clarence Darrow in Defense of the American Dream,* by Phyllis Vine. Surely the finest and most famous play about any of Darrow's trials is *Inherit the Wind* (1955), by Jerome Lawrence and Robert E. Lee, based loosely on the 1925 Scopes trial. Both the play and the 1960 movie based on the play are American classics.

Finally, a number of scholars have closely analyzed various aspects of Darrow's impact. Among the works of these scholars, two notable books are *Clarence Darrow and the American Literary Tradition* (1962), by Abe C. Ravitz, and *Clarence Darrow: Public Advocate* (1978), by James Edward Sayer. From this starting point readers can begin exploring Darrow's complex life and legacy.

About the Editors

EDWARD J. LARSON is University Professor in history and holds the Hugh and Hazel Darling Chair in Law at Pepperdine University and retains a professorial appointment at the University of Georgia, where he has taught for twenty years. The author or coauthor of twelve books and more than 120 published articles, Larson received the Pulitzer Prize in History for *Summer for the Gods: The Scopes Trial and America's Continuing Debate over Science and Religion*. Larson lives in Athens, Georgia, and Malibu, California.

JACK MARSHALL is a lawyer, ethicist, writer, and teacher. An adjunct professor of legal ethics at American University in Washington, D.C., he is a nationally recognized legal ethics specialist and trainer whose firm, ProEthics, Ltd., presents ethics seminars for bar associations, law firms, government agencies, and corporations. He is also an award-winning stage director and playwright, and the author of the play *A Passion for Justice: The Clarence Darrow Story*. Marshall lives in Alexandria, Virginia.

A NOTE ON THE TYPE

The principal text of this Modern Library edition
was set in a digitized version of Janson, a typeface that
dates from about 1690 and was cut by Nicholas Kis,
a Hungarian working in Amsterdam. The original matrices have
survived and are held by the Stempel foundry in Germany.
Hermann Zapf redesigned some of the weights and sizes for
Stempel, basing his revisions on the original design.